Four Princes

Four Princes

Henry VIII, Francis I, Charles V,
Suleiman the Magnificent and the
Obsessions that Forged Modern Europe

JOHN JULIUS NORWICH

Atlantic Monthly Press
New York

First published in Great Britain in 2016 by John Murray (Publishers), an imprint of Hachette UK

Published simultaneously in Canada
Printed in the United States of America

First Grove Atlantic hardcover edition: April 2017

Library of Congress Cataloguing-in-Publication data available for this title.

ISBN 978-0-8021-2663-4
eISBN 978-0-8021-8946-2

Atlantic Monthly Press
an imprint of Grove Atlantic
154 West 14th Street
New York, NY 10011

Distributed by Publishers Group West

groveatlantic.com

17 18 19 20   10 9 8 7 6 5 4 3 2 1

For Moll

Contents

Preface

Bluff King Hal was full of beans;
He married half a dozen queens.
For three called Kate they cried the banns,
And one called Jane, and a couple of Annes.

I LEARNED THOSE LINES, and the several stanzas that followed them, when I was about four years old. They came from a wonderful book called *Kings and Queens*, by Herbert and Eleanor Farjeon, in which each spread bore on the left a full-colour picture of each monarch in turn, and on the right a humorous verse. My mother bought two copies, cut them up and pasted the lot on to a large screen in the nursery; thus I was almost literally brought up with them, and cannot remember a time when I didn't recognise them all, as well as the order in which they came. Since we started with William the Conqueror and there were six kings or queens to a column, Henry VIII was the second one down in the fourth; I felt I knew him well.

Getting to know Francis I took me a bit longer. The Farjeons, alas, never got around to doing for French history what they had done for English, and in those pre-war days primary historical education in England was almost unbelievably blinkered: never were we told what was going on in Europe, except on those occasions when we won a battle abroad, like Agincourt or Blenheim. We knew nothing about Italy, where the British hardly ever fought a battle before the twentieth century – that of Maida (which gave its name to Maida Vale) in 1806 is the only one I can think of offhand, and we were certainly never told about that – and only a very little about Spain – principally the story of the Armada. As for the Byzantine Empire, which lasted over a thousand years and dominated the civilised world for centuries, I think I had barely heard of it before I went to Oxford. Francis, anyway, had to wait until we settled in France, when my parents and I always stopped at Fontainebleau on our way to the south and I went on a bicycle tour among the châteaux of the Loire.

Charles V was still more of a challenge. During my formative years I suppose we thought of him – when we thought of him at all – as a German; and since we were at war with Germany we would have cold-shouldered him on principle. (Of course, he was also Spanish, but then we weren't terribly keen on Spain either.) Nor, it must be said, did we like the look of him, with that dreadful Habsburg jaw and chin. Besides, he was against Martin Luther, on whom most Anglican schools were rather keen. I obviously learned a certain amount about him when I was writing about the Papacy. 'He had little imagination', I wrote, 'and no ideas of his own' – which now strikes me as a bit unfair. He was certainly a lot more intelligent than his majestically boring son Philip II. I suspect in any case that he still remained a somewhat shadowy figure in my mind until I came to tackle the book that you now hold in your hands.

And so to Suleiman the Magnificent. Of course, he was always an outsider. But did those English preparatory and public schools ever mention the Ottoman Empire? Did they ever tell us about the Battle of Mohács – one of the greatest military encounters that Central Europe has ever seen? Or of how the Turks twice reached the gates of Vienna and – surely most surprising of all – of how in 1543 they besieged and plundered the city of Nice, of all places, enthusiastically supported by a French army? Of course they didn't. I think I first came to know Suleiman – insofar as I know him at all, since none but his very few intimates knew him well – in the 1970s, when I made a series of six films for the BBC about the antiquities of Turkey, the last of the series being devoted to the Ottomans. Biographies of him are in short supply. Antony Bridge, a former Dean of Guildford, produced one, but the definitive biography in English remains to be written – and the task won't be easy. Since Kemal Atatürk introduced the Latin alphabet in 1928, the old Arabic alphabet has not even been taught in Turkish schools. The result is that no one in Turkey, apart from a few scholars, can read any book published before that date.

Henry, Francis, Charles and Suleiman – when did I begin to see them as the single phenomenon that they collectively were, and the possible subject of a book of their own? First, I think, ten or twelve years ago, when I was writing about the Mediterranean; but the idea was then a pretty nebulous one and I had other things on my mind. It began to assume a rough shape only five years later, when – although I was principally concerned with the Popes – it struck me once again what giants those four men had been, how completely they had overshadowed their predecessors and successors and, finally, how deep was the imprint they left on the century in which they lived. There was, I felt reasonably sure, a book there somewhere. I only hope this is it.

John Julius Norwich
April 2016

Author's Note

FAR TOO MUCH, I believe, is sacrificed on the altar of consistency. The attentive reader will notice several inconsistencies in these pages: French dukes, for example, may sometimes be 'duc' and sometimes 'duke'; foreign names are sometimes anglicised (Francis for François, for example) and sometimes not – it would be ridiculous to translate 'Jacques' into 'James' or 'Ivan' into 'John'. In every case I have been guided by what sounds right to my ear – and will, I hope, sound right to the reader.

SCOTLAND

NORTH SEA

Flodden

IRELAND

ENGLAND

Hamburg

Brandenburg

Elbe

Berlin

London

Hampton Court

Ghent · Antwerp

Calais

Boulogne

Seaford

Isle of Wight

Solent

Tournai

HESSE

Cologne

SAXONY

Nuremberg

BOHEMI

Rhine

Seine

Paris · Montreuil

Fontainebleau

Augsburg

Danube

AUS

Vie

ANJOU

Loire

BURGUNDY

Amboise

Chambéry

SWISS
CONFEDERATION

Munich

ATLANTIC
OCEAN

FRANCE

Geneva

Novara · Milan

Marignano · Venice

SAVOY

Turin

Pavia

Genoa

ADRIAT

Aigues-Mortes

Rhône

Toulon

Nice

Florence

PAPAL-
STATES

Corsica

Rome

NAP

Ebro

Douro

Barcelona

Madrid

SPAIN

Balearic Is

Mahon

Minorca

Sardinia

Naples

Tagus

PORTUGAL

Lisbon

Guadalquivir

MEDITERRANEAN SEA

Sicily

Algiers

Tunis

ROM

ALGERIA

TUNISIA

Djerba

Tripoli

══════ Boundary of the Holy Roman Empire

0   300

miles

L I B

EUROPE, c.1500–1550

POLAND

RUSSIA

Dniester

Dnieper

Don

Volga

MOLDAVIA

NGARY

ged

TRANSYLVANIA

s

Belgrade

k

CRIMEA

Danube

BULGARIA

BLACK SEA

O

Sofia

Adrianople

Constantinople

alona

Iznik

Bursa

Nicopolis

eza

Lepanto

N

ANATOLIA

M

Manzikert

Nauplia

Konya

Tigris

P

I

Malvasia

R

E

Rhodes

Euphrates

Crete

Cyprus

S

Y

R

I

A

Damascus

Baghdad

Alexandria

Jerusalem

Cairo

E G Y P T

The Hollow of Their Hands

THE BEGINNING OF the sixteenth century was an exciting time to be alive. The feudal Europe of the Middle Ages was changing fast into a cluster of national states; the unity of western Christendom was endangered more than it had ever been before, and was indeed to be lost before the century had run a quarter of its course; the Ottoman Turks, thanks to a succession of able and ambitious sultans, were surging westward on all fronts; the discovery of the New World had brought fabulous wealth to Spain and Portugal, causing vast disruption to the traditional European economy. And in no other period was the entire continent overshadowed by four such giants, all born in a single decade – the ten years between 1491 and 1500. They were, in order of age, King Henry VIII of England, King Francis I of France, the Ottoman Sultan Suleiman the Magnificent and the Holy Roman Emperor Charles V. Sometimes friends, more often enemies, always rivals, the four of them together held Europe in the hollow of their hands.

The most colourful was Francis. When he was born, in Cognac on 12 September 1494, he seemed a long way from the throne. His father Charles, Count of Angoulême, was only the first cousin of the reigning king, the already ailing Louis XII, who in his determination to produce a male heir married three wives, the last being Henry VIII's younger sister Mary Tudor. The French were shocked that this ravishingly beautiful eighteen-year-old with luscious golden hair to her waist should be handed over to a gouty and toothless old dotard three times her age; but Mary bore her fate philosophically, knowing that it could not possibly last very long. And she was right. After their wedding night on 9 October her battered bridegroom boasted to all who would listen that 'he had performed marvels', but nobody believed him. As he watched Francis jousting during the wedding celebrations, he was heard to murmur: '*Ce grand jeunehomme, il va tout gâcher.*'* He died on New Year's Day 1515, less than three months after the marriage – exhausted, it was generally believed, by his exertions in the bedchamber. Mary found it hard to disguise her relief. She had long been passionately in love with Charles Brandon, Duke of Suffolk, and was now at last free to marry him – which she lost no time in doing, despite a warning by two English priests in Paris that he regularly cast spells and trafficked with the Devil. Francis, meanwhile, assumed the throne. In the previous year he had married King Louis's daughter Claude, and on 25 January 1515, in Rheims Cathedral, he was crowned and anointed the fifty-seventh King of France.

His new subjects were delighted. The country had recently suffered a whole series of drab and sickly monarchs; here now was a magnificent figure of a man, bursting with youthful energy. A Welshman who saw him at the Field of the Cloth of Gold in 1520 describes him as being six feet tall, the nape of his neck unusually broad, his hair brown, smooth and neatly combed, his beard (of three months' growth) darker in colour, his eyes hazel and somewhat bloodshot, and his complexion the colour of watery milk. His buttocks and thighs were muscular, but his lower legs were thin and bandy. He was not, it must be said, strictly

---

* 'That big lad – he'll ruin everything.'

handsome – his perfectly enormous nose earned him the nickname of *le roi grand-nez* – but he made up for it with his grace
and elegance, and with the multicoloured silks and velvets which
left his courtiers dazzled. He had beautiful manners and irresistible charm. He loved conversation, and could discuss any subject
relating to the arts and sciences – not so much because he had
studied them all deeply as because of his quite extraordinary
memory: it seemed that he remembered everything that he ever
read, or was ever told. Always laughing, it was clear that he loved
every moment of his kingship, revelling in all the pleasures that
it could provide – hunting, feasting, jousting and, above all, the
ready availability of any number of beautiful women.

He was quintessentially a man of the Renaissance, with a
passion for art and a degree of wealth that enabled him to
indulge it to the full. Before long he was celebrated as one of
the greatest patrons of his age. He brought Leonardo da Vinci
from Italy, installing him in splendid apartments at Amboise,
where the great man lived till his death. At various times he also
welcomed Andrea del Sarto, Rosso Fiorentino (known to the
French as *Maître Roux*) and countless other Italian painters,
sculptors and decorators, including Benvenuto Cellini, who
carved the medallion from which Titian was later to paint his
famous portrait. Of them all, however, his favourite was Francesco
Primaticcio, whom he employed – particularly at Fontainebleau
– with spectacular success. Fontainebleau was always his favourite
residence; it was indeed his home – insofar as he had one. But
Francis was restless by nature, and he was also a compulsive
builder. He largely reconstructed the châteaux of Amboise and
Blois, and created Chambord – that most magnificent of all
hunting-boxes – quite possibly with the help of Leonardo himself.
In all of them, again and again, we see his emblem, the salamander, often surrounded by flames; its legendary attribute of
being impervious to fire made it the perfect symbol of endurance.
In Paris itself he transformed the Louvre from a medieval fortress

into a vast Renaissance palace, and personally financed the new Hôtel de Ville in order to have full control over its design.

Then there was literature. Francis was a dedicated man of letters, with a reverence for books which he had inherited from his mother, Louise of Savoy. She had taught him fluent Italian and Spanish; his weak spot was Latin, with which he was never entirely at ease. He was a personal friend of François Rabelais, for whose unforgettable giant Pantagruel he is said to have provided the inspiration.* To be his chief librarian he appointed Guillaume Budé, who at the age of twenty-three had renounced a life of debauchery and pleasure to become the greatest French scholar of the day; and he employed special agents all over north Italy to seek out manuscripts and the relatively new printed books, just as others were seeking out paintings, sculptures and *objets d'art*. In 1537 he signed a decree, known as the *Ordonnance de Montpellier*, providing that one copy of every book published or sold in France should be lodged in the Royal Library – a right that is now enjoyed by the Bibliothèque Nationale, of which that library formed the nucleus. At the time of his death it was to contain over three thousand volumes (many of them looted from the Sforza Library in Milan) and was open to any scholar who wished to use it. Another decree, the *Ordonnance de Villers-Cotterêts*, of 1539, made French – rather than Latin – the official language of the country and instituted a register of births, marriages and deaths in every parish.

To be Chancellor of a new college for Greek, Latin and Hebrew, Francis invited the greatest humanist of his day, Erasmus of Rotterdam; and Budé wrote a letter urging him to accept the invitation. 'This monarch', he wrote,

---

* His philosophy, according to Rabelais, was rooted in 'a certain gaiety of mind pickled in the scorn of fortuitous things' – whatever that may mean.

is not only a Frank (which is in itself a glorious title); he is also Francis, a name borne by a king for the first time and, one can prophesy, predestined for great things. He is educated in letters, which is unusual with our kings, and also possesses a natural eloquence, wit, tact, and an easy, pleasant manner; nature, in short, has endowed him with the rarest gifts of body and mind. He likes to admire and to praise princes of old who have distinguished themselves by their lofty intellects and brilliant deeds, and he is fortunate to have as much wealth as any king in the world, which he gives more liberally than anyone.

Erasmus, though flattered and tempted, did not allow himself to be persuaded. (The fact that he was receiving a regular pension from the Emperor may have had something to do with it.) The invitation was declined, and the project shelved. Only a little more successful was the King's short-lived Greek college in Milan. His great educational triumph, on the other hand, came in 1529 when, to the fury of the Sorbonne, he founded the Collège des Lecteurs Royaux, the future Collège de France. In short, it seems hardly too much to say that modern French culture and all it stands for was virtually originated by Francis I. He was the personification of the Renaissance. Hunting and fighting were no longer enough for a nobleman; education was now required as well. Before him the French world was still essentially Gothic, obsessed by war; during his reign war might still be important – Francis himself was a fearless fighter on the battlefield and loved nothing more than staging mock battles for the amusement of his friends* – but

---

* A particularly ambitious one took place at Amboise in 1518, when six hundred men led by the King and the Duc d'Alençon defended a model town against an equal number led by the Dukes of Bourbon and Vendôme. 'It was the finest battle ever seen', wrote the young Maréchal de Fleuranges, 'and the nearest to real warfare, but the entertainment did not please everyone, for some were killed and others frightened.'

the art of elegant living was more important still. In Baldassare Castiglione's *Book of the Courtier* – which was begun in 1508, though it was not published until twenty years later – it is Francis who is seen as the great white hope who brings civilisation to France at last. 'I believe', says Count Ludovico,

> that for all of us the true and principal adornment of the mind is letters; although the French, I know, recognize only the nobility of arms and think nothing of all the rest; and so they not only do not appreciate learning but detest it, regarding men of letters as basely inferior and thinking it a great insult to call anyone a scholar.

But the Magnifico Giuliano replies:

> You are right in saying that this error has prevailed among the French for a long time now; but if good fortune has it that Monseigneur d'Angoulême, as it is hoped, succeeds to the throne, then I believe that, just as the glory of arms flourishes and shines in France, so also with the greatest brilliance must that of letters. For when I was at the Court not long ago I set eyes on this prince . . . And among other things I was told that he greatly loved and esteemed learning and respected all men of letters, and that he condemned the French themselves for being so hostile to this profession.

The Magnifico, as we know, was not disappointed; and it is no surprise that, of all their kings, it is Francis whom – with Henry IV – the French most love today. They love him for his swagger and his braggadocio; for his courage in war and his prowess in the bedchamber; for the colour and opulence with which he surrounded himself; and for the whole new civilisation that he left behind. They pass over with a shrug his financial recklessness, which by June 1517 had led him into a debt roughly equal to his annual income. In the following year he paid Henry VIII 600,000 gold *écus* for the return of Tournai, which was French anyway; the imperial election meant the throwing away of another 400,000, while the Field of the Cloth of Gold could not have cost him less than 200,000 *livres tournois*.* There is admiration, too, for the sheer zest that he showed in his lifelong struggle with the House of Habsburg – all too easily identified in French minds with Germany, France's traditional enemy for the next four hundred years. Only his increasing persecution of the Protestants, mostly (though not entirely) in the last decade of his reign, do they find harder to forgive.

For the first decade the most important woman in Francis's life was unquestionably his mother, Louise of Savoy. On two separate occasions while he was fighting in Italy, in 1515 and 1524–6, she served as Regent, but even when he was at home her influence was considerable – greater by far than that of either of her daughters-in-law. Next came his sister Margaret. Beautiful, elegant, intelligent and graceful in all her movements, to her brother she was everything that a woman should be. When she was eighteen she was forced to marry the Duc d'Alençon, in theory 'the second nobleman in France'. The marriage, however, was not a success – first, because Alençon was 'a laggard and a dolt', and second, because she was at the time passionately in love with the dashing Gaston de Foix, Duke of Nemours, known as 'the Thunderbolt of Italy'. There were, fortunately, no children; and after Alençon's death in 1525 she married King Henry II of Navarre.

Francis had two wives. His first, as we have seen, was Claude, the daughter of Louis XII and Anne of Brittany. Her name is still remembered in the Reine–Claude plum, or greengage, and

---

* Gold *écus* were actual coins, *livres tournois* money of account. It's no good even trying to give modern equivalents.

she did her duty by bearing Francis seven children;* but since she was 'very small and strangely corpulent', with a limp and a pronounced squint, she never interested him much. For all that, she was a good, sweet-natured girl; an ambassador reported that 'her grace in speaking greatly made up for her want of beauty'. She died in 1524, in her twenty-fifth year. The King's second wife, whom he married after six years of riotous bachelorhood, was Eleanor of Austria, sister of Charles V; for three brief years she had been the third wife of King Manuel I of Portugal. Alas, she proved to be no great improvement on her predecessor: tall and sallow, with the jutting Habsburg chin and a curious absence of personality. A lady-in-waiting was subsequently to report that 'when undressed she was seen to have the trunk of a giantess, so long and big was her body, yet going lower she seemed a dwarf, so short were her thighs and legs'. Already four years before her wedding to Francis it was reported that she had grown corpulent, heavy of feature, with red patches on her face 'as if she had elephantiasis'. Francis largely ignored her; there were no children. She was certainly no match for her husband's regiment of mistresses† – of whom the loveliest of all was Anne d'Heilly, one of the thirty children of Guillaume d'Heilly, Sieur de Pisseleu ('worse than wolf') in Picardy. Later Francis was to make her Duchesse d'Etampes. Well read, highly cultured and ravishingly beautiful, she was, as he used to say, '*la plus belle des savants, la plus savante des belles*' ('the most beautiful of the scholars, the most scholarly of the beauties').

Even when Francis was not on campaign, he was constantly

---

* Of their three sons, the first and third, Francis and Charles, both died before their father; the second, Henry, named after the King of England, was to become King Henry II.

† To this he apparently even tried to recruit his predecessor's wife, Queen Mary Tudor, who complained that he had been 'importunate with her in divers matters not to her honour'.

on the move. 'Never', wrote a Venetian ambassador,* 'during the whole of my embassy, was the court in the same place for fifteen consecutive days.' This appears still more remarkable when one considers the logistical problems involved. When the court was complete, it took no fewer than 18,000 horses to move it; when the King visited Bordeaux in 1526, stabling was ordered for 22,500 horses and mules. The baggage train normally included furniture, tapestries (for warmth) and silver plate by the ton. And the finding of suitable accommodation, as may be imagined, was a constant nightmare. Often there were rooms only for the King and his ladies; everyone else slept in shelter often five or six miles away, or under canvas. But whatever hardships they were called upon to suffer, they were always expected to be ready for the elaborate ceremonies that were staged by the major cities and towns through which they passed. In Lyon in 1515 Francis was entertained by a mechanical lion designed by Leonardo da Vinci; at Marseille in 1516 he sailed out to meet a Portuguese ship carrying a live rhinoceros, a present from King Manuel to the Pope. These royal visits, however, did not always pass without a hitch: in 1518 the captain of Brest was obliged to pay one hundred gold *écus* 'following artillery accidents during the King's entry . . . as indemnity to the wounded and to the widows of the deceased'.

Appalled by the vast new wealth that was flooding from the New World into the coffers of his brother-in-law and rival the Emperor Charles V, Francis was determined that Charles should not have it all his own way. He sent several major expeditions across the Atlantic, as a result of which he was able to claim

---

* Venice was the first state to have a fully organised diplomatic service, with resident representatives in the principal capitals; and the Republic's State Archives are the most comprehensive and complete in the world. No wonder then, that we rely so much on the Venetians for contemporary reports such as those in this book.

Newfoundland for France, together with the city of New Angoulême on the island of Manhattan.* It was named by a certain Giovanni da Verrazzano, an Italian navigator sailing under the French flag, who in April 1524 became the first man since the ancient Norsemen thoroughly to explore the Atlantic coast of the New World between New Brunswick and Florida.† In 1534 and 1535 Jacques Cartier was the first to describe the Gulf of St Lawrence and the shores of the St Lawrence river, but his reputation suffered greatly after the gold and diamonds that he had brought back with him were tested and found to be worthless. Meanwhile, Jean Parmentier of Dieppe – a town that later became famous for its mapmaking – sailed to the coasts of North and South America, west Africa and, in October 1529, the island of Sumatra.

Where religion was concerned, Francis's reign coincided almost exactly with the Reformation. Initially, he had tended to sympathise with Protestantism – so long as it remained well this side of heresy – if only because by doing so he made trouble for Charles. (His sister Margaret had still stronger reformist tendencies, and was known, though not altogether deservedly, as *la mère poule de la Réforme.*) In 1534 he was even to send a mission to Germany, to establish friendly relations with the reformers. All the time, however, he had to contend with the Sorbonne, which remained vigorously pro-Catholic and, in 1521, issued a violent condemnation of Martin Luther. In 1523 it went further still and, shocked by the recent publication of a French version of the New Testament, even tried to ban foreign translations of the Scripture altogether; but this

---

* It was later to become a Dutch colonial settlement, named New Amsterdam after 1625. In 1664 it was conquered by the English and renamed New York.
† He might have gone even further, had he not in 1528 had the misfortune to be eaten by a Carib tribe on Guadaloupe.

time Francis stepped in. Its author, he pointed out, was no less than Maître Jacques Lefèvre d'Etaples, a highly respected scholar, celebrated and esteemed throughout Europe. Any objection to his works was henceforth forbidden.

Despite the opposition there is every reason to suppose that Francis might have continued to regard the new movement with sympathy, had it not been for what became known as the *affaire des placards,* a full account of which will be given in Chapter 4. Wholesale persecutions and executions began, and the country was plunged into a religious civil war which did much to poison the last years of the King's life and was to continue till the end of the century, fifty years after his death. Oddly enough, however, while his Protestant and Catholic subjects were at daggers drawn, the Most Christian King – a special title granted by the Pope – was, for the last twenty years of his reign, in extremely friendly contact with the infidel Sultan Suleiman. The friendship was, it need hardly be said, born of politics rather than religion; but it was to do severe damage to the King's reputation in the rest of Christian Europe.

~

Like Francis, King Henry VIII of England was not born to be king. The second of Henry VII's sons – he first saw the light of day on 28 June 1491, at Greenwich – he grew up expecting the crown to pass to his elder brother Arthur. This is probably why we know so little about his youth; everyone was far more interested in Arthur than they were in Henry. All we are left with is the mildly ridiculous catalogue of titles which were almost immediately bestowed on him: Constable of Dover Castle and Warden of the Cinque Ports before his second birthday; Earl Marshal of England before his third; Lieutenant of Ireland before his fourth. On 30–31 October 1494, still aged three, he was admitted to the Order of the Bath by his father, who commanded the Duke of Buckingham to attach a spur to his right heel before dubbing him. The next day he was proclaimed Duke of York, a month later Warden of the Scottish Marches, and on 17 May 1495 he received the Garter. Despite these distinctions he enjoyed no real prominence until 14 November 1501, when he headed the procession which escorted his brother's young bride, the Princess Catherine, daughter of King Ferdinand of Aragon and Queen Isabella of Castile, to St Paul's for her marriage. It was only when Arthur died of consumption in 1502 at the age of fifteen – leaving young Catherine a widow – that Henry found himself heir to the throne. In the following year he was formally betrothed to his sister-in-law – she was by now seventeen, while he was nearly twelve – and in 1506, after the granting of a special papal dispensation, they were married.*

His childhood, both before and after his engagement, seems to have been a nightmare. According to a Spanish envoy who came to England in 1508, the seventeen-year-old was confined to a single room, the sole access to which was through the chamber of the King; he could go out only into a private park, and even then had always to be accompanied by one of the few officials authorised to do so. The Spaniard may of course have been exaggerating – he later reported that the young prince spent his days tilting at Richmond – but Arthur was a sickly boy and his father, who had already lost five of his eight children, may well have suspected that his second son might soon succeed his eldest, and must therefore be kept on a short leash.

King Henry VII died on 22 April 1509. Strangely, he had made no effort to train his son and heir in the art of kingship. Thus it was that, when young Henry was himself proclaimed king on

---

* According to Professor Scarisbrick, she was 'certainly of a quality of mind and life which few queens have seriously rivalled'.

the following day, he had surprisingly little idea of what to expect. This, however, did not stop him embracing his new role with tremendous, unashamed gusto – as well he might. Thanks to his father he had inherited a throne more secure than ever it had been, a very considerable fortune and the best-governed kingdom in Christendom. Like his French rival, he made an impressive figure: a good six feet in height and always magnificently dressed. 'His fingers were one mass of jewelled rings', wrote the Venetian ambassador, 'and around his neck he wore a gold collar from which hung a diamond as big as a walnut.' 'His Majesty', opined another Venetian, 'is the handsomest potentate I ever set eyes on.' He was better-looking than Francis, and he knew it. From the beginning, however, he was conscious of the bitter rivalry between them; and he knew too that he was beginning with a serious disadvantage. His forebears had been simple Welsh squires; those of Francis had been kings since the tenth century. Soon after his accession, that same Venetian envoy reported to his government:

> His Majesty came into our arbour and, addressing me in French, said 'Talk with me awhile. The King of France, is he as tall as I am?' I told him there was but little difference. He continued, 'Is he as stout?' I said he was not; and he then inquired, 'What sort of leg has he?' I replied 'Spare.' Whereupon he opened the front of his doublet and, placing his hand on his thigh, said: 'Look here: I too have a good calf to my leg.'

As a builder, Henry was no match for Francis. He tried hard enough, first with a palace at Bridewell – which subsequently became a prison – and then another at Oatlands in Surrey; only when these were completed did he start work on Nonsuch, near Ewell, the largest and most splendid of them all, which he intended as a proclamation of Tudor wealth and power – a rival, he hoped, to Francis's Chambord. Alas, while Chambord remains as glorious as ever, of Nonsuch not one stone remains on another. Henry's only major building that still stands is St James's Palace in London; but even if all his buildings had survived, they still could not hold a candle to what Francis achieved in Paris, Fontainebleau and on the banks of the Loire.

Both physically and intellectually on the other hand, Henry in his youth seems to have been more than a match for the French King. He was a prodigious horseman, and when at the hunt is said to have regularly worn out eight or ten horses in the course of a day. He wrestled; he played tennis; he threw the javelin further than any of his court; at the jousts he was prepared to take on any knight in his kingdom; when he practised archery with the archers of his guard, 'he cleft the mark in the middle and surpassed them all'. He was a considerable scholar too, and no mean theologian. He spoke French fluently, his Latin was very nearly as good, and thanks to Catherine he was to pick up more than a smattering of Spanish. He enjoyed close contact with Erasmus, who kept him abreast of European culture. On clear nights he would go up on to the palace roof with Sir Thomas More to study the stars.

Above all, he loved music. He regularly employed foreign as well as English musicians, among them the celebrated Dionisio Memo, sometime organist of St Mark's in Venice; he himself played beautifully on the virginals. He was an accomplished singer and wrote several love songs,* which he sang to his own accompaniment on the lute, and at least two Masses, both in five parts. These came straight from the heart, since he was deeply and sincerely religious, hearing Mass at least once a day. He was in fact that strange combination, a Catholic and a puritan; it was he who authorised the English Bible, ordering that a copy should be kept in every parish church 'for all to read on that would';

---

* But not, alas, 'Greensleeves', with which he is commonly credited, but which is almost certainly Elizabethan in date.

yet he was also the first English iconoclast, replacing the crucifixes in the churches with the Royal Arms, while the damage he inflicted on English art and literature by his dissolution of the monasteries is beyond computation. His quarrel with the Catholic Church was not doctrinal but essentially personal – directed against the Medici Pope Clement VII, who consistently refused to grant the annulment on which he had set his heart. By this time Henry genuinely believed that marriage to a dead brother's wife was an offence against canon law, and that Catherine's continued failure to bear him a son – after countless miscarriages and still-births – was a proof of divine displeasure. Even after the establishment of the Church of England he continued to see himself as a champion of Catholicism – always confident that he was right and the Pope was wrong, and that it was he, not Clement, who was doing God's will.

Only where government was concerned did Henry betray a certain lack of self-confidence. He was content to leave most political decisions to three supremely competent advisers. They followed each other in swift succession, and each in turn wielded more power than any others during the entire Tudor dynasty. First came his wife, Catherine of Aragon, of whom there will be more to say in the next chapter. Next, Thomas Wolsey. Born in Ipswich in about 1473, Wolsey was long thought to have been the son of a local butcher, thanks probably to the unkind stories deliberately circulated about him by his enemies during his lifetime; his father is actually more likely to have been a prosperous cloth merchant. We know for a fact, however, that in 1507 he entered the service of King Henry VII, who soon afterwards appointed him Royal Chaplain; by 1514 he was the controlling figure in the government, and in the following year – while still in his early forties – he became Archbishop of York and a cardinal. For some fifteen years he was the most powerful man in England after the King himself. But it was all too good to last. Try as he might, Wolsey failed utterly to arrange the annulment of Henry's marriage. In consequence he fell out of favour and was stripped of his government posts. Charges of treason were put forward, but he died – of natural causes – before he could answer them.

Henry's third adviser was Thomas Cromwell. He indeed was of humble origins, the son of a blacksmith and innkeeper. From around 1516 to 1530 he was a member of Wolsey's household and by 1529 his secretary; but that was the very year of the cardinal's downfall. Less than twelve months later, Cromwell had effectively replaced his former master in the King's favour and trust. When Henry took the most fateful step in his career – his break with Rome, in order to divorce Queen Catherine and to marry Anne Boleyn, subsequently setting himself up as head of the Church of England – it was Cromwell, not Wolsey, who made it all possible. He also played a key role in the dissolution of the monasteries, which began in 1536. But he was to end his life in still worse disgrace than his predecessor. Wolsey at least died in his bed; in July 1540 Thomas Cromwell was beheaded on Tower Hill.

In the early years of his reign Henry was loved by his subjects, being seen as a welcome contrast to his avaricious old father; and despite the excesses and brutalities of his later life, much of his popularity endured. The sixteenth century was less easily shocked than we are today; executions – usually public – were fairly frequent occurrences. Little sympathy was shown for Anne Boleyn or Catherine Howard, the two wives whom the King beheaded; they were generally believed to have been unfaithful – indeed, in Catherine's case, wildly promiscuous. As for the divorce, everyone understood that a male heir was the only guarantee of future tranquillity; and since the Pope's refusal to allow the dispensation was known to be entirely political – he did not dare to offend the Emperor Charles, who was Queen Catherine's nephew – nobody could blame Henry for taking the law into his own hands. He was fortunate indeed that his 'great matter' – the putting aside of Catherine – should have coincided so neatly with the beginnings of the Reformation; it was much easier to quarrel with Rome when half of northern Europe was doing much the same thing.

Doubtless because of his remarkable matrimonial history, Henry has the reputation of having been a great lover of women. In fact, he seems to have been, if anything, the reverse; here was another field in which he could not begin to equal his rival Francis. He is known to have had two affairs. One – with Elizabeth Blount, a lady-in-waiting to Queen Catherine – produced a son, whom Henry subsequently acknowledged and made the Duke of Richmond; the other, with Anne Boleyn's sister Mary, may also have been fruitful, but the jury is still out.* Of his wives, Anne is probably the only one whom he genuinely loved – though even with her he was quite often stricken with impotence – and even she ended on the block.† With Anne of Cleves he was unable to perform at all. The other four, in varying degrees, he saw primarily as potential mothers. The problem of the succession became slightly less acute with the birth to Jane Seymour in October 1537 of the future King Edward VI; but infant mortality in those days was such that two or three sons were necessary if the succession were to be even half guaranteed. Edward in fact was to survive for only sixteen years – and, unlike Prince Arthur, had no younger brother to

---

* The importance of Henry's affair with Mary unfortunately meant that he was henceforth technically related to her sister in the same degree of affinity as he was to Catherine; if the law forbade him Catherine, it also forbade him Anne. He devised a quibble to get out of the difficulty, though it satisfied few people other than himself.

† By 1535 there is reason to believe that Henry seriously suspected her of witchcraft. What other reason could there be for impotence, in a man as lusty and virile as he believed himself to be?

take his place. In Henry's eyes, it need hardly be said, princesses were no substitute; England had never had a ruling queen, apart from the twelfth-century Matilda, whose reign — largely spent battling with King Stephen for the crown — had been, to say the least, undistinguished.

~

For most of his life Charles V was by far the most powerful man in the civilised world. Born in Ghent in 1500 and consequently the youngest of our four princes, he was the grandson of the Emperor Maximilian, the son of Philip the Handsome of Austria and Joanna the Mad of Aragon and Castile. He had inherited neither of his parents' primary attributes. His appearance was unattractive and ungainly, with the characteristically immense Habsburg chin and protruding lower lip; and he was fully aware of the fact. He used to say with a smile that he couldn't help being ugly, but that, as artists usually painted him uglier than he was, strangers on seeing him for the first time were agreeably disappointed. He suffered also from an appalling stammer. He was serious, and deeply religious; one never gets the feeling that he enjoyed his monarchy in the way that Francis and Henry did — indeed it is doubtful whether the idea of doing so ever entered his head. Not for him were the roistering and the feasting, the glowing velvets and the brocades; at least in his youth, he ate sparingly and usually alone,* and while there were obviously occasions when he was obliged to dress

---

* An exception was a dinner Charles gave in his youth to the Chapter of the Golden Fleece. Most of the Knights present missed the subsequent service of Vespers, either because they were incapable or were still at table — possibly both.

richly – as when Titian first painted him at the age of thirty-three – he always appears vaguely uncomfortable; it is only in the master's third and last portrait, painted fifteen years later, that he looks at his ease. He is then dressed entirely in black, with the Golden Fleece around his neck providing the only touch of brilliance.

Apart from his religion, his life was dominated, as it had to be, by politics. A little less intelligent and a lot less cultivated than Henry or Francis, he was far more industrious than either. Unlike them, he had no real interest in literature: most serious books were still written in Latin, and his mastery of the language, like that of Francis, was always surprisingly weak. As a boy he had devoured the *Mémoires* of Olivier de la Marche, a fifteenth-century member of the Burgundian court whose surprisingly salacious tales of chivalry and derring-do on the part of former dukes had enjoyed immense success in court circles; later in his life, what little spare time he possessed was devoted to music, for which he had a lifelong passion. He played the spinet, the flute and several other instruments; he sang, we are told, like an angel.

His inheritance was greater than that of any European ruler in history. It began with the Burgundian Low Countries, which had come to him through his grandmother Mary of Burgundy and where he spent his childhood. Since both his parents had left for Spain when he was still a baby, he was put under the guardianship of Margaret of York, the childless widow of Duke Charles the Bold of Burgundy and the sister of the English kings Edward IV and Richard III; after her death in 1503 his upbringing was entrusted to his father's sister Margaret of Austria – also childless after two marriages – who ruled as Regent until, at fifteen, he took over the reins himself. His father Philip was long dead; his mother Joanna, though already hopelessly insane, was still technically Queen of Castile, with her father, Ferdinand of Aragon, acting as Regent; but shortly after

Ferdinand's death in 1516 – rumoured to have been due to dropsy, brought on by an aphrodisiac given him by his second wife, Germaine of Foix,* in the hope of begetting a child – Charles was proclaimed King not only of Aragon and Castile, but also of Naples, Sicily and Sardinia. Then, in January 1519, his grandfather Maximilian died of a massive stroke at the age of fifty-nine. Since the Empire remained elective, the succession of his grandson was by no means a foregone conclusion; Charles, however, was determined to secure it at any cost – if only to prevent it from falling into the hands of Francis, who was initially supported by the reigning Pope, Leo X. From his point of view the election of Francis would have been a catastrophe; it would have spelt the end of his hopes of regaining Burgundy, and might even have called into question the hereditary Habsburg lands in Germany and Austria. Fortunately for Charles, however, the German electors hated the idea of a French Emperor almost as much as he did himself; the Fuggers – that hugely rich and influential banking family from Augsburg – lined as many pockets as was necessary; and Charles was elected – unanimously – Holy Roman Emperor. The whole operation probably cost him rather more than half a million gold florins. He was to remain in debt for the rest of his life.

Maximilian had never thought much of him. If it was not for the boy's love of hunting, he used to say, he would have questioned his parentage. He made no secret of the fact that he vastly preferred Charles's younger brother Ferdinand, who with his easy ways, charm and gregariousness was by a long way the more attractive of the two; he was also much better-looking. It may well be, indeed, that his grandfather's disapproval lay at the

---

* She was a niece of Louis XII. According to Prudencio de Sandoval, Bishop of Pamplona, she also taught the hitherto abstemious Spanish grandees the joys of the table, which they enjoyed so much that several of them died in consequence.

root of the difficulties that Charles always had with his German subjects, in whose language he was never really happy. His first language had been French, and since his childhood he had also spoken fluent Flemish – though this was not at the time considered a 'polite' language. When he first went to Spain at the age of seventeen to claim his inheritance, he still possessed not a word of Spanish – though it was rapidly to become his second tongue. 'The divine language' he called it, and he used it always when speaking or writing to his wife and children (though he wrote to his brother's family in French). He is frequently quoted as saying that he spoke French to his friends, German to his horses, Italian to his mistresses and Spanish to God.*

Strange as it may seem, Charles had spent all his early youth in Flanders; never once had he visited the old Habsburg lands. Now, in addition to his already vast domains, there devolved on him with his election all the old patrimony of the Habsburgs, comprising most of modern Austria, Germany and Switzerland. Milan, Bohemia and western Hungary were to follow a little later. For a man whom most people believed – mistakenly, as it turned out – to be of modest talents and frankly mediocre abilities, here was an inheritance indeed. Sensibly enough, he soon decided to entrust the central European part of the Empire to his brother the Archduke Ferdinand, despite the fact that the Archduke had been born and brought up in Spain and never set foot in the old Empire until his eighteenth year. In 1521 he married Ferdinand to Anne, the sister of King Louis of Hungary; and in the following year Louis married his and Ferdinand's sister Mary. Thus, if Louis were to die without issue, the Empire would be extended to the frontiers of the Slavonic world, and Charles's position vis-à-vis the Ottoman threat would be at least

---

* It is only fair, however, to add that much the same remark has also been attributed to Frederick the Great, though this seems highly unlikely: mistresses were not Frederick's *forte*.

to some degree strengthened. Even so, his life involved almost constant travelling; and travelling in the early sixteenth century, even if one was an Emperor, was an uncomfortable and exhausting business. Backwards and forwards he went, principally between Spain and the Low Countries, but also to Italy, France, England and even north Africa. He travelled up and down the Rhine, through Württemberg, Bavaria and Austria. All in all, he probably spent several years of his life on the road, and several months at sea.

Soon after his election, his vast dominions were still further increased. In the space of a single decade Hernán Cortés defeated the Aztec Empire of Mexico and Francisco Pizarro the Inca Empire of Peru. Within a year or two, Spanish galleons were bringing untold wealth back across the Atlantic. These successes, combined with Ferdinand Magellan's circumnavigation of the world in 1522 – Magellan was Portuguese, but Charles had provided all five of his ships and most of the finance – left the Emperor in no doubt about his destiny: it was clear that he had been divinely ordained to be the leader of Christendom.

Charles's election as Emperor brought Spain into the heart of Europe. Spanish soldiers were henceforth to fight in Germany and the Netherlands; Spanish writers and philosophers imbued themselves with the new humanism of Erasmus and his followers. At the same time Spain was acutely conscious of being the one firm rock of the True Faith, its chief defence against the vile Protestant heresies springing up in the north. The election also – and this was perhaps still more important – resulted in the polarisation of continental Europe. France was now trapped as in a vice, virtually encircled by the Empire; conversely, Charles found himself sovereign of a divided dominion, its two parts cut off from each other by a hostile state between them. The result was inevitable: a lifelong struggle between the two men for dominance in Europe and mastery of the western Mediterranean.

The new Emperor had two principal ambitions. The first

involved the Duchy of Burgundy. By the accession in 1467 of Charles the Bold, the last of its four great Dukes,* Burgundy had become, with Venice, the most powerful state on the continent of Europe. True, the Duke was a vassal, who owed homage to the King of France for his traditional Duchy together with Flanders and Artois, and to the Emperor for the remainder; but his court was more splendid than either of theirs, and when his contemporaries called him 'the Grand Duke of the West', it seemed no more than his due. Duke Charles, however, though undoubtedly bold, had also been dangerously over-ambitious. He had foolishly set himself up against France, at whose hands he had suffered a whole series of defeats before being killed at the Battle of Nancy in 1477. Most of his lands had subsequently reverted to the French crown. The Emperor, as the grandson of Mary of Burgundy and great-grandson of Charles the Bold, was deeply conscious of his Burgundian blood, and was determined to restore the Duchy to what it had been only a quarter of a century before his birth, serving also as an invaluable buffer state between France and Germany. As late as 1548 we find him, in his political testament, charging his son Philip never to abandon the claim to *nuestra patria* – 'our country'.

His second ambition was still only a dream; yet it was a dream that he believed might easily come to pass. He longed to win back the ancient Empire of the East. Old men were still alive who remembered that dreadful day in 1453 when Constantinople had fallen to the young Sultan Mehmet II – and the Byzantine Empire, after more than eleven centuries, had come to an end. Throughout western Europe the defeat still rankled. As early as 1396, in an effort to save the already doomed city, Charles's great-great-great-grandfather John the Fearless had been captured

---

* They were Philip the Bold (*le Hardi*, 1363–1404), John the Fearless (*Sans Peur*, 1404–19), Philip the Good (*le Bon*, 1419–67) and Charles the Bold (*le Téméraire*, 1467–77).

when a Christian army estimated at a hundred thousand – the largest ever launched against the infidel – was smashed by Sultan Bayezit I at Nicopolis on the Danube. And in the much more recent past had not his rival Francis, while canvassing for the imperial election, declared that if he were successful, then within three years he would be either dead or in Constantinople? Sultan Suleiman was a formidable warrior indeed; but against the combined forces of the Christian West there was no reason to think that he was invincible.

The difficulty was, as Charles well knew, that comparative military strength was not really the point. In Spain, thanks to the long years of Muslim occupation, men could still talk seriously of launching a Crusade; in northern Europe they knew in their hearts that it was out of the question. Crusades belonged to the long-ago days of feudal Europe; now that the continent had become divided into individual nations and states – and in particular with the Reformation threatening to divide it even further – the sort of political unity necessary for such vast expeditions was no longer possible. For that very reason the question was never put to the test. Charles remained preoccupied with the affairs of Europe and the religious disputes by which, as a deeply pious Christian, he was obsessed. As a result, Emperor and Sultan were never to confront each other. Charles would never enter Constantinople; Suleiman would never occupy Vienna or Rome.

Was Charles interested in women? Not, certainly, as Francis was, or even Henry. (Suleiman, for obvious reasons, was in a class by himself.) He worked too hard, he travelled too much, and – while she lived – he loved his frail and beautiful Portuguese wife Isabella to distraction. Of his four illegitimate children, three were born well before his marriage; the fourth – who was to achieve fame as Don John of Austria, hero of the Battle of Lepanto – was born to a singer named Barbara Blomberg on his father's own birthday, 24 February 1547, eight years after Isabella's death.

Charles was the only one of our four princes to abdicate. He did so piecemeal: Naples and Sicily first, then the Netherlands, and finally Spain. Physically and mentally exhausted and tortured by gout, he withdrew to the monastery of Yuste in Extremadura, where, on 21 September 1558, he died of malaria.

~

The Sultan was sitting on a very low couch covered in carpets and cushions of exquisite workmanship. His bow and arrows lay next to him . . . We gestured to kiss his hand and were led along a wall which faced his seat, being careful never to turn our backs on him. There were high-ranking officers, troops of the Imperial Guard, *sipahi** and janissaries in the room . . .

Look now at the immense sea of turbans with countless folds of the whitest silk, the bright clothes of every kind and colour, and everywhere the glitter of gold, silver, silk and satin. Words cannot give a clear impression of that strange spectacle: never have I seen a more beautiful ceremony. What most struck me about that crowd was its silence and discipline. The janissaries, lined up apart from the other troops, were so still that I wondered whether they were soldiers or statues until I greeted them as I had been advised, and they all bowed their heads to me.

Thus does the Archduke Ferdinand's ambassador to the Sublime Porte, Ghislain de Busbecq, describe the court of the last, arguably the greatest and unquestionably the richest member of our quartet. The Ottoman Sultan Suleiman, normally known to us as 'the Magnificent', stands a little apart from the other three. To begin with, he was a Muslim, and in consequence sublimely

---

*   Cavalrymen.

unconcerned with the Church of Rome. His people, the Turks, were comparative newcomers to the land that now bears their name: the first wave of Turkish invaders, the Seljuks, had burst into Asia Minor only in 1071. The Byzantine Emperor Romanus IV Diogenes had personally led an army against them, but had been soundly defeated and taken prisoner at the Battle of Manzikert in the same year. The Seljuk leader, Alp Arslan – whose moustaches, we are told, were so long that he had to have them tied behind his back while hunting – had treated him handsomely and sent him back with an escort to Constantinople, but the damage had been done. By the end of the century the Turks had spread all over Anatolia, leaving only parts of the coast in Byzantine hands.

The Seljuks left behind them an extraordinary architectural heritage, much of which still survives: superb mosques, bridges of soaring grace and elegance and magnificent caravanserais – one every twenty miles along the main caravan routes. But as rulers they did not last long, their army being effectively destroyed by the Mongols in 1243. During the years of confusion that followed, a number of small Turkoman states – some of them hardly larger than the tribes they represented – rose from the ruins. Among them was that of a young warrior named Othman (or Osman), who after a whirlwind campaign had declared his independence as ruler in the ancient Bithynia, at the extreme western end of Anatolia. In 1354 his grandson Suleiman Pasha* crossed the Dardanelles to capture the fortress of Gallipoli, the first Turkish base on European soil. Almost at once the Ottomans – as they had come to be called – began their relentless progress, at the culmination of which, almost exactly a century later, on 29 May 1453 – it was a Tuesday – the twenty-one-year-old Mehmet II, after one of the great sieges of history, rode in triumph into Constantinople.

---

* Suleiman Pasha never became Sultan, as he died before his father.

Suleiman was Mehmet's great-grandson. He was born a few weeks after Francis, probably on 6 November 1494, in Trebizond (the modern Trabzon) on the Black Sea. It was under him that the Ottoman Empire, though it was to continue for another three and a half centuries, reached the apogee of its political, military and economic power. By the time of his death he ruled over much of Eastern Europe and the Middle East together with north Africa as far west as Algeria, while his navy dominated most of the Mediterranean, the Red Sea and the Persian Gulf. To Henry of England he was usually too remote to be of much serious concern; to both Francis and Charles, however, his ever-threatening shadow loomed immense throughout their reigns. There are, so far as we know, no portraits of him taken from life; but we possess several descriptions, largely by Venetians, which enabled Albrecht Dürer to draw and Titian to paint his portrait. 'He is tall but thin', wrote the Venetian ambassador Bartolomeo Contarini, 'with a delicate complexion. His nose is a little too long and aquiline, his features fine. He has the shadow of a moustache and a short beard. His general appearance is pleasing, although he is a little pale.' Pleasing, perhaps; but as both portraits make all too clear, forbidding too, with that outsize turban worn low over his eyes, giving him what seems to be a perpetual frown.

When Suleiman succeeded to the Ottoman throne at the age of twenty-five, he was already an experienced ruler. At fifteen he had been appointed Governor of Caffa in the Crimea, a major trading post where he had remained for three years; subsequently his father, the aptly named Sultan Selim the Grim, had appointed him Governor of Istanbul. But it had been an unhappy time: eight years during which Selim had instituted a reign of terror. He had been intelligent and cultivated enough – some of his verses are, we are told, among the loveliest in all Ottoman poetry – but he seemed to conceive of government solely in terms of executions. When he had dethroned (and

subsequently murdered) his own father, Bayezit II, in 1512, his
first act on his accession had been to have his two young brothers
and five orphan nephews strangled by the bowstring. Thus it
was that, by the time of his succession, Suleiman was the only
male member of his entire family left alive.

Nor were Selim's executions by any means confined to his family.
He had thought nothing, for example, of condemning to death
four hundred Turkish merchants who had disobeyed his edict by
trading with Persia. It was therefore hardly surprising that his son's
accession was universally greeted as a new dawn. And so it was:
unjustly held captives were released, trade with Persia re-established,
corrupt or sadistic officials brought to justice and hanged. From
the very beginning, however, the young Sultan made it clear that
he was an autocrat through and through: his rule was to be just,
but it would also be uncompromisingly firm. 'My sublime
commandment', he wrote to the Governor of Egypt, 'as inescapable
and as binding as fate, is that rich and poor, town and country,
subjects and payers of tribute – everyone must hasten to obey. If
some of them are slow to do their duty, be they emirs or fakirs,
do not hesitate to inflict on them the ultimate punishment.'

Suleiman was, from the start, sublimely confident of his power
to govern his vast Empire. He was, however, also constantly aware
of the world beyond it. He had spent many hours studying the
major powers of western Europe and their respective rulers, and
he knew that the Emperor Charles, to whom he always referred
as 'the King of Spain' – how, after all, could there be more than
one empire? – was determined on a Crusade which, if successful,
would drive him and his subjects back into the Asian steppe.
He knew too that his own forces were comfortably stronger
than those of any single European state; but a vast Christian
alliance would be another matter – if it could ever be got
together. Fortunately Christendom was at this moment bitterly
divided, principally by the Christian religion itself; and religion,
he also knew, was the most divisive force of all. At any rate,

however great or however negligible the danger, opposition was the best defence; and the further he could advance the territories of Islam to the west, the safer his Empire would be.

Above the central door of the great mosque in Istanbul that bears his name – the Suleimaniye – are inscribed the words 'Propagator of the Imperial Laws', and to the Turks he is known not as the Magnificent, but always as *Kanuni*, 'the Lawgiver'. The title was well merited: Suleiman went a long way towards a complete revision of the legal system of his Empire, instituting radical changes in society, education, taxation and criminal law. He collected all the judgements issued by the nine previous sultans and condensed them into a single clear code, while taking care every step of the way not to violate the *sharia*, the basic law of Islam – which, incidentally, gave special protection to Christian and Jewish subjects of the Empire and was to endure in his Empire for the next three hundred years. In the field of education, he founded fourteen large primary schools and eight *medreses* (colleges) in Istanbul alone, while countless other schools attached to mosques and funded by religious foundations provided a largely free education to boys, long before such a thing was known in the west.

But Suleiman was also, like our other princes but in his own oriental way, a son of the Renaissance: a man of wide culture, virtually bilingual in Turkish and Persian – in both of which languages he was a gifted poet – to which he added fluent Arabic, with serviceable Greek and Bulgar and a smattering of Hungarian. Himself an expert goldsmith, he was a hugely generous patron of the arts; under him the imperial potteries of Iznik (the ancient Nicaea) were at their most inspired, and the imperial architects – above all the celebrated Mimar Sinan – adorned the cities of the Empire with mosques and religious foundations, schools and caravanserais, many of which still stand today. He also established an institution known as the *Ehl-i Hiref*, the Community of the Talented, which gave artists and craftsmen official and professional status and attracted all the Empire's most talented artists, both oriental and European, to his court. Though a sincere and conscientious Muslim – his passionate prayer before the Battle of Mohács has come down to us – he was not especially pious, as was, for example, Charles V. He was notably tolerant of his Christian and Jewish subjects – as long as they paid their taxes – and allowed them freedom of worship throughout his dominions. He showed, too, considerable sympathy, at least at the beginning of his reign, towards the few of his Shi'a subjects that his father had not massacred – though in his later years his attitude towards them was appreciably to harden.

Suleiman had three known consorts, who bore him altogether ten children; but the only one whom he deeply loved – and indeed made his wife – was Haseki Hürrem Sultan, the daughter of an Orthodox priest from Ruthenia, then part of Poland. It was because of these origins that she became known as Roxelana, 'the Russian woman'. Captured in her infancy by Crimean Tartars,* she had been sold as a slave in Istanbul, had entered the imperial harem and – perhaps largely owing to her good humour and playfulness (*Hürrem* means 'the merry woman' in Turkish) – had soon become the Sultan's favourite. She sang him haunting Slav songs to her guitar and was to bear most of his children;† in consequence she was eventually freed from slavery to become his legal wedded wife, something that no Ottoman Sultan had possessed since Orhan, two centuries earlier. As such, she was in an even stronger position to look after her own interests – as she most meticulously did.

~

* I know that the correct word is Tatars. But I have always called them Tartars – a word I much prefer – and it is too late to change now.

† According to Busbecq, she retained her husband's affections 'by love charms and magical means'.

Francis, Henry, Charles, Suleiman: here are our four princes. Individually, they could hardly have been more different; together, they dominated the world stage and moulded the continent of Europe. None perhaps – not even Suleiman – was a truly great man; but they all possessed elements of greatness, and each left a huge and indelible footprint on the land or lands over which he ruled. Their mutual relations shifted unceasingly. Often they were actively hostile; occasionally – *very* occasionally – they were almost embarrassingly friendly. Always there was an element of wariness and suspicion – total trust was impossible – but always too there was a healthy respect; never did any one of them make the mistake of underestimating another.

This, then, is their story.

2

'The flower and vigour of youth'

THE YOUNG PRINCESS Catherine's first years in England had not been happy. Widowed after only five months of marriage to the fifteen-year-old Prince Arthur, she had soon afterwards been betrothed to his brother Henry, now Prince of Wales; but for the next seven years she had been left in a ghastly limbo. At one moment Henry's father the King had considered the possibility of marrying her himself; he was still only in his middle forties, and it was by no means unreasonable that he should try to beget more sons to ensure the continuation of his dynasty. But his proposal was, not surprisingly, vetoed by Queen Isabella. She was determined that her daughter should have diplomatic and political influence over her husband – something that would have been out of the question with an experienced monarch like Henry. Moreover, by marrying a man well over twice her age she would have been almost certainly condemned to spend a good half her life as Queen Dowager – always a thankless position.

King Henry did not press the point; neither, however, did he make any effort to marry her off to his son as promised. There were, it seemed, all sorts of problems: first of all, Catherine's marriage to Arthur had put her, canonically speaking, in the first degree of affinity to her intended husband, which meant that their marriage would require a papal dispensation; second, the King continued to insist that he had received only half her dowry; third, it had been agreed that the marriage, even with the dispensation, could not take place before the groom's fifteenth birthday in June 1506, and then only if the second half of the dowry were paid. Meanwhile poor Catherine was installed in the empty London palace of the Bishops of Durham on the Strand, where she settled with a few mostly Spanish attendants and was, to all intents and purposes, ignored and forgotten. Not only was she no longer invited to court; she was not even permitted to see her future husband – whose fifteenth birthday, which should have been her wedding day, passed without notice. Her father Ferdinand hardly ever wrote to her, and when he did it was never more than a few lines. Nor did he ever send her any money, while the trickle that came from the eternally avaricious King Henry was both irregular and inadequate. She and her ladies desperately needed a few new dresses; Durham House, already in a fair state of dilapidation when she moved in, was becoming more threadbare by the day. Sometimes there was not even enough to pay her few servants' wages; even food ran short.

Then, in April 1509, Henry VII died of tuberculosis at Richmond, and all was changed. His austerity, suspiciousness and above all his avarice had created a fearful, joyless atmosphere in which even minor offences could be punished with savage fines, and where the ubiquity of the royal agents had brought the country down almost to the level of what nowadays might be called a police state. Now, under his splendid young son, freedom returned, and with it a new spirit of gaiety and optimism. Life once again was fun. And, suddenly, Catherine found herself in another world. Of course she was to marry, and as soon as possible. The papal dispensation would cause no difficulty; as to the remainder of the dowry, the matter was quite without importance. In early June she and her betrothed sailed down to Greenwich, where on the 11th they were married in the church of the Observant Friars outside the Palace.

Less than a fortnight later, on Midsummer Day, Sunday 24 June, they were anointed and crowned together at Westminster, Catherine riding to the Abbey on a litter of cloth of gold slung between white palfreys, herself all in white satin, the costume of a virgin bride, with her gleaming hair 'hanging down her back, of a very great length, beautiful and goodly to behold'.

It was perhaps only then that Henry began to realise the sort of wife he had married. Ferdinand and Isabella had educated their daughters well; all three of them were destined to be queens, and their parents had spared nothing to make them worthy of their title. Catherine's Latin, for example, he soon realised to be far better than his own; she had no difficulty in improvising extempore replies to the flowery speeches of foreign ambassadors – which was particularly fortunate since she was an ambassador herself; her father had appointed her, well before her marriage, the official Spanish Plenipotentiary to the Court of St James. And to no less a judge than Erasmus of Rotterdam, her scholarship was on a completely different level from that of the King. She was soon to speak excellent English, though she never lost a faint Spanish accent, which many young Englishmen – who had probably never before heard a foreigner speaking their language – found curiously attractive. In 1518 she made a tour of all the Oxford colleges, dining at Merton and being received 'with as many demonstrations of joy and love as if she had been Juno or Minerva'.* But, more important than any of that, Henry loved her. In his letter to Ferdinand, thanking him for his congratulations, he leaves him in no doubt of the fact and adds: 'If I were still free, I would choose her for wife before all others.'

❧

* It is a curious fact that, despite his much-vaunted respect for learning and scholarship, Henry never once visited either Oxford or Cambridge.

Henry VII had hated war; Henry VIII enjoyed it enormously. It was typical of him that he saw himself as a great warrior, the successor to Edward III and Henry V; as far as he was concerned, the Hundred Years War was still in progress. There were still men around him whose grandfathers had fought at Agincourt; the extreme north-east corner of France was already English territory; the rest, so far as Henry was concerned, was still waiting to be conquered by an English king. And was not one of the foremost duties of a king to lead his army in battle? As early as 1513, he had Catherine proclaimed Governor of the Realm; then, allied with the Emperor Maximilian,* he led a vainglorious and mildly ridiculous campaign across the Channel, at the head of an invasion army estimated at forty thousand. Besides these soldiers he took with him a household of nearly three hundred, with over a hundred clergy and a body of musicians from the Chapel Royal. In August 1513 he laid siege to the utterly inconsequential town of Thérouanne – 'an ungracious doghole' was how one parliamentarian described it – where Maximilian's grandson Charles, still six years from the imperial throne, crossed the frontier to greet him.

It was on 13 August 1513, during the siege of Thérouanne, that Maximilian himself arrived at Henry's camp, offering to put himself and the small force accompanying him under the King's command. Henry received him in as great a state as was possible in the circumstances, in a tent heavily adorned with cloth of gold. The weather, the chroniclers tell us, was 'the foulest ever', but the meeting seems to have been a success; Henry reported every detail to Catherine, who in turn wrote to Wolsey that it was not only a great honour for her husband; it would also do wonders for the reputation of Maximilian, of whom she clearly

---

* 'Through whose head the grandest schemes of European domination chased in rainbow glory while he dodged from one German town to another to avoid his creditors' (Mattingly).

held a not very high opinion. He would henceforth, she wrote, 'be taken for a nother man that he was befor thought'.

On the morning of the 16th a small force of French cavalry suddenly found itself – to its surprise and considerable alarm – opposite the allied army; it turned and fled, with the English and Burgundian cavalry in hot pursuit. There was no actual engagement, but the French left behind six standards together with a number of distinguished gentlemen who had been unable to gallop quite as fast as the rest; they included a duke, a marquis and the Vice-Admiral of France. This fortunate chance enabled Henry to present what was at most a minor skirmish as a heroic battle – the so-called Battle of the Spurs. Francis, who was present with the French army though not yet king, chanced to be bathing at the time and was consequently caught without his armour. Wisely, he also fled.

Thérouanne fell on 22 August, and on the orders of Maximilian the whole town – except for its church – was razed to the ground. After a few days' celebrations at Lille, Henry then turned his attention to Tournai – which, having seen what had happened to Thérouanne, soon surrendered in its turn. It was to remain English for the next six years. The King was tempted to continue his successes; but autumn was fast approaching and he judged it better to return to England. It was only when he reached London that he heard of the momentous victory that had been gained during his absence. King James IV of Scotland – husband of Henry VII's daughter Margaret – had seized the opportunity to cross the Tweed and do battle with what he believed to be a much-diminished English army. Catherine, to whom Henry had fortunately given the additional title of Captain-General of the Forces for Home Defence, had sprung into action. She was already working flat out to keep her husband's army properly supplied; she now had the additional responsibility of resisting the invasion in the north, where the seventy-year-old Thomas Howard, Earl of Surrey, was advancing against it. In case Surrey should be defeated, she quickly prepared a second line of defence in the Midlands; meanwhile she ordered the immediate seizure of all Scottish property in England. No one – not Wolsey, not Cromwell – could have handled the situation better.

It had soon become clear to King James that he had seriously underestimated his opposition. The two armies had met at Flodden on 9 September, and it had been the old story of the English longbow against the Scottish spear – the longbow, as always, proving victorious. During just three murderous hours King James himself was killed together with much of the Scottish nobility and higher clergy. The latter included the Archbishop of St Andrews, two bishops and two abbots. It was typical of Catherine that on hearing the news her first thought should have been of the widowed Queen Margaret. She was, after all, Henry's sister, who now found herself Regent for her son James V, still only one year old; not only for family reasons, she needed all the help she could get. Even before Henry had returned to England a Franciscan friar was on his way to Edinburgh, with affectionate and consolatory messages.

In comparison with Flodden Field, the Battle of the Spurs had been little more than a schoolboy scrap; and indeed it is hard to take Henry VIII's invasion of France in 1512 very seriously. He had been only three years on the throne; he was young, ambitious and bursting with energy; he needed adventure and excitement, and longed for an opportunity to show himself off on the international scene. All his life he was to love the spotlight; and while Louis XII was his antagonist, he had understandably felt that he was in no danger of having to share it. King Francis was, however, a very different sort of article: from all Henry had heard, a serious competitor with himself and quite possibly a dangerous one. Henry had received an invitation to attend his coronation at Rheims but had politely declined; when he first heard that Francis, within a few months of that coronation, was planning an invasion of Italy, he was frankly incredulous: 'You may assure your master', he said to the

Spanish ambassador Bernardino de Mesa, 'that the French will not attack Milan without my leave.' But later, on further consideration, he may perhaps not have been entirely surprised: for by the beginning of 1515 France had lost all the territories in the peninsula that had once been hers. Genoa – which had been under French domination for fifteen years – was once again an independent republic; the Kingdom of Naples was in the hands of the House of Aragon; Milan – which Francis claimed through his predecessor's grandmother Valentina Visconti, and about which he felt more strongly than anywhere else – was back with its old rulers the Sforzas. To the young King it seemed nothing less than a sacred duty to regain the lost ground and to avenge France's recent military disasters.

In any event there was nothing much that Henry could do about it; *his* first duty was to congratulate Francis on his accession, for which purpose he sent Charles Brandon, Duke of Suffolk, to the French court. But Brandon had another mission too, a good deal more important from Henry's point of view: to bring back the jewels given to his sister Mary by her late husband, Louis XII. Predictably, this did not prove so easy. The French politely explained that the jewels had not been given to Mary for the sake of her blue eyes; they were hers only in her capacity as Queen of France and could in no circumstances be taken out of the realm. This was probably as much bad news to Brandon as it was to Henry; after all, he and Mary were to marry in the very near future. But the two were probably too much in love to care.

Francis was also preoccupied by the preparations for his forthcoming Italian campaign, the principal object of which would be to recover Milan. The city had been lost in 1513 after the Battle of Novara, fought between a French army of some ten thousand and bands of Swiss pikemen, mercenaries of Duke Maximilian Sforza. On this occasion the Swiss had won hands down, the French losing almost half their men, and Sforza had returned victorious to Milan – though the real power had remained

with the Swiss. It was they, therefore, who were Francis's chief
enemy when he invaded Italy two years later. He met them
on 13 September 1515 at Marignano – now Melegnano – some
ten miles south-east of Milan, and had his revenge. What
followed was one of the great victories in the history of France.
The fighting was long and hard: beginning in mid-afternoon,
the battle raged throughout the night until the morning sun
was high in the sky. The King fought with his usual courage,
and had himself knighted on the battlefield by Bayard, the
almost legendary *chevalier sans peur et sans reproche*. Effectively,
the battle had won him Milan; and a deputation from the city
made its submission on the 16th, though Sforza held out
heroically in the castle until 4 October. Finally Francis promised him a pension if he settled permanently in France – which
he agreed to do. And so at last, on 11 October, the King rode
in triumph into Milan, beside himself with joy and pride.
Never again, he wrote to his mother, could his men-at-arms
be called 'hares in armour', as they had been after the Battle
of the Spurs. Seven weeks later he left Milan to meet the
Pope at Bologna.

Leo X had been the Supreme Portiff for the past two years.
On his election, he had written to his brother, 'God has given
us the Papacy, let us now enjoy it' – and enjoying it he certainly
was. The second son of Lorenzo de' Medici, he had been
throughout his life more a Renaissance prince than a man of
the Church. Homosexual like his predecessor Julius II, he was
a cultivated and polished patron of the arts, far more magnificent
than his father had ever aspired to be. A passionate huntsman,
he would ride out with an entourage of up to three hundred;
an insatiable gourmet, he gave prodigiously lavish banquets and
willingly attended those given by his friends. Having decided at
an early stage to support the Emperor against French ambitions,
he had not taken the news of Marignano well; if Francis could
unseat Sforza in Milan, what was to prevent his similarly removing

the Pope's Medici cousins from Florence? In fact, Francis would never have done anything of the kind; if he were ever to establish a permanent foothold in Milan and Naples, he knew that he could do so only with papal cooperation, and at Bologna he was anxious to give Leo all the assurances he needed. The conference lasted four days, after which the Pope celebrated High Mass in the great church of San Petronio. When the two separated, he gave Francis a superb golden crucifix, containing within it a piece of the True Cross. What the King offered the Pope in return is not known; we are informed, however, that the presents he distributed to Leo's retinue gave less satisfaction. The papal master of ceremonies was apparently disgusted to receive only 100 gold *écus*.

After the Bologna meeting, Pope Leo had no more misgivings where Francis was concerned; but he now began to be haunted by another, far greater, anxiety: the westward expansion of the Ottoman Turks. It was now well over half a century since they had penetrated deep into the Balkans and had captured Constantinople, and since then they had continued their steady advance. As recently as August 1516, under the Sultan Selim the Grim, they had conquered Syria, and in the following year they had invaded Egypt. 'It is time', said Leo, 'that we awake from our sleep, lest we be put to the sword unawares.' He accordingly proposed a new Crusade, to be led jointly by the Emperor and the King of France, with the other Christian powers participating according to their abilities. The general reaction, however – even after he had proclaimed a five-year truce throughout Christendom and sent out four cardinals to the principal courts to drum up support – was at best lukewarm. It was not that the Turkish danger was unrecognised, simply that the princes of Europe had more immediate problems on their hands.

~

Charles's association with Spain had begun early: in Valladolid, at the age of six, and then again in Madrid four years later he had been invested *in absentia* as Prince of Asturias, heir apparent to his mother Joanna, Queen of Castile. There was at that time no need for him to visit the country itself; his grandfather Ferdinand was Regent, and was coping admirably. But Ferdinand died in 1516, and by then Queen Joanna was incurably insane.

Joanna was a tragic figure. From the day of her arrival in Flanders she had been desperately in love with the man she was to marry, Philip of Burgundy; but it was a love that she had been utterly unable to control. Philip, an easy-going *roué*, was irritated and occasionally infuriated by her frenzied jealousy, her unceasing demands, sometimes even her physical attacks on one or the other of his several mistresses. Since he was incapable of showing her the love she craved, he understandably took to avoiding her as much as possible. Gradually her once happy personality seemed to disintegrate; sudden outbursts of fury or hysterical weeping would alternate with long hours of silent depression. It was a state that would now instantly be recognised as a severe nervous breakdown, but in her day poor Joanna could expect no treatment – and very little sympathy.

Then, in September 1506, Philip fell ill at Burgos, apparently of typhoid fever, and on the 25th he died. Joanna, naturally convinced that he had been deliberately poisoned, had never left his bedside; and after his death, when his body lay in state in the cathedral, she resumed her vigil beside the bier, refusing to answer questions or to give orders for the funeral and flying into a fury if any attempt were made to move her away. Eventually the coffin was surreptitiously removed while she slept, and taken to a nearby convent; she was there by dawn on the following day, when she had it opened and gazed for hours upon the dead man's face. What happened then is best described by Garrett Mattingly:

Suddenly she took alarm. With a little, worried suite she appeared at the gate of the monastery, beat down all objection, had the coffin removed and raised on the shoulders of bearers and, as night fell, like a thief stealing a holy relic, she was off through the mountains towards distant Granada, a few alert counsellors spurring anxiously behind her. Thereafter, from time to time, astonished peasants saw from their mountain fastnesses a weird procession winding through the night; monks chanting a *miserere*, a wavering line of torches, a horse litter with sable plumes, and behind it, swathed in black, a solitary figure. Whoever liked, whoever was strongest, might rule now in Castile. Joanna had only one thought. She would never be parted from Philip again.

She was, of course. In 1509 her son settled her in the convent of Tordesillas, near Valladolid, where he conscientiously visited her whenever possible. There she remained for nearly half a century, convinced that the nuns were plotting to kill her, constantly refusing to eat, sleep, wash or change her clothes. She died on 12 April 1555. It was Good Friday.

In September 1517, leaving his aunt Margaret of Austria to resume the regency of the Low Countries and accompanied by his elder sister Eleanor, who was betrothed to King Manuel of Portugal and would one day marry Francis I, Charles took ship for Spain. His first impressions of his new kingdom were not altogether favourable. Several days struggling through the roadless mountains of Asturias in torrential rain were enough to dampen the highest spirits; it soon became clear, moreover, that his accession would not be as automatic as he had been led to believe. His younger brother Ferdinand had been living in Spain since the age of three, and there were many noblemen of power and influence who would have preferred him to this villainously ugly new arrival, who spoke not a word of their language. All this would have been tactfully explained by the celebrated Cardinal Ximénes de Cisneros, Ferdinand's successor as Regent, who was similarly struggling – though in the opposite direction – on his way to receive him; but Ximénes died the day before the two were due to meet. (Foul play was inevitably, though groundlessly, suspected.)

Charles was to spend more than two and a half years on his first visit to Spain. One of his first priorities was to get his brother Ferdinand out of the way by sending him to Flanders; after that he made an extensive tour of the country, spending long periods in Castile, Aragon, Catalonia and Galicia – unfortunately he devoted twelve months to Catalonia and only six to Castile, causing angry mutterings in Valladolid – learning pretty thoroughly the language and customs of his Spanish subjects. When he finally set sail for Flanders in May 1520, he was all too well aware that he had not yet won the country's heart; he had, on the other hand, been elected King of the Romans. In all but name, he was now Holy Roman Emperor.

The Holy Roman Empire had never managed to follow the example of the rest of Europe and convert its elective monarchy to a hereditary one. The advantages of the latter should be plain enough: so long as the principle of primogeniture is also accepted, it operates automatically and eliminates all doubts about the succession.* The elective system, by contrast, can spin out the uncertainty over months – even years – with, inevitably, adverse effects on the government and administration. In this particular case, the fundamental reason for its preservation was to emphasise not only the importance of the Empire but also its uniqueness: it was not to be handed down like any other piece of property, but could be bestowed only after a solemn and considered election by seven of the

---

* Heredity without primogeniture spells disaster. In the Ottoman world, as we have seen, it frequently led to the massacre by the bowstring of most male members of the imperial family.

highest dignitaries in Christendom, and then sanctified by coronation at the hands of the Pope himself. In a perfect world this might have been an effective enough procedure; in sixteenth-century Europe it meant bribery on a massive scale. The imperial election of 1519 proved just as much a contest between Charles and Francis as the two were ever to know on the field of battle. If Charles was resolved to win it in order to keep it from Francis, Francis was every bit as determined to withhold it from Charles. He had two basic reasons. First, although the Empire was based in Germany, it carried immense international prestige; it was – insofar as anything could be – the secular counterpart of the Papacy. Second was the likely consequence of its remaining under Habsburg control. 'You understand', he wrote,

> the reason which moves me to gain the Empire, which is to prevent the said Catholic King from doing so. If he were to succeed, seeing the extent of his kingdoms and lordships, this could do me immeasurable harm; he would always be mistrustful and suspicious, and would doubtless throw me out of Italy.

He was perfectly right; but what it took him some time to learn was that for the Electors the question was not who would be the best Emperor; it was, quite simply, how much they could get for their vote. That was why they had encouraged him to join the contest. He, of course, should have seen what was going on and pulled out while he could; instead, he plunged in ever deeper, paying out huge sums that he could ill afford. In England King Henry refused him a loan of 100,000 crowns – though he managed to obtain one of 360,000 from Italian bankers in London. In France he sold royal lands and a number of high offices – all to no purpose whatever.

On 8 June 1519 the seven Electors gathered in Frankfurt: the Archbishops of Mainz, Trier and Cologne, the King of Bohemia, the Count Palatine of the Rhine, the Duke of Saxony and the Margrave of Brandenburg. Conditions were far from favourable. The city was roasting in a savage heatwave; plague was everywhere. Outside the walls, the army of the Swabian League stood at the ready. It was said that this was for the protection of the Electors, but none of them could have been in much doubt that their ultimate safety depended on their making the right choice. If any were still uncertain, Count Henry of Nassau made the matter clearer still: no Frenchman, he declared, would enter Germany except on the points of spears and swords.

And the Electors got the message. Pope Leo at last gave his reluctant approval to Charles; on 26 June Francis withdrew his candidature; and on the 28th Charles was unanimously elected. Finally, on 23 October 1520, he was crowned – not in Rome but in the old Carolingian capital, Aachen – as the Emperor Charles V. Henry and Francis accepted their respective defeats with a good grace. Francis actually sent his congratulations, which Charles received with rather overdone gratitude. The new Emperor also quite unaccountably sent his thanks to Henry, ostensibly for the King's supposed help in his election. In fact, Henry had not helped at all; there could be no doubt, on the other hand, that the election had vastly improved his international position. Before it there had been four major powers in western Europe: France, Spain, the Empire and England. Now there were only three. Of these, two – France and the Empire – were roughly equal in strength; the third – England – controlled the balance between them.

~

By 1520 Henry VIII had been eleven years on the throne, Francis I five; yet still the two greatest Renaissance princes of their time had never met face to face, and it was generally considered to be time they did. So it was that Cardinal Thomas Wolsey settled down to prepare for their first summit meeting.

Wolsey was now at the summit of his career. Energetic, industrious, immensely intelligent and utterly confident in all he did, he had quickly made himself indispensable to his master. He knew how easily bored Henry became in meetings of the Council and would encourage him not to bother with affairs of state, leaving himself, Wolsey, to look after everything. The King was only too pleased to do so; and off he would go, hawking, hunting or otherwise amusing himself for days at a time, leaving the cardinal to read and write his letters and to take the decisions – virtually all the decisions – on his behalf.

Then, suddenly, his mood would change. He would, as it were, seize control. On such occasions he would astonish those around him, not only by his industry but also by his knowledge of domestic or foreign affairs and by the soundness of his judgement. As with everyone, he had certain subjects in which he showed particular interest: the navy, for example, and war, and – perhaps most of all in the early years of his reign – King Francis. Later, of course, he was to become obsessed with the problem of his divorce; and he then showed time and time again that he could discuss the relevant issues of theology and canon law as knowledgeably and as intelligently as anyone in his kingdom. His temperament was, in short, quite astonishingly mercurial, governed by whatever mood he happened to be in at the time; and no one understood this better – or handled it more skilfully – than Thomas Wolsey.

Wolsey liked peace; he also liked money, and, as he constantly emphasised, war was the quickest way to lose it. Henry's war in France had cost some £700,000, nearly half of it in the single week of 5–12 June 1513. In 1518 the cardinal had negotiated the nearest thing the world had ever seen to a United Nations Charter – a general treaty of peace signed by no fewer than twenty states, with the blessing of Pope Leo X. Its chief provisions had been: first, that if any of the signatories suffered aggression, the others would collectively demand the aggressor to withdraw and, if he did not do so, go to war against him; and second, that all previously concluded treaties contrary to this basic act of union would be abrogated. There would thus be formed a perpetual league, of which the Pope would be president. England and France would henceforth enjoy permanent peace, each helping the other against any aggressor. Wolsey also inserted in the text a special reference to the two young kings, recommending that Henry should soon visit France, since 'the said serene princes of England and France be like in force corporal, beauty and gifts of nature right expert, and having knowledge in the art militant, right chivalrous in arms, and in the flower and vigour of youth'. To cement their friendship, it was agreed that Francis's son and namesake, the Dauphin – who had been born only a few months earlier – should eventually marry Henry's daughter Mary, then aged two. After long and careful diplomatic negotiations, the date of the proposed meeting between the two monarchs was eventually fixed for 7 June 1520.

But there now arose an embarrassing complication. The new Emperor Charles sent ambassadors to Henry proposing that as a mark of special friendship he should personally call at the English court on his way back from Spain to northern Europe; England would thus be the first foreign nation that he would visit as Emperor. This would, he assured Henry, be in no sense a state visit; no extensive ceremonial would be required. But since he would in any case be passing up the Channel, he would very much appreciate the opportunity of renewing his acquaintance with His Majesty and paying his respects.

Henry could clearly not refuse to receive him; nevertheless, the timing could hardly have been worse. It was already mid-May; he would need at least a week in France before he was ready for his meeting with Francis. The early summer weather was notoriously unpredictable; the Emperor had already been delayed for weeks in Corunna by a violent north-easterly, and though he was well aware of the King's commitments, he could give no clear indication of the date of his arrival. The days passed, and Henry's anxiety steadily increased. It would be a diplomatic disaster if the Emperor were to arrive in England only to be informed that the King had left for France; on the other hand, to be obliged to postpone the projected meeting would be a humiliation that – even though Francis might relish it – he himself would find almost impossible to bear.

Charles eventually landed at Dover on 26 May, just – but only just – in time. Henry hurried down to meet him, arriving late in the night, going straight to his bedchamber and embracing him. The following day, Whit Sunday, the party rode to Canterbury, where, for the first time in his life, Charles met his aunt, Queen Catherine, in the Archbishop's Palace. Two days later, after various sessions of banqueting and dancing – which Henry loved but the Emperor hated – a close compact was signed between the two monarchs. It was agreed that, as soon as possible after Henry's forthcoming meeting with Francis, he and Charles should meet again, perhaps somewhere in the Low Countries. On 1 June they parted, with much show of affection, Charles heading for Sandwich and thence for Germany, while Henry, Catherine and their entourage took ship to Calais, still in those days English soil. Finally, after nearly a week spent in further frenzied preparation, Henry and Francis came together – for the first time in their lives – at the Field of the Cloth of Gold.

It was a magnificent name, and the occasion was more magnificent still, with each of the two protagonists determined to outdo the other in splendour. Henry brought with him a suite of well over five thousand men, together with nearly three thousand horses; another six thousand artisans from both England and

Flanders – builders, stonemasons, carpenters, glaziers and the rest
– had been working flat out for months, transforming the castle
of Guînes and surrounding it with temporary structures so
elaborate and fantastical that they seemed to have come straight
out of a fairy tale. Francis, we may be sure, kept a close eye on
their work; whatever Henry could do, he was determined to do
better. According to the near-contemporary description by
Edward Hall,* the two were to meet in a valley called the Golden
Dale, midway between Guînes (which was English) and Ardres
(which was French). Here Henry had pitched his Great Tent
– said to have been made, literally, of cloth of gold. Near by he
had erected a vast prefabricated castle, its walls crenellated, its
gatehouse decorated with Tudor roses. In front of it two foun-
tains flowed with wine.†

> The foregate of the same palace . . . with great and mighty
> masonry was arched, with a Tower on every side of the same
> portered by great craft, and inbatteled was the gate and Tower,
> and in the fenesters and windows were images resembling men
> of warre redie to cast great stones; also the same gate or Tower
> was set with compassed images of ancient Princes, as Hercules,
> Alexander and other, by entrayled worke, richly limned with
> gold and Albyn colours . . . also the tower of the Gate as seemed
> was built by great masonry . . . for the sundrie countenances of
> every Image that there appeared, some shooting, some casting,
> some ready to strike, and firing of gonnes, which shewed very
> honourably.‡

---

* A government official under Henry VIII. Hall began *The Vnion of the
Two Noble and Illustre Famelies of Lancastre and York* around 1530.
† These proved a mistake, being soon surrounded by piles of prostrate
drunks.
‡ Richard Grafton, *A Chronicle at Large* (1568).

Francis's tent was also of gold, with three horizontal stripes of blue velvet, each sewn with golden *fleurs-de-lys*. It was crowned by a six-foot-high wooden statue of St Michael, trampling the dragon underfoot. But this was only the beginning. Altogether there were nearly four hundred such tents, all of them sumptuously decorated. Seldom in history has there been so vast and gratuitous a display of wealth.

When the great day dawned, Henry and Francis were each attended by five hundred horsemen and some three thousand infantry. A great gong was sounded, and the entire company was ordered to stand stock still, on pain of death, as the two kings spurred on their horses and rode at full gallop towards each other. An embarrassing collision seemed inevitable; but at the very last moment they reined in, embraced, dismounted and, doffing their hats, embraced again. They then walked arm in arm to yet another magnificent tent, where toasts were drunk and the principal nobles on each side presented to their respective Majesties. A pleasant story is told by Robert de la Marck, Seigneur de Fleuranges, one of Francis's closest friends, who was present throughout the festivities. He tells us that when the English herald,* reading a formal proclamation, began with the words 'I, Henry, King of France', Henry immediately stopped him. 'That I cannot be', he said to Francis, 'while you are here.' He ordered the herald to begin again, and this time to say 'I, Henry, King of England'.

There were virtually no political discussions – but politics was not the point. The next fortnight was spent in jousting, feasting and general carousing. Perhaps not surprisingly, the two kings won most of the jousts; in his encounter with the Earl of Devon, however, Francis sustained a wound in the eye serious enough to force him to wear a piratical black patch for several days. His

---

* According to another version, it was Wolsey himself who read out the proclamation.

honour was saved when, after watching a series of wrestling matches, Henry suggested that they should have one of their own, and Francis promptly threw him.* Henry took it in good part, and asked for a return bout, which Francis rather unsportingly declined. Then on Sunday, 17 June, there came another memorable moment. Early that morning Francis appeared in Henry's chamber, unexpected and unannounced, and taking over from his valet helped him to dress. Henry, deeply touched by this display of affection, presented him on the spot with a collar of rubies worth 30,000 Venetian ducats. Francis reciprocated with something even more expensive, but refused to stay for breakfast. That night he and the heavily pregnant Queen Claude entertained Henry and Catherine to dinner, with a masque to follow. Other nights saw a number of different entertainments but ended almost always with a banquet. At one of these Francis proved his well-known gallantry by going, cap in hand, round the hall, kissing every English lady present, 'save four or five that were old and not fair'.

The programme ended on Sunday, 24 June. At noon the day before, Wolsey had rather hesitatingly celebrated a Pontifical High Mass – something he had not done for many a long year – with five other cardinals and more than twenty bishops. The service was unexpectedly enlivened when an immense firework in the shape of a dragon, intended for the St John's Eve festivities a few hours later, was accidentally exploded half-way through the service; but order was soon restored, and the cardinal limped his way through to the end. The royal couples then together attended yet another banquet, more sumptuous even than its predecessors. On Sunday, after a further exchange of presents, the English made their farewells and retired to Calais. Francis travelled on to his château of Saint-Germain-en-Laye, where on 10 August

---

* This incident is reported in the French accounts of the festivities but not, for some reason, in the English.

Queen Claude gave birth to a daughter. The two kings vowed to build a chapel to Our Lady of Peace at the place where they had met, but unfortunately they never got around to it.

~

The Field of the Cloth of Gold, having quite seriously impoverished both countries, had in fact amounted to little more than an immense charade. But it had had its uses. It is hard for us nowadays to understand the measure of hatred that normally existed in the sixteenth century between the English and the French.* This hatred, at least among the nobility on each side, was now significantly – if temporarily – reduced. The meeting had also to some extent put an end to the mutual suspicions of the two monarchs, and had provided a spectacle that no one fortunate enough to be present would ever forget. Politically, it had achieved nothing; but that had never been the purpose of either king. Francis had made no serious attempt to persuade Henry to join him as an ally in his coming struggle with Charles. In any case, he was perfectly well aware that his two fellow-monarchs had arranged to meet in the very near future – even before the King returned to London.

When Henry met Charles on 11 June between Calais and Gravelines, the atmosphere was very different. Despite appearances, he had never really taken to Francis – who offered, apart from anything else, too much serious competition. For Charles, on the other hand – who was still only twenty – he felt a genuine affection. After his visit to England the young man had

* On his return to England, the brother of the Marquis of Dorset was heard to remark to a friend that, if he had a drop of French blood in his body, he would cut himself open and get rid of it; to which the friend replied that he would do the same.

written a letter thanking him and Catherine warmly for their hospitality, and in particular for the advice Henry had given him 'like a good father when we were at Cantorberi'; and it may well be that the King, who was, after all, already his uncle, did feel in some degree paternal – or at least protective – towards him. What seems abundantly clear is that Charles endeared himself not only to Henry but to all who were with him, in a way that Francis, with all his swagger, had completely failed to do. Not, however, that Henry forgot his recent undertakings with the French King, or the provisions of the international treaty of two years before. He said nothing to betray Francis, agreeing only that neither he nor the Emperor should make any further marriage arrangements with France without consultation. It was Charles who tried to tempt Henry into an anti-French alliance and to break the marriage contract between his daughter Mary and the Dauphin; but Henry refused to listen to 'any such exhortation tending to the violation of his said promise'. Throughout 1520 and early 1521, as relations between France and the Empire grew steadily worse, he saw himself as a perpetual peacemaker, urging both sides to do nothing provocative and warning them enigmatically that if war should indeed break out, he would be bound 'to give aid and assistance either to the one party or the other'.

For all that, he was well aware that if he had to choose France or the Empire as an ally, it would have to be the Empire every time. An alliance with Francis had very little to offer him; one with Charles, on the other hand, carried the promise of as much French territory as his army could conquer, and also vastly improved the ever ambitious Wolsey's chances of obtaining the one prize on which he had set his heart, the Papacy. It was now, in 1521, that Henry – despite his protestations of the previous year – broke the marriage contract binding Mary to the Dauphin, engaging her instead to Charles, who agreed to marry her when she reached the age of twelve. He was sixteen years older than his intended bride, but such differences were by no means uncommon in royal marriages and would certainly not have bothered Henry, who was thrilled to welcome the Emperor as a prospective son-in-law. At the same time he promised a new military expedition to France, to assist in recovering 'all that was held by the King of France but rightfully belonged' to Charles. This, in the minds of the contracting parties, meant above all the Duchy of Burgundy but also included Provence and all France east of the Rhône. Thus no one was surprised that when, in November 1521, the fighting began between Charles – who was also backed by the Pope – and Francis, Henry sided firmly with the Emperor; four months later he himself declared war.

The principal bone of contention was, however, not France but Italy. Charles's interest in the peninsula was based on the fact that he had inherited from his grandfather King Ferdinand the crowns of Naples, Sicily and Sardinia, all of which he was determined to pass on intact to his successors. He had no wish to acquire further Italian territory, and was perfectly content that the local rulers should remain in charge of their states, provided, of course, that they recognised the Spanish claims and showed them due respect; French influence, on the other hand, could not be tolerated. King Francis, for as long as he remained in Italy, constituted a challenge to the imperial hold on Naples.* He was also a danger in the north, where the Duchy of Milan – claimed at his coronation in 1515 and won back at Marignano the same year – had become something of an obsession.

The Emperor was deeply grateful for King Henry's support – so grateful indeed that on his way back to Spain in 1522 he spent six weeks in England. His visit got off to a shaky start. He arrived at Dover on 26 May – two years to the day after

---

* The House of Anjou had held the Kingdom of Naples from 1266 until its capture by Alfonso I of Spain in 1442, though the last of the Angevins, René, had remained titular king until his death in 1480.

his first visit – and had to wait there three days for his baggage. Only then did he travel to Greenwich – where he met his six-year-old fiancée, Princess Mary – and thence to Richmond and Windsor. By now the festivities had begun in earnest; Henry was determined to make up for the hurried informality of 1520. It was in England, incidentally, that on 3 July Charles made his first will – at Bishop's Waltham in Hampshire, where the now ruined palace in which he stayed can still be seen. He also concluded two more treaties, binding Henry to a joint attack on France. Not until 6 July did he embark for Santander.

But Charles had other preoccupations besides France, and a number of seemingly unanswerable questions on his mind. Five years earlier, in 1517, Martin Luther had nailed his Ninety-Five Theses to the church door at Wittenberg; three years after that, he had publicly burned the papal bull excommunicating him; and in 1521, at the Diet of Worms, he had effectively raised the standard of revolt against Pope and Emperor alike. The only hope of satisfying him, in Charles's view, lay in calling a General Council of the Church to discuss reforms; but what was the use of a General Council if neither France nor her allies were represented?

And there was more bad news on the way.

~

The more we read of Sultan Suleiman, the readier we are to believe that, determined as he may have been that the Emperor Charles should not become ruler of the world, he would have been far from averse to the prospect of assuming the title himself. Thanks to his warlike predecessors, most of the former Christian enemies of the Turks in eastern Europe had ceased to exist: the Serbian and Bulgarian empires had been annihilated at the end of the fourteenth century, the Byzantine in the mid-fifteenth.

That left only the Kingdom of Hungary. Under its two great fifteenth-century rulers, John Hunyadi and his son Matthias Corvinus, the kingdom had played a stalwart part in the resistance against the infidel; but after the death of Corvinus in 1490 it had notably declined in power and prestige, which its present King Louis II – the Emperor's brother-in-law – seemed unlikely to regain.

It was against Hungary, therefore, that the Sultan now marched, leaving Istanbul on 6 February 1521 at the head of an army estimated at a hundred thousand men with some three hundred cannon. Accompanying him was his right-hand man, Ibrahim Pasha, still on the threshold of his extraordinary career. Born in a small fishing village in what is now Albania, Ibrahim appears to have been captured during a pirate raid and somehow to have found his way to Istanbul and the Sultan's court. There he so impressed everyone by his charm, his intelligence and his striking good looks that he was sent to the palace school, and in due course was appointed one of the Sultan's personal pages. Since this brought him into the constant company of Suleiman, further promotion came fast. Before long he was Chief of the Bedchamber, one of the most important positions at court. He was also his master's closest friend, accompanying him everywhere, often as his only companion. Inevitably, people started talking: was the Sultan's obvious intimacy with his servant altogether healthy? If permitted to continue, might it not harm his prestige and reputation? Ibrahim himself seems to have thought so; he is said to have protested to his master that he had been promoted quite far enough. But Suleiman brushed all his objections aside, and in 1523 appointed him his Grand Vizier. Ibrahim was now, after the Sultan himself, the most powerful man in the state. When he married Suleiman's sister Hatice Sultan, he became if anything more powerful still. 'Neither the Sultan nor any of his courtiers takes any decisions without Ibrahim', wrote the Venetian ambassador, 'yet Ibrahim does everything, without consulting the Great Lord or anyone else.'

The Sultan's first objective on his new campaign was Belgrade, the mighty fortress standing at the confluence of the Sava river and the Danube, the effective gateway to Hungary and the Danube valley through which he could take his armies straight to Buda and Vienna. In 1456 John Hunyadi had successfully defended it against his great-grandfather Mehmet II, who had been seriously wounded in the fighting – a disaster that Suleiman was determined to avenge. The siege of Belgrade lasted for three weeks, until the Turkish sappers managed to blow up the principal tower of the fortress. The garrison, part Serbian and part Hungarian, attempted to fight on, but the Orthodox Serbs hated the Catholic Hungarians and eventually concluded a separate peace on condition that their lives were spared. The Hungarians were massacred to a man; the Serbs were taken back to Istanbul and settled in a woodland site to the north-east of the city – still known today as the Forest of Belgrade. Then the Turks poured in; and before long Belgrade, now with a population of more than a hundred thousand, was the second largest city in the Empire, surpassed only by Istanbul itself.

When the news reached western Europe that one of the greatest Christian strongholds of the east had fallen to the forces of Islam and that its largest church had been converted into a mosque, there was general consternation. Where would the Sultan attack next? Probably, it was thought, he would march on Budapest; after that he might even press on along the Danube to Vienna. But Suleiman was in no hurry; the Hungarians were not his only enemy. He now turned his attention to another, very different adversary, in a very different direction: the Order of St John of Jerusalem.

A military order originally established in Palestine in the eleventh century to tend sick pilgrims, the Knights of St John had been evicted with the last of the Crusaders from the Holy Land in 1291. After a long search for a suitable new headquarters, followed by a two-year siege, they had captured Rhodes, which in 1310 they had made their base and which, by a subsequent papal decree, became their property. In these circumstances they were not only an order of knighthood; they were a sovereign state. One of their very first tasks on their arrival had been to start work on their new infirmary. It was soon to become the most celebrated – and by far the best – hospital in the world. The great ward – which remains today almost exactly as it was when the Order left it nearly five centuries ago – could accommodate no fewer than eighty-five patients, all tended by the Knights themselves. With their hospital completed, they returned to their other preferred occupation. Now at last they could resume their continuing war against the infidel, with its avowed object of 'reducing to silence the enemies of Christ'.

Like all the early Ottoman Sultans, Suleiman was a pious Muslim, so that after his accession it was only a question of time before he turned his attention to the Knights, whose island fortress lay at his very doorstep, ten miles off the Anatolian coast. They were comparatively few, with neither an army nor a navy that was any match for his own; but, as his great-grandfather Sultan Mehmet had discovered to his cost, they were by no means easy to dislodge. In 1480 Mehmet had led an army of some 70,000 against them, carried in a fleet of about 50 ships. Also on board there had been a number of those formidable cannon that had smashed the walls of Constantinople twenty-seven years before. Against this huge host the Knights had opposed some 600 members of their Order, together with perhaps 1,500 paid foreign troops and local militia. After the first three weeks of the siege the walls

began to crumble and their Grand Master was seriously
wounded, but somehow the defenders held firm; then,
suddenly, panic spread through the Turkish lines; the *bashi-
bazouks** turned and fled, the rest of the army behind them.
Why this occurred remains a mystery; but whatever the reason,
the Turks' triumph was transformed from one moment to
the next into disaster. The furious Sultan had immediately
begun preparing a fresh army, but in the spring of 1481, as he
was riding through Asia Minor to take command, he was
struck by a violent attack of dysentery; a day or two later he
was dead.

Thus for forty years one of Mehmet's few defeats had
remained unavenged. During those years the Knights had worked
unceasingly on their defences, building huge angled towers that
would permit covering fire along exposed sections of the walls
and strengthening the ramparts against the heavy cannon by
which they had been so nearly defeated in 1480. Their Grand
Master, Philippe Villiers de l'Isle Adam, a deeply pious French
nobleman of fifty-seven who had spent most of his life in
Rhodes, had received – within a week or two of assuming
office in 1521 – a letter from the Sultan. In it Suleiman had
boasted of the conquests he had already made, including those
of Belgrade and 'many other fine and well-fortified cities, of
which I killed most of the inhabitants and reduced the rest to
slavery'. Its implications were all too clear, but de l'Isle Adam
refused to be intimidated; in his reply he proudly reported
his own recent victory over Cortoğlu, a well-known Turkish
pirate who had tried unsuccessfully to capture him on his return
to Rhodes.

Then, in the early summer of 1522, there came another letter:

---

* Irregular and largely undisciplined Turkish troops, who fought for plunder
rather than pay.

To the Knights of Rhodes:
The monstrous injuries that you have inflicted upon my most long-suffering people have aroused my pity and my wrath. I command you therefore instantly to surrender the island and fortress of Rhodes, and I give you my gracious permission to depart in safety with your most valued possessions. If you are wise, you will prefer friendship and peace to the cruelties of war.

Any Knights who wished – the letter continued – might remain on the island, without paying homage or tribute, provided only that they acknowledged the sovereignty of the Sultan. To this second letter the Grand Master returned no answer.

On 26 June 1522 the first ships of the 700-strong Ottoman fleet appeared on the northern horizon. More and more were to join this vanguard over the next two days, including the flagship carrying Suleiman himself, his Grand Vizier Ibrahim and his brother-in-law Mustafa Pasha, who had marched down with the army through Asia Minor. Such was its size – we are told that it was not far short of 200,000 – that it took over a month to disembark and assemble: an overwhelming force, it might be thought, when measured against some 700 Knights, even after their numbers had been swollen by contingents from the various commanderies of the Order throughout Europe, by 500 Cretan archers, by some 1,500 other mercenaries and, of course, by the Christian people of Rhodes, determined to defend their homes and families. On the other hand, the city's defences were so strong as to be thought by many to be literally impregnable; and the Knights had spent the previous year laying in sufficient supplies of food, water and munitions to hold out for many months.

In this type of warfare, moreover, life was always a good deal harder for the besiegers than for the besieged, since they had little protection either from the sweltering summer sun or from the cold and rain of winter. For the defenders, forced as they were into a passive role, the principal strain was psychological; fortunately, however, there was endless work to keep them occupied. They had to maintain a constant vigil over every foot of the wall, repairing damage as soon as it was inflicted and watching for any sign among the enemy below that might suggest the activity of sappers: mining had become something of a speciality with the Ottoman armies, who well understood that many an impressive fortification was a good deal more vulnerable from beneath than from the front.

By the end of the month the heavy bombardment had begun in earnest, the cannon being even more powerful than those used in the earlier siege, capable of hurling cannonballs almost three feet in diameter a mile or more. The Turkish army was now drawn up in a huge crescent to the south of the city; that of the Knights was divided among their eight 'tongues',* each of which was responsible for the defence of its own section of the wall. By mid-September their worst fears were realised: they had found no fewer than some fifty tunnels – all the work of Turkish sappers – running in various directions under the wall. Fortunately they had been able to secure the services of the greatest military engineer of his day, an Italian named Gabriele Tadini. Tadini had constructed his own warren of tunnels, from which he could listen – with the aid of tightly stretched drums of parchment capable of picking up every blow of a Turkish spade – and frequently deactivate the enemy fuses. But he could not hope to succeed every time, and early in September a mine exploded under the English section, creating a gap in the wall over thirty feet across. The Turks poured in, and there followed two hours of bitter hand-to-hand fighting before the defenders somehow prevailed and the exhausted survivors retired again to their camp.

---

* These were essentially national divisions: those of Aragon, Auvergne, Castile, England, France, Germany, Italy and Provence.

By December, however, the Knights were at the end of their tether. Well over half their fighting force was now either dead or hopelessly disabled. Although the Sultan was still offering honourable terms, for a long time the Grand Master kept his resolve. Rather than surrender to the infidel, he argued, every last Knight must perish in the ruins of the citadel. It was the native Rhodiots who finally persuaded him that if he continued to resist the result could only be a massacre, of Knights and people alike. And so at last de l'Isle Adam sent a message to the Sultan, inviting him personally into the city to discuss terms – and Suleiman accepted. It is said that as he approached the gates he dismissed his bodyguard with the words 'My safety is assured by the word of the Grand Master of the Hospitallers, which is more sure than all the armies of the world.'

Negotiations were protracted. It was finally agreed that the Order would leave Rhodes within twelve days, leaving fifty hostages, twenty-five Knights and twenty-five islanders; meanwhile the Turkish army would retreat a mile from the town. For five years the local population would be exempt from taxes, and from the *devşirme*, the conscription of Christian children into the imperial Ottoman service. Suleiman also promised that the city would be spared; but somehow a group of janissaries managed to force their way in and – despite their legendary discipline in battle – to show just how impious and barbaric they could be. 'They proceeded', wrote an eyewitness, 'to the great church of St John, where they defaced the frescos, broke up the tombs of the Grand Masters, scattered the ashes of the dead, dragged the crucifix in the dust, and turned the altars upside down.' And all this, he adds, occurred on Christmas morning.

On the following day the Grand Master made his formal submission. Suleiman is said to have treated him with all the respect he deserved, congratulating him and his men on their tenacity and courage. It was the fate of princes, he said, to lose towns and provinces from time to time. A week later, on the evening of 1 January 1523, the survivors of one of the great sieges of history sailed for Crete. It is reported that the Sultan, as he watched them depart, turned to Ibrahim Pasha. 'It saddens me', he murmured, 'to force that brave old man to leave his home.'

Nor was it easy for the Knights to find another. After Crete they tried Messina, then Viterbo, and finally Nice, but all without success, Then, in 1530, the Emperor Charles offered them Malta, with its neighbouring island of Gozo and, as an additional bonus, the city of Tripoli on the north African coast. The fee was a single falcon – 'the Maltese Falcon' – payable every year on All Souls' Day. The Knights accepted with alacrity, and started work at once on their new hospital. Malta was to be their home for the next 268 years.

But, as we shall see, they had not heard the last of the Sultan.

3

'All is lost, save honour'

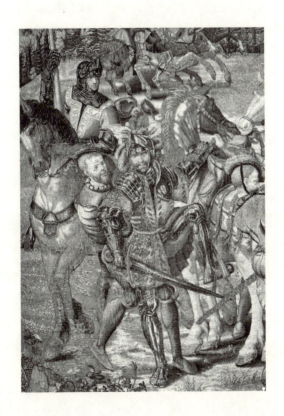

For the past five or six years King Henry had been badgering Rome for a special title to match those of his fellow-monarchs, the Most Catholic King of Spain and the Most Christian King of France; and Rome was not averse to the idea. As early as 1512 Julius II had been on the point of transferring the schismatic Louis XII's title to Henry, but had ultimately decided against it. Nothing much actually happened until 1521, when a magnificently bound copy of a book that the King had just written, the *Assertio Septem Sacramentorum* – a refutation of Luther's recent book on the Babylonian Captivity – was presented to Leo X. Perhaps surprisingly, Leo was deeply impressed by it. He read it with rapt attention, regularly expressing surprise that such a book could have been written by a king,[*] and praised it *super sidera,* 'to the skies'. No longer could he defer the question of the King's new title; and so *Fidei Defensor* was decided on, 'Defender of the Faith'. Theoretically it was awarded to Henry only, and not to his successors; but in 1543, by act of Parliament, it was joined in perpetuity to the English crown. The whole

---

[*] Henry had doubtless had a good deal of help from his friends, but seems to have written much of it himself.

thing seems a little incongruous, considering that the faith in question is the Roman Catholic one which Henry and his successors did remarkably little to defend;* but its abbreviation – *Fid Def* or, more often, the simple *F D* – regularly appears on British coinage to this day.

In that same year of 1521, to strengthen his hand against Francis in Italy, the Emperor Charles had signed a secret treaty with Pope Leo, as a result of which a combined papal and imperial force had expelled the French from Lombardy, restoring the house of Sforza in Milan and, incidentally, enabling the Papacy to regain Parma and Piacenza, lost six years before. For Leo, here was a splendid reason for celebration; but it the course of the ensuing banquet, which seems to have been more than usually riotous and to have continued all night, he caught a chill that rapidly turned into a fever, and on 1 December he died. As a Renaissance prince he was superb; as Pope he was a disaster. In seven years he is estimated to have spent some five million ducats, and at his death he was well over 800,000 in debt. Such was the state of the treasury that the Vatican did not even buy new candles for his funeral; those used were left-overs from the obsequies of a cardinal who had died a few days before.

Conclaves were well known to be uncomfortable things, but the one that now took place must have been among the worst in history. In the depths of a bitter winter, the Vatican was entirely unheated; several windows had lost their glass and had to be roughly boarded up, with the result that there was also very little light. Most of those present had spent the greater part of their lives in conditions of extreme luxury; now they found themselves herded together, shivering in the encircling gloom, with little to eat – their food was passed to them 'at a round turning wheel made in the wall' – still less to drink and only the most rudimentary sanitation. On the sixth day, by which time one elderly

* Apart from James II; but much good did it do *him*.

72

cardinal had been carried out half-dead, the meagre rations were still further reduced. Few better ways, one might have thought, could have been devised to encourage a quick decision; but Their Eminences found agreement impossible and the deadlock continued.

A few days later, however, a letter arrived from the Emperor Charles V, warmly recommending his erstwhile tutor, a sixty-two-year-old Dutchman from Utrecht named Adrian Florensz Dedal. Hardly anyone in Rome had even heard of him, but there: he had no enemies in the city and, given his age, was unlikely to last too long. Moreover, after Pope Leo a compromise candidate with (so far as anyone knew) a spotless reputation might be no bad thing. And did not a vote for him represent the best chance of escaping from a freezing Vatican back to their own warm palaces? Thus it came about that on 9 January 1522, after fourteen nightmare days of conclave, Pope Adrian VI – he made no attempt to adopt a papal name – was elected Vicar of Christ on Earth.

Having travelled by sea, he arrived in Rome only in the following August. He spoke no Italian, his Latin was incomprehensible and before the end of the year he had antagonised everyone: the populace, who considered him a northern barbarian; the Curia, who were furious at his refusal to distribute the usual benefices; Charles V, who had expected him to join his league against Francis I; and Francis himself, when the Pope arrested and imprisoned one of his cardinals for secretly plotting to hand over Naples to the French. Meanwhile Adrian lived like a monk. Gone were the courtesans, the catamites and the banquets with which the Renaissance Papacy had made so free. Adrian spent precisely one crown a day on catering and employed as domestic staff only his old Flemish housekeeper, who did all his cooking, washing and cleaning. For the art and architecture of the Renaissance he cared not a jot; he threatened to have the Sistine Chapel whitewashed, and the *Laocoön* cast into the Tiber.

It need hardly be said that his promised reforms all came to nothing. He failed to control the cardinals, who continued to live like fighting cocks; nor could he do anything to check the sale of indulgences, without which the Church would have faced bankruptcy. All his initiatives ended in disaster: his attempts to form a European coalition against the Sultan; his handling of the Reformation, whose importance he consistently failed to recognise (just as Pope Leo had before him); even his proposal – after the expulsion of the Knights from Rhodes – for a three-year truce over the whole of Christendom. When he fell sick and died in September 1523, little more than a year after his arrival in Rome, there was nothing but relief all round. It was another four and a half centuries before the election of the next non-Italian pope.

That relief was tempered, however, by the grim prospect of another conclave. Fortunately it opened in autumn rather than winter, but it proved even worse in the end: this time it was only after fifty days that the cardinals finally made up their minds. Their final choice fell on Pope Leo's cousin Giulio de' Medici, who took the name of Clement VII.* The two could hardly have been more different. Leo had been unusually ugly, with a huge head and a fat, red face; on the other hand, he had possessed a charm that many found irresistible. Clement, now forty-eight, was tall and slim; he might have been good-looking but for his thin, tightly compressed lips, haughty expression and almost perpetual frown. He was pious, conscientious, industrious; but nobody liked him much. His contemporary Francesco Guicciardini went so far as to describe him as 'somewhat morose and disagreeable, reputed to be avaricious, far from trustworthy and naturally disinclined to do a kindness'.

---

* Leo was the son of Lorenzo the Magnificent, Clement the bastard son of Lorenzo's brother Giuliano, who had been assassinated by the Pazzi in Florence in 1478.

It might reasonably be supposed that such a man, however lacking he might be in the social graces, would prove at least a competent pope. Alas, Clement was nothing of the kind. He was vacillating and irresolute, terrified whenever he was called upon to make a decision. He also turned out to be a good deal less intelligent than had first appeared. He might have made a moderately good major; as a general he was a disaster. His record speaks for itself: the eleven years of his pontificate saw the worst sack of Rome since the barbarian invasions, the establishment in Germany of Protestantism as a separate religion and the definitive breakaway of the English Church over Henry VIII's divorce.

~

In the winter of 1522–3 some interesting and intriguing news was brought to King Henry at Greenwich. It concerned Charles, 3rd Duke of Bourbon and Constable of France, a man as grand – and at the same time as proud and arrogant – even as the French nobility could produce. He had commanded the vanguard of the French army at Marignano, and had been rewarded by King Francis with the Governorship of Milan. Later he had carried the King's sword at the Field of the Cloth of Gold. But Francis, who was never entirely at ease with him, shortly afterwards relieved him of his military command, transferring it to his own brother-in-law the Duke of Alençon. For Bourbon this was quite bad enough, but worse was to come. The year 1521 had seen the death of his wife (and second cousin), Suzanne; she too had been born a Bourbon and had inherited from her father virtually all the immense family estates, which she had bequeathed in her will to her husband. We can therefore easily imagine his reaction when he heard that these estates were now being claimed by the King's mother, Louise of Savoy, on the grounds of 'proximity in blood' – her mother having been the daughter of the first Bourbon duke – and by Francis himself, who argued that they had escheated to the crown.

There was a further complication in that Suzanne had left no children; it was thus essential that the Duke should remarry, to preserve the safety of his line. Louise, who had loved him for years, proposed to settle the problem by herself becoming his second wife; but at forty-four she was fourteen years older than he was, and he not unreasonably turned her down. She, however, took her rejection as an insult, as did Francis; henceforth Valois–Bourbon relations could hardly have been worse. And so the Duke turned to Francis's enemies: to the Empire and to England. Secret negotiations were put in train. At the end of June the English ambassador to the Low Countries was instructed to put on heavy disguise, seek out Bourbon and offer him terms, and a week or two later a treaty was signed between Henry, Charles and Bourbon committing all three to a joint invasion of France.

The year was dangerously far advanced – most campaigns began at the first signs of spring – but the opportunity seemed too good to miss; and in August 1523, almost exactly a decade after Henry's first French adventure, the Duke of Suffolk led an army of ten thousand men across the Channel. His principal target was Boulogne, possession of which would greatly facilitate the much more ambitious campaign that was being planned for the following year; alas, his masters changed their minds. Some three weeks after his arrival at Calais, Wolsey – pointing out that 'there shall never be such or like opportunity given hereafter for the attaining of France' – proposed an immediate attack on Paris. King Henry at first objected: the year was too old, the problems of victualling a fast-moving army too great; Francis might swiftly recall his army from Italy, leaving the invaders to face a vastly superior force. But at last he allowed himself to be persuaded, and Suffolk duly ordered his men to march into the heart of France. By the end of October they were only some fifty miles from the capital. Then, suddenly, disaster struck on every side. Bourbon's projected march from Besançon collapsed almost as soon as it had started; Suffolk's Burgundian allies deserted him; an unseasonal cold snap wrought havoc throughout the army – particularly among the horses – and this was followed by a sudden thaw which turned everything to mud, making the heavy guns impossible to move. It was difficult enough even to pitch a tent. There was nothing for it but an ignominious retreat. Meanwhile Francis formally stripped Bourbon of all his offices and declared him a traitor – which indeed is exactly what he was.

King Henry, it need hardly be said, took the news of the disaster very badly indeed. At first he refused absolutely to accept it, demanding that his by now despairing army should return and continue the fight. Finally he accepted that nothing more could be done during the coming winter; but he insisted it was only a question of *reculer pour mieux sauter* ('step back for a better jump') and at once set about the preparations for a new campaign in the spring. Meanwhile he despatched an ambassador, Richard Pace, to conclude a new treaty with Bourbon, who received him warmly and swore an oath of allegiance to Henry. 'I promise you on my faith', he declared, 'that I will . . . put the crown of France upon the King our common master's head, or else my days shall be cut off.' He followed up with a magnificent advance through Provence to Marseille, but once again he failed to achieve anything permanent. Suddenly – we are not sure why – he abandoned the siege of Marseille and slipped over the border into Italy. Charles and Henry might have been forgiven for thinking that their glamorous new ally possessed feet of clay.

~

The Emperor Charles had concluded a secret treaty with Pope Leo X in 1521, which had committed the Pope fairly and squarely to the imperial side in its struggle with the King of France; and he naturally supposed that Leo's cousin Clement VII would respect it. Clement, however, did nothing of the kind. Instead, he tried to make peace between the two parties – an attempt that failed utterly, just as everyone had told him it would; Charles would yield Milan only in return for Burgundy. Francis, meanwhile, was as determined as ever to launch a new Italian campaign – on which, in the absence of any clear papal opposition, the way was now clear for him to go ahead; and in the summer of 1524, with an army of some twenty thousand, he marched back over the Mont Cenis pass into Italy. In late October 1524 he recaptured Milan.

He then turned south to Pavia. This city proved a tougher nut to crack than he had expected; its garrison of six thousand Germans and Spaniards made it clear at the start that they proposed to give as good as they got. At one moment he even tried to divert the Ticino river, which washes the walls on the southern side; but his dam was swept away by torrential rains. His most sensible course would have been to retire to Milan for the winter, but no: never, he somewhat absurdly claimed, had a French king besieged a city or town without taking it. He would maintain the siege until the defenders starved – which, however, they seemed in no hurry to do. He and his men suffered an extremely cold and uncomfortable winter as a result, and they were still there in late February, when an imperial army appeared on the horizon, led not – as might have been expected – by an Austrian or a Spaniard, but by his former friend and now his arch-enemy, Charles, Duke of Bourbon.

The two armies met in the great hunting preserve of Mirabello Castle, just outside the walls of Pavia; and on the morning of Tuesday, 24 February 1525 – it happened to be the Emperor's twenty-fifth birthday – battle was joined. The ensuing engagement proved to be one of the most decisive in European history. It was also, perhaps, the first to prove conclusively the superiority of firearms over pikes. The Swiss pikemen, who were this time fighting for Francis, struggled valiantly; but their weapons, fearsome as they were, were no match for Spanish bullets. When the fighting was over, the French army had been virtually annihilated; some fourteen thousand soldiers – French and Swiss, German and Spanish – lay dead on the field. Francis himself had shown, as always, exemplary courage; after his horse had been killed under him, he had continued to fight on foot until at last, overcome by exhaustion, he had allowed himself to be captured. 'All is lost', he wrote to his mother, 'save honour, and my skin.'* Having sustained nothing more than a bruised leg and a scratched hand and cheek, he was indeed lucky to be alive; the best estimates suggest that of the fourteen-hundred-odd French men-at-arms on the field, not more than four hundred survived.

Francis was taken first to the castle of Pizzighettone on the Adda river, where he remained for some three months. The news of his capture was received by his fellow-monarchs in widely differing ways. Charles, we are told, to whom the news was brought on 10 March in Madrid, ordered services of thanksgiving and then withdrew to pray alone. He also sent instructions to the Viceroy of Naples to take good care of his prisoner and to send regular reports to the King's mother. Henry, on the other hand – to whom the news was delivered on the previous day – leaped from his bed, pulled on some clothes, gave a shout of joy and then fell on his knees to give his own thanks. 'All the enemies of England', he declared, 'are now gone.' He then called

---

* The King's capture was largely due to a brilliantly executed attack by the Spanish general Fernando Francisco Avalos, Marquis of Pescara. We should have heard much more of him had he not died that December – his death having been caused, according to the contemporary historian Paolo Giovio, by his reckless habit of drinking water.

for wine and invited the messenger – whom he had improbably compared to the Archangel Gabriel at the Annunciation – to celebrate with him. Beacons blazed over England, and Wolsey sang a special celebratory High Mass in St Paul's.

But celebration was not enough. Now was the time for what Henry called the Great Enterprise – for Charles and himself, assisted by the Duke of Bourbon, to invade France and partition it between them; not a moment was to be lost. An embassy was immediately sent to Spain to plan the details. Francis's capture was divine punishment 'for his high orgule', his pride and his insatiable ambition. There must be no question, Henry suggested, of the King's ransom or restoration, even to a reduced kingdom; 'rather let his whole line and succession be abolished, removed and utterly extinct'. The two allied forces must now march on Paris, where Henry would be crowned King of France 'by just title of inheritance'. He and Charles would then march together to Italy, where he would assist Charles in the recovery of his rights and even witness his final coronation in Rome.

Alas, he was in for a serious disappointment. Charles, desperately short of money, was in no mood to redraw the map of Europe. Henry's ambassadors who returned to England with Charles's reply were not inclined to mince matters. The Emperor, they reported, intended 'little or nothing . . . to your commodity, profit or benefit'. And there was worse to come. In April there arrived in London a special ambassador from the Emperor, the Knight Commander Peñalosa, to say that unless the Princess Mary could be sent at once to Spain, with a substantial part of her dowry in ready money, his master must ask the King to release him from the engagement so that he would be free to marry another cousin, King Manuel I of Portugal's daughter Isabella. (He doubtless refrained from adding that Isabella would be bringing with her 900,000 golden ducats in cash.) He was keen to marry sooner rather than later, since he was anxious to return to northern Europe and wanted to leave an Empress ruling in Spain.

For Henry, this was betrayal. He had been genuinely fond of Charles, had helped him, advised him, lent him money. He and Catherine had looked forward to the day when he would be not only their nephew but their son-in-law as well. Now there was nothing he could do but reply that he expected the immediate repayment of all the Emperor's debts to him, and that he considered all treaties between them to be null and void. Wolsey meanwhile was instructed to conclude, as a matter of urgency, a separate peace with France.

It may have been part of his anger and frustration that induced Henry to turn on his wife. The two of them had now been married sixteen years. Their first passion – if passion it had been – had long since burned itself out, and Catherine's continued failure to produce a son had not improved their relationship. Henry's son by her lady-in-waiting Bessie Blount, little Henry Fitzroy, had meanwhile attained the age of six, and – perhaps because he saw him as a possible future monarch – his father decided to bring him into the public eye. On 18 June 1525 the boy was brought down the river to Henry's recently built Bridewell Palace at Blackfriars. There, in the presence of the entire court and much of the nobility of England, he was first knighted, then granted a peerage; finally he rose from his knees to be acclaimed Duke of Richmond and Somerset. By evening he was also Lord Admiral of England, Wales and Ireland, of Normandy, Gascony and Aquitaine, Knight of the Garter, Keeper of the City and Castle of Carlisle and prime peer of England. It was the first time since the twelfth century that a king of England had ennobled a bastard son.*

The feelings of Catherine, who had been obliged to witness

---

* The first occasion had been in 1188, when Henry II made his son William Longespée Earl of Salisbury.

all these successive ceremonies, may well be imagined. Here was a deliberate insult, both to herself and to her daughter, and one that she did not propose to take lying down. She protested to her husband, to Wolsey, to all with whom she came in contact; but her protests were ignored. Soon afterwards, without any advance consultation, Wolsey summarily dismissed several of her waiting-women on the grounds that they had encouraged her outburst. And even that was not all. Henry now ordered his daughter, the little Princess Mary now nine years old, to take up residence in the castle of Ludlow – 150 miles from London, a good week's journey – there to assume her responsibilities as Princess of Wales. Her mother, who had brought her up, educated her and had seldom left her side, was expressly forbidden to accompany her.

There was one single crumb of comfort. Mary was still Princess of Wales. Where the succession was concerned, Henry's mind was clearly still not made up.

~

Francis remained at Pizzighettone till May. After that he had been destined for a prison in Naples, but the prospect was so unpleasant that he begged the imperial viceroy, Charles de Lannoy, to send him instead to Spain. Lannoy agreed, and so it was to Spain that the captive King sailed from Genoa on the 31st. He arrived in Barcelona to find a letter from the Emperor – whom, surprisingly, Lannoy had not bothered to inform of his decision; Charles was in Madrid and had first learned of it only by chance. He showed, however, no sign of anger, being content to welcome the King to Spain and to express the hope that peace would be the result.

Thenceforward, from the very moment of his arrival until he reached Madrid, Francis found himself treated like the king he was. In Barcelona he attended Mass at the cathedral and even touched for the king's evil. At Valencia he was so mobbed by the populace that the Spanish captain responsible for his safety, Fernando de Alarçon, had to remove him to a comfortable villa outside the town. The last stage of his journey to Madrid was more than ever like a royal progress. There were banquets; there were bullfights; there were visits to hospitals and universities. But a bitter disappointment awaited him in Madrid: on his arrival in the capital on 11 August he was given lodging in the tower of the Alcázar, standing on the site of the present royal palace.* The Duc de Saint-Simon, who visited it two centuries later, describes it in his *Mémoires*:

> The room was not big, and had only one door, through which one entered. It was made a little larger by an embrasure on the right as one came in, facing the window. The latter was wide enough to give some daylight, it was glazed and could be opened, but it had a double iron grill, strong and stiff, which was welded into the wall . . . There was enough room for chairs, coffers, a few tables and a bed.

From the window, the duke added, there was a drop of more than a hundred feet, and the tower was guarded day and night by two companies of troops. Here Francis, having made one unsuccessful attempt to escape disguised as a black servant, was made to wait, his only exercise the occasional mule ride under heavy escort, while preparations were begun for the peace talks – which could clearly not be very long delayed.

The decisiveness of the Emperor's victory had sent a tremor through the entire Italian peninsula, where peace – even comparative peace – depended on the balance of power; but Italy was not Charles's main anxiety. The fact was that, for all their mutual

---

* It was destroyed by fire in 1734.

hostility, he *needed* Francis. However insuperable their differences, the two must combine their forces, not only against Martin Luther but now also against Suleiman. Where, Charles was wondering, would the dread Sultan strike next? There was no doubt that he would continue his advance against the forces of Christendom; how could he be halted except by a concerted Crusade, led by Charles himself and backed by all the Christian powers? But how, in the prevailing circumstances, could Francis be persuaded to lend his support to such an effort? How, in short, was such a Crusade to be launched while Europe was so bitterly and brutally divided against itself?

The peace talks – which were attended, on the French side, by both Francis's mother, Louise of Savoy, now Regent, and by his sister Margaret of Alençon – began in Toledo in July 1525 unpromisingly enough, with Burgundy remaining as always the principal bone of contention. They were still dragging on by 11 September – on which day, however, Francis suddenly fell ill: so ill indeed that his life was despaired of. For twenty-three days he lay inert and, for most of the time, unconscious; the Emperor, who till now had shown no desire to meet his fellow-monarch, came hurrying to his bedside; it was their first meeting. According to the doctors, the root of the trouble was 'an abscess in the head', but sixteenth-century diagnoses were far from reliable and we shall never know. In any event the King suddenly began to recover, and as soon as he was well enough he was moved to the capital, where the negotiations continued until he declared himself ready to agree to the proposed treaty.

The first thing to be said about the Treaty of Madrid, which a convalescent Francis signed on 14 January 1526, was that he had not the faintest intention of observing it – despite the fact that he was prepared to leave his two sons as hostages for his good behaviour. He had even taken the precaution of signing another, secret declaration, nullifying the surrender of Burgundy as having been extracted from him by force. How otherwise could he so readily have renounced all his long-held claims, not only to Burgundy but also to Naples and even to Milan?* He was still far from well: on Sunday, 29 January he had to be carried to church on a litter. But he returned riding on a mule, and the next day he was well enough to attend a luncheon given in his honour. Afterwards, we are told, he visited a convent where he touched thirty scrofulous nuns.

On 13 February Charles V joined him in Madrid. It had been arranged as part of the treaty that Francis should marry Charles's sister Eleanor, widow of King Manuel I of Portugal, and the Emperor now introduced the pair for the first time. She tried to kiss his hand, but he – not uncharacteristically – insisted, as her husband, on a proper kiss on the mouth. Next day she performed a Spanish dance for his benefit. The day after, the two sovereigns separated – Charles to Lisbon, there to marry his own Portuguese princess, King Manuel's daughter Isabella; Francis to return to Paris, whither it was arranged that his new bride should follow him in due course.

But there was one unhappy little ceremony to be completed before he did so. It occurred on the little River Bidasoa, which constituted – as it still does – part of the frontier between France and Spain. There was no bridge; it could be crossed only by boat. Early on the morning of 17 March 1526, two rowing boats made their way to a pontoon in mid-stream. One carried the King, the Viceroy of Naples and Alarçon; the other, two little boys, the eight-year-old Dauphin and his brother Henry, Duke of Orleans, aged seven. Both of them still recovering from serious attacks of measles, they were on their way to Spain for an indefinite period as hostages for their father's good behaviour. When the two boats reached the pontoon, they changed passengers,

---

* He also, incidentally, restored all the disputed lands to the Duke of Bourbon, 'on condition that we never see him again'; but the restoration never took place in the Duke's lifetime.

while a tearful Francis made the sign of the cross over his children and promised – with how much hope, one wonders – to send for them as soon as he could. The exchange completed, the boats then returned to their original moorings.

~

Henry VIII had welcomed the news of Francis's capture at Pavia; that of his capitulation in Madrid caused a very different reaction in London. Cardinal Wolsey simply could not believe what he was being told. Imagine if Charles should recover Burgundy while his sister Eleanor was Queen of France! And what was to happen if Charles and his brother Ferdinand died without legitimate issue? Their whole inheritance would devolve upon their sister and her husband, Francis. The future of Europe looked perilous indeed.

Francis on the other hand spent a delightful summer riding gently though his realm and arrived in Paris only in the autumn, by which time some of the initial indignation at the terms of the Treaty of Madrid had begun to die down – though the Estates of Burgundy were still vociferously protesting that the King had no right to alienate a province of the kingdom without the consent of its people. Francis replied, quite simply, that he had no intention of doing so. It was surely well known that promises extorted in prison had no binding force. He had no wish to antagonise Charles more than he had to; apart from anything else, he wanted to recover his sons. At the same time the balance of power had become seriously upset; the Emperor was once again too powerful, and it was plain that something must be done to cut him back to size.

As for Pope Clement, he was aghast: without a French presence anywhere in Italy, how could he hope to defend himself against imperial pressure? Hastily he recruited Milan, Venice and

Florence to form an anti-imperialist league for the defence of a free and independent Italy – and invited France to join. Though the ink was scarcely dry on the Treaty of Madrid, and though he and the Pope held widely differing views on Milan – the Pope favouring the Sforzas while Francis still wanted the city for himself – on 22 May 1526 the King, with his usual flourish, signed his name to what was to be called the League of Cognac. It meant, he knew, that it would be a long time – perhaps another three or four years, unless he could persuade Charles to accept a cash ransom – before he saw his sons again, but there: they would be well looked after. They would also learn Spanish and make a number of contacts which might be of considerable use to them in the future.

For Charles, this was, of course, nothing less than a betrayal. There could now be no question of a ransom, if indeed there ever had been. Francis's breach of faith had horrified him, and shocked him deeply: crowned heads simply could not behave so shamelessly. He had been planning to go to Italy for his coronation by the Pope; now that journey would clearly have to be indefinitely postponed. 'He is full of dumps', reported an English envoy, 'and solitary, musing sometimes alone three or four hours together. There is no mirth or comfort with him.' To the French ambassador he did not conceal his anger:

I will not deliver them [the two little princes] for money. I refused money for the father: still less will I take money for the sons. I am content to render them upon reasonable treaty, but not for money, nor will I trust any more the King's promise; for he has deceived me, and that like no noble prince. And where he excuses that he cannot fulfil some things without grudge of his subjects, let him fulfil that that is in his power, which he promised by the honour of a prince to fulfil; that is to say, that if he could not bring all his promise to pass he would return again hither into prison.

The League of Cognac – which King Henry warmly encouraged but was careful not to join – introduced an exciting new concept into Italian affairs. For perhaps the first time, here was an agreement dedicated to the proposition that Milan, and so by extension all the other Italian states, should be free of foreign domination. Liberty was the watchword. Clearly there could not yet be liberty for Italy as a whole, since Italy was still no more than a geographical expression; at the same time, it was clear to all the Italian signatories of the League that the only hope of resistance to the power of Charles V (or Francis I, come to that) lay in a settlement of their own internal differences, a pooling of their resources and the presentation of a firmly united front to any would-be invader. The *Risorgimento* was still more than three centuries away; but here, perhaps, were the first glimmerings of the national sentiment that gave it birth.

Francis, however, still felt threatened. Charles and his brother Ferdinand seemed determined to control the whole of Europe, while his own kingdom was already surrounded by potentially hostile territory. If it were to survive unconquered, its best hope lay in finding a new ally in the east – and that could only be the Ottoman Sultan. The first French diplomatic mission to Suleiman set out early in 1525 – immediately after Pavia – on the orders of the Queen Mother, even before the King's return from captivity. The name of its leader has not come down to us; we do know, however, that he carried many precious gifts – too precious, as it happened, because he and his entire suite were set upon and killed *en route* by the Pasha of Bosnia, who seized all their treasures for himself. When Francis, now released, heard of the disaster, he seems to have accepted it philosophically. He immediately ordered another mission, this time led by John Frangipani, a Croatian nobleman in the French service who, if the Pasha remained in a murderous mood, would at least be able to remonstrate with him in his own language. In fact, Frangipani – who carried a letter from his master hidden in the sole of his boot – was to arrive in December safely

in Istanbul, where he received the warmest of welcomes. The penitent Pasha was summoned to the Sublime Porte and obliged to return all that he had stolen, while Suleiman readily agreed – though without making any definite promises – that he and his new French friends should spare no efforts to ensure that the Emperor should not become 'the ruler of the world'.

Frangipani also had a number of minor requests, all of which the Sultan instantly granted, except for a church in Jerusalem which had been converted into a mosque and which he declined to restore to its original purpose. The laws of Islam, it was politely explained, did not permit a mosque to change its function. But even this pill was carefully sugared:

> The places other than the mosque will remain in Christian hands. No one will molest those who remain there during our just reign. They will live in tranquillity under the wing of our protection . . . they may retain in complete security all the oratories and other buildings which they occupy at present, without anyone being permitted to oppress them or to torment them in any way.

By establishing such friendly relations with the Porte, Francis doubtless improved the lot of Christians in the east; but he never lost sight of his primary object – to enlist Ottoman help against Charles. His negotiations with the Sultan were by now common knowledge throughout Europe; as Thomas Cromwell once remarked, no Christian scruple would deter the King of France from bringing the Turk and the Devil into the heart of Christendom if this could help him recover Milan. Francis himself admitted as much:

> I cannot deny that I keenly desire the Turk powerful and ready for war, not for himself, because he is an infidel and we are Christians, but to undermine the Emperor's power, to force heavy expenses upon him and to reassure all other governments against so powerful an enemy.

To his enemies, 'the Most Christian King' had now become 'the Executioner of Christendom'. If, as was widely rumoured, the Turks were planning another campaign along the Danube, the French were sure to be behind it. Francis thus found himself on a tightrope. He was obliged to convince Europe of his utter loyalty to the Christian cause; at the same time it was vital to keep the Sultan reassured, and to persuade him that such public statements as he was obliged to make from time to time were of no real significance. He was aware too that he needed Suleiman far more than Suleiman needed him; without the Sultan's help, what chance had he of resisting the immense power of the Empire, which hemmed him in both to the east and to the west? And how else, finally, could he ever achieve the old Valois dream of ruling Italy?

~

Frangipani's mission was a success as far as it went; but by then Suleiman had other things on his mind. For one thing, he had unfinished business in Hungary; the time had now come to return to the charge. And so it was that, on Monday, 21 April 1526, he and Ibrahim Pasha – by now his Grand Vizier – led another huge army out of Istanbul's Adrianople Gate and headed west. Their route was familiar enough, passing once again through Sofia and Belgrade, and thence along the Danube to Buda. The weather was dreadful; Suleiman was unlucky with it all his life. The rivers were swollen, many bridges had been swept away and the roads, such as they were, consisted for the most part of thick, deep mud which made the cannon almost impossible to move. Yet somehow the army managed to advance, with the Sultan always maintaining the iron discipline for which he was famous: soldiers who trampled on sown fields or failed to respect the townspeople and villagers as they passed were executed on the spot. When they reached the town of Osijek, they were obliged to build a bridge over the Drava river; 332 metres long, it was completed in five days. The moment the last soldier had crossed it, it was destroyed: retreat was never an option. At last they reached the Mohács plain, some fifteen miles from the confluence of the Drava and the Danube, where King Louis – the Emperor's brother-in-law – was waiting for them.

For Louis, the situation was grave indeed. His country was deeply divided, many of the peasants living in such misery that they were prepared to welcome the Turks as liberators. Meanwhile an ambitious nobleman named John Zápolya had his eye on the crown, and most of his fellow-boyars had no interest at all in strengthening the King's position, or that of the Habsburgs. The Germans indeed they detested to the point where they demanded their expulsion, at the very time when the country needed all the help it could get. Louis had done his utmost to find support elsewhere in Europe: 'If assistance from Your Majesty does not arrive soon,' he wrote to Henry in England, 'my kingdom is lost'; Henry, it need hardly be said, did not lift a finger. Charles V was equally disobliging: he was in Spain anyway, and had other problems on his mind. In any case, matters such as this were the responsibility of his brother – why else had he split the Empire? In his desperation Louis had even begged the Shah of Persia to create a diversion in the east, but had received no reply. As a last resort he had appealed to the Diet of German Princes, but they made any help conditional on the calling of a general council to settle their religious problems. After long discussions and in return for a promise that such a council would indeed be held in eighteen months' time, they agreed to send twenty-four thousand men; but by then it was too late; the Battle of Mohács had been fought – and lost.

On the Hungarian side, Mohács provided the perfect illustration of how not to fight a battle. To begin with, none of Louis's boyars heeded his call to the colours. He had summoned them to assemble on 2 July, but on the appointed day not one of them showed up. Nor, incidentally, did Louis himself; it was only after his arrival a day or two later that the army began to form. Those members of the nobility who were prepared to fight at all pressed the King to engage the enemy at once, without even waiting for the armies of John Zápolya or the Croatian Count Christoph Frankopan – perhaps another thirty to forty thousand men in all – which were only a few days' march away. The supreme command had for some reason been given to a Roman Catholic monk, Archbishop Pál Tomori of Kalocsa, whose astonishing over-confidence was probably due to his blind belief in the Hungarian cavalry, of which both horses and riders were so completely encased in armour that they were practically unable to move when their lightly armed Turkish counterparts slipped in and out and methodically destroyed them. The archbishop had forgotten too – if indeed he had ever understood – the power of the Turkish artillery with its huge cannon, firing cannonballs of iron that exploded on impact.

The battle began at around two o'clock in the afternoon, and probably ended at around six. During much of that time it was pelting with rain. Both sides fought with conspicuous bravery and the Sultan, always in the thick of the fray, narrowly escaped with his life. Several of his bodyguards were killed, and he himself survived only when a body of his own janissaries surrounded him and hamstrung the horses of his assailants. And few were braver than the Archbishop. In the unimprovable words of Kemalpashazade, a Turkish historian:

Like cast iron, the more the battle struck him, the more he steeped himself in it and drew strength from it. Like a viper or an elephant, he held his own against the claws of combat or the stones cast in battle. Covered with wounds, like a mad dog he recovered himself. When he rushed into the attack, impetuous as the Nile, he uttered screams like the trumpeting of elephants when tigers and lions flee before them.

Unable or unwilling to follow their leader's example, most of his compatriots fled for their lives. King Louis left the field as dark was falling, but was thrown from his horse while crossing a river. The weight of his armour did the rest. Among the fifteen thousand who died with him were most of the Hungarian nobility. Until midnight, we are told, the Turkish fanfares rang out in honour of the victory. The next morning Suleiman, seated on a golden throne in a scarlet tent, received congratulations and distributed rewards; before him was a pyramid of two thousand human heads, including those of seven Hungarian bishops. Summoning his Grand Vizier to his side, he personally pinned to his turban a heron's feather decorated with diamonds, 'whose shadow covered him like the wing of Felicity'.

The Battle of Mohács effectively put an end to Hungary as a single independent state for generations to come. All western Europe was horrified, but also conscious of its collective failure, a repetition of that which had lost Constantinople seventy-three years before: despite increasingly desperate appeals from King Louis, no one had come to his aid. The country never entirely recovered, and its most memorable defeat entered its folklore. An old Hungarian song tells of a series of domestic disasters; after each comes the chorus: *Több is veszett Mohácsnál* – 'but no matter; more was lost on Mohács field'. In modern Hungarian the line has become a proverb.

~

It was a few months before Mohács, in March 1526, that the Emperor Charles – all thoughts of his English princess forgotten – married his first cousin Isabella, daughter of King Manuel I of Portugal, in the Alcázar in Seville. She had been named after her maternal grandmother, Queen Isabella of Castile. It had started as a purely political union – Charles simply needed a member of his dynasty to govern Spain, Castile and Aragon during his long absences, and the couple had never seen each other before they met to be married – but it turned rapidly into a love match. An eyewitness noted that during what passed for their honeymoon 'when they are together, although there are many people around, they do not notice anyone else; they talk and laugh, and nothing else distracts them'. On 21 May 1527 Isabella gave birth to a son, the future Philip II, which her husband celebrated as a Spaniard should, with a *corrida*. We are told that he himself stepped forward as matador, killing the bull by his own hand.

Two more of Isabella's children, Maria and Juana, grew to adulthood. She herself remained all her life in Spain, spending with her husband little more than half their thirteen years of marriage; but the Emperor, despite his long absences, loved her dearly and seems to have remained faithful to her until her death. That death, however, was to come all too soon. The lovely Empress died, after her sixth pregnancy, in 1536 at the age of only thirty-three, and it broke her husband's heart. He never remarried, and was to dress in black for the rest of his life.

~

On 30 August 1525 King Henry VIII had signed a treaty of peace with France. He had done so much against his will. He would greatly have preferred to take advantage of the French King's captivity to invade the country and conquer what he could, had he only been able to do so; but it was not only Charles's lack of enthusiasm that had prevented him. There was also a problem of finance. The cost of such an operation had been estimated at £800,000 – and Parliament had put its foot down. The King's earlier adventures in France had not been particularly profitable; it had no intention of financing any more of them. Cardinal Wolsey had therefore tried an alternative with what he called an 'Amicable Grant' – in fact, a levy of one-third of the goods of the clergy and between one-sixth and one-tenth of those of the laity. The result had been far from amicable; there were furious demonstrations up and down the country, and in many places an outright refusal to contribute. At Lavenham in Suffolk, ten thousand men planned to converge in active protest; it was said that they failed only because the clappers had been removed from the church bells that were to signal the start of the uprising.

Wolsey was on shaky ground, and he knew it. With no parliamentary authority for his scheme, he had no course but to abandon the idea – a humiliating climb-down which may well have indirectly contributed to his fall four years later, since it was the first occasion on which he had significantly failed to do his master's will. It was at this point, in an attempt to strengthen his position, that he made the King a present of Hampton Court – though from all that we know of Henry we can be sure that, however grateful he may have been, the frustration of his French ambitions would have continued to rankle. For the moment, however, peace it would have to be; and in April 1527, with Francis back again in Paris after his captivity and the situation looking very different from what it had been two years before, that peace was converted into an alliance, which was ratified when Wolsey met Francis at Amiens the following August. Soon afterwards, England and France declared war on the Empire; but Charles had too much else on his plate and seems to have taken little notice.

Henry too had other preoccupations. He had come to the conclusion that he must leave his wife. He dreaded breaking the news to her, and put the evil day off as long as he could; but one day in the high summer of 1527 he sought out Catherine in her closet. He had been advised, he told her, that their marriage was invalid: for the past eighteen years they had been living in sin. The book of Leviticus (xx, 21) made it all too clear: 'And if a man shall take his brother's wife, it is an unclean thing. He hath uncovered his brother's nakedness; they shall be childless.'* He and Catherine had no choice but to separate at once, while he sought an official annulment from the Pope. Meanwhile, of course, he had every desire that she should continue to live in comfort; where, precisely, would she like to go?

For a long time Catherine stared at him in silence; then she burst into a flood of tears. They were tears, however, not of sorrow but of anger: anger that she should be condemned as an adulteress, anger that her daughter was being declared a bastard, but anger too at the ridiculous excuse she had been given for the proposed separation. As yet she knew nothing of Anne Boleyn; taking her husband's words at their face value, she herself had no doubts that her marriage to him had been legitimate. It was the first ceremony, to young Prince Arthur, which had been null and void, simply because it had never been consummated. She had come to Henry a virgin, as he could himself have attested, had he been willing to do so; she had married him – and indeed been crowned with him – in the presence of the greatest and most learned churchmen of both England and Spain, and for the past eighteen years no one had voiced any doubts. If he had simply been honest with her, telling her that he had fears for the succession and felt that he must remarry to engender a son, she would at least have understood, even though her answer

---

* The King was less inclined to quote Deuteronomy xxv, 5: 'Her husband's brother shall go in unto her, and take her to him to wife . . .'

might have been the same. So far as she was concerned, she was
the legal wife of her husband and the rightful Queen of England,
and would continue so to be until she died. As to where she
would like to go, she had every intention of remaining where
she was; if she was obliged to move, she would choose to go to
the Tower; then at least the people of England would know what
had become of her, and would offer up their prayers on her
behalf. In any case there could be no question of an annulment.
As she wrote to her nephew the Emperor:

> For the present Pope to undo what his predecessors have done
> would reflect on his honour and conscience, and bring grave
> discredit to the Apostolic See, which should stand firmly on the
> Rock which is Christ. Were the Pope to waver now, in this case,
> many might be led astray into thinking that right and justice are
> not with him.

Catherine of Aragon was a woman of steel. She might bend to
her husband, as far as her sense of duty required; but she would
never break.

~

The League of Cognac had failed catastrophically to drive the
imperialists out of Italy, but Charles had been unable to pay the
soldiers who had fought so successfully against it. The result was
that some thirty-four thousand deeply discontented men went
on the rampage, out to plunder the richest city they could find
– and that city was Rome. Early in 1527 the army under the
command of the Duke of Bourbon – who had had little choice
in the matter – advanced on the Papal States. Despite his treachery
to his King, Bourbon remained a charismatic figure, universally

admired for his courage. He never shirked an engagement and
could always be found where the fighting was thickest; he was
also immediately distinguishable by the silver and white surcoat
that he always wore and by his black, white and yellow standard
emblazoned with the word *Espérance*. Ignoring the several important towns along his route, he led the army directly to Rome,
drawing it up on the Janiculum hill, immediately to the north
of the city wall; and at four o'clock in the morning of 6 May
1527 the attack began.

In the absence of heavy artillery, Bourbon had decided that
the walls would have to be scaled – a technique far more difficult and dangerous than that of simply pounding them till they
crumbled. He himself was one of the first of the casualties; he
was actually positioning a scaling-ladder against the wall when
he was shot through the chest by an enemy arquebus – fired, if
we are to accept the man's own testimony, by Benvenuto Cellini
himself. Thirst for revenge spurred on his men, and soon after
six in the morning the imperial army, now commanded by
Philibert of Chalon, Prince of Orange, burst into the city. The
Romans rushed from the wall to barricade their homes, and
many of the papal troops joined the enemy to save their own
skins. Only the Pope's personal Swiss Guard fought heroically
on until it was slaughtered *en masse* on the steps of St Peter's.

As the invaders approached the Vatican, the Pope was hustled
out of his apartments and led along the Passetto di Borgo – the
covered way that still links the Vatican City to the Castel
Sant'Angelo – which was already thronged with panic-stricken
families seeking refuge. Such were the crowds that it was only
with the greatest difficulty that the portcullis could be lowered.
One cardinal had to be pushed in through a window; another
was pulled up in a basket. Outside, in the Borgo and Trastevere,
despite specific orders by their commanders, the imperial army
– hungry and unpaid – embarked on an orgy of killing. Cardinal
Giovanni Maria Ciocchi del Monte, the future Pope Julius III,

was hung up by his hair. Almost all the patients in the Hospital of Santo Spirito were massacred; of the orphans of the Pietà, not one was left alive.

Just before midnight the invaders crossed the Tiber. The sack that followed has been described as 'one of the most horrible in recorded history'. The bloodbath continued unabated; to venture out into the street was to invite almost certain death, and to remain indoors was very little safer: scarcely a single church, palace or house of any size escaped pillage and devastation. Monasteries were plundered and convents violated, the more attractive nuns being offered for sale in the streets. The Vatican Library was saved only because Philibert had established his headquarters there. At least two of the cardinals who had failed to escape to the Castel Sant'Angelo were dragged through the city and tortured; one of them, who was well over eighty, subsequently died from his injuries. 'Hell', reported a Venetian eyewitness, 'has nothing to compare with the present state of Rome.'

Not till 10 May, with the arrival of Cardinal Pompeo Colonna – a sworn enemy of Pope Clement – and his two brothers with eight thousand of their men, was a semblance of order restored. By this time virtually every street in the city had been gutted and was strewn with corpses. One captured Spanish sapper later reported that on the north bank of the Tiber alone he and his companions had buried nearly ten thousand and had thrown another two thousand into the river. Six months later, thanks to widespread starvation and an epidemic of plague – due probably to the thousands of bodies lying unburied during the hottest season of the year – the population of Rome had been reduced to less than half of what it had been before the siege. Culturally, too, the loss was incalculable. Paintings, sculptures and libraries were ravaged and destroyed, the pontifical archives ransacked. The painter Parmigianino was imprisoned, saving his life only by making drawings of his jailers. And Pope Clement remained in the Castel Sant'Angelo, a prisoner of the imperialists.* Far away in Spain the Emperor had no idea of what had happened in his name until it was over. He was naturally appalled, but there was nothing he could do.

It was now that Wolsey saw his opportunity. By this time his thoughts, like Henry's, were dominated by what was always referred to as 'the King's great matter'. He knew that Clement was unlikely – to put it mildly – to confirm the annulment of the Queen's marriage while he was effectively the prisoner of her favourite nephew; consequently, if such confirmation were ever to be granted, it would have to be while the Pope was still in the Castel Sant'Angelo. On 22 July he took ship for France. His plan was ambitious, to say the least. He would meet a group of favourably minded cardinals in Avignon, take advantage of the Pope's incarceration to seize control of the Church administration and then rush through an official approval to the King's annulment and remarriage. He even drew up a commission, to be signed by Clement, granting to himself absolute power 'even to relax, limit or moderate divine law'. But Clement, though still in captivity, was apparently able to retain at least a degree of control; sensing danger, he had forbidden any of his cardinals to move from the Vatican. Wolsey heard the news before he had got further than Compiègne; but the frustration he doubtless felt can have been as nothing to his alarm when he found one of the King's secretaries, William Knight, on his way to Rome, with a letter from Henry to the Pope. This sought nothing less than a dispensation for the King to marry again even if his marriage to Catherine were not annulled – a licence, in fact for

---

* It was during his half-year's captivity that Clement grew a bushy black beard, as a sign of mourning for the sack of Rome. Heretofore Catholic canon law had required priests to be clean-shaven, but Clement's example was followed by his successor Paul III and by the twenty-four popes who followed him – right down to Innocent XII, who died in 1700.

bigamy. It was a foolish enough request, but for the cardinal it carried a yet more sinister message: it had been sent without his knowledge or approval. Henry, it seemed, was taking policy into his own hands.

Wolsey managed to stop the letter; but a day or two later it was followed by another, with a further proposal: if his first marriage were annulled, the King requested that he be permitted to marry any woman, even if she were related to him in the first degree of affinity, even one whose affinity sprang from illicit intercourse and even one with whom he himself had had intercourse already. It was in many ways a remarkable document, strongly implying, as it did, the King's intention to marry Anne Boleyn and implicitly confessing his affair with her sister. It had, of course, no effect, but it struck further terror in Wolsey's heart. Even in matters of the greatest moment Henry was no longer taking his advice. His fears grew even greater when, hurrying back to London, he found the King closeted with Anne; now, for the first time, he found himself debarred from his sovereign, who refused absolutely to receive him until his mistress allowed him permission to do so.

～

Peace between France and the Empire, when it was finally concluded, was the result of negotiations begun during the winter of 1528–9 between Francis's mother, Louise of Savoy, and her sister-in-law (and the Emperor's aunt) Margaret of Austria. The two met at Cambrai on 5 July 1529, and the resulting treaty was signed in the first week of August. The Ladies' Peace, as it came to be called, was a surprisingly long and complicated document, but it confirmed imperial rule in Italy. Francis renounced all his claims to Milan, Genoa and Naples, for which he and his predecessors had fought so hard for the best part of forty years. Charles for his part ransomed the King's sons after all – though demanding no less than a million ducats* – and promised not to press his claims to Burgundy, Provence and Languedoc. For Francis himself, and for his allies in the League of Cognac who had not been consulted during the negotiations and felt that he had betrayed them, it was a sad and shameful settlement. But at least it brought peace to Italy and put an end to that long and unedifying chapter in her history, a chapter that had brought the Italians nothing but devastation and destruction.

The imperial army had suffered almost as much as the Romans. It too was virtually without food; its soldiers – unpaid for months – were totally demoralised, interested only in loot and pillage. Discipline had broken down: Germans and Spaniards were at each others' throats. Pope Clement, however, had no course open to him but once again to capitulate. The official price he paid was the cities of Ostia, Civitavecchia, Piacenza and Modena, together with 400,000 ducats – a sum that could be raised only by melting down all the papal tiaras and selling the jewels with which they were encrusted. The Papal States, in which an efficient government had been developing for the first time in history, had crumbled away. Clement himself had escaped from the Castel Sant'Angelo in early December 1527. Rome was still uninhabitable, so the unhappy Pope, disguised as a poor pedlar, struggled off with a few cardinals to Orvieto, where he settled as best he could in the draughty, dilapidated and bitterly cold palace of the local bishop. It was there that he received ambassadors from King Henry. One of them reported:

> The Pope lieth in an old palace of the bishops of the city, ruinous and decayed; as we came to his privy chamber we passed three chambers, all naked and unhanged, the roofs fallen down and,

---

* They finally returned on 1 July 1530.

as one can guess, 30 persons – riffraff and others – standing in the chambers for a garnishment. And as for the Pope's bedchamber, all the apparel in it was not worth twenty nobles . . . It were better to be in captivity in Rome than here at liberty.

Here was an opportunity to repair at least some of the papal finances. Clement had but to agree to the King of England's annulment; Henry would be only too happy to pay liberally for it. But still the Pope havered. Decisions were always difficult for him, but this one was harder than most because, quite apart from political considerations, he was afraid – afraid of the Emperor and his loathsome *Landsknechte*, who had already wrought havoc once in the Holy City and would be only too pleased, if given the opportunity, to repeat the process. Finally the English ambassadors produced a draft that went nowhere near far enough, but they felt was the most that the Pope might possibly accept; the cardinals fell on it 'as though there were a scorpion under every word'. The resulting document, still further emasculated, was sealed on 13 April 1528. The ambassadors warned Clement that there was no chance of their master accepting it, but the Pope replied that even this was a declaration against the Emperor, for which he fully expected to be punished.

Charles, by contrast, found himself in an unusually strong position – strong enough to demand his imperial coronation. This was no longer the indispensable ceremony that it had been in former centuries; his grandfather Maximilian had ignored it altogether. He himself, since his first coronation at Aachen, had been nearly ten years on the throne, deprived throughout that time of this final confirmation of his authority. The fact remained, nevertheless, that until the Pope had anointed him and laid the crown on his head, he was not technically Holy Roman Emperor; to one possessing so all-pervading a sense of divine mission, both title and sacrament were important.

Imperial coronations were traditionally performed in Rome.

On landing at Genoa in mid-August 1529, however, the Emperor received alarming news. Sultan Suleiman, at the head of a large army, was steadily advancing on Vienna. It was clear that in such circumstances a projected journey so far down the Italian peninsula would be folly; it would take far too long, as well as leaving him dangerously cut off in the event of a crisis. Messengers sped to Pope Clement, who agreed that in the circumstances the ceremony might be held in Bologna, a firmly papal city that remained considerably more accessible. Even then the uncertainty was not over: while on his way to Bologna in September, Charles received an urgent appeal for help from his brother Ferdinand in Vienna, and came near to cancelling his coronation plans there and then. Only after long consideration did he decide not to do so. There was no point: by the time he reached Vienna, the city would have fallen or the Sultan would have retired for the winter. In either case the small force that he had with him in Italy would have been insufficient to tip the scales.

And so, on 5 November 1529, Charles V made his formal entry into Bologna, where, on the steps of the great basilica of San Petronio, Pope Clement was waiting to receive him. There was much to be done, many outstanding problems to be discussed and resolved before the coronation could take place. It was, after all, only two years since papal Rome had been sacked by imperial troops, with Clement himself a virtual prisoner of Charles in the Castel Sant'Angelo; somehow, friendly relations had to be re-established. Only when peace had been restored throughout the peninsula would Charles feel justified in kneeling before the Pope to receive the imperial crown. Coronation Day was fixed for 24 February 1530; Emperor and Pope had given themselves a little under four months to settle the future of Italy.

It proved enough. Peace was signed. Clement's League of Cognac and Charles's sack of Rome were, if not forgotten, at least dismissed from mind; and on the day appointed, in San Petronio, Charles was first anointed and then received from the

Pope's hands the sword, orb, sceptre and finally the crown of the Holy Roman Empire. Something of a cloud was cast over the proceedings when a makeshift wooden bridge linking the church with the palace collapsed just as the Emperor's suite was passing across it; but, once it was established that the many casualties included no one of serious importance, spirits quickly revived, and celebrations continued long into the night.

It was the last time in history that a pope was to crown an emperor; on that day the seven-hundred-year-old tradition, which had begun in AD 800, when Pope Leo III had laid the imperial crown on the head of Charlemagne, was brought to an end. The Empire was by no means finished, but never again would it be received, even symbolically, from the hands of the Vicar of Christ on Earth.

~

Sultan Suleiman was riding high. After Mohács he had plundered Buda. He did not take possession of the city, but he destroyed the palace, which boasted a collection of Renaissance art as magnificent as anything in Italy, removing its superb library together with the collections of Matthias Corvinus, which were sent back to Istanbul. It was the first great victory of the Turks in the heartland of Latin Christendom. The question now was who was to rule in Hungary. King Louis had died without issue, and the way seemed clear for John Zápolya – who had been careful not to intervene at Mohács – to place himself under the Sultan's protection and to persuade Stephen Podmaniczky, the senior Hungarian bishop surviving after seven of his fellow-prelates had been killed in the battle – to crown him King. When, however, on 22 October 1526, Louis's brother-in-law the Archduke Ferdinand was elected, first as King of

Bohemia and then as King of Hungary, Podmaniczky decided that Zápolya's coronation had been unwise: on 17 December he crowned Ferdinand as well. The result was that there were now two kings of Hungary: one recognised by the Sultan, the other by the Emperor.

The desire to destroy Ferdinand – and thus to reunite all Hungary under his domination – may have been an additional reason for the Sultan's decision to attack Vienna in 1529, but he would probably have done so in any case as part of his grand plan for the conquest of eastern Europe. Vienna, Suleiman believed, was despite its importance surprisingly weakly defended and would soon be forced to submit. It lay only ninety miles from the Turkish frontier; the campaign promised to be relatively easy. Perhaps for this reason he seems to have been in no hurry, leaving Istanbul only in May and spending a fair time in Hungary, first for a formal meeting with John Zápolya and then for a successful attack on Buda, where the imperial troops surrendered within a week. As a result, the army took the road to Vienna far too late in the year, and was further seriously delayed – as always – by the atrocious weather that continued throughout the summer. The heavy artillery was often immobilised for days at a time, axle-deep in mud. Many of the several thousand camels intended to pull them simply gave up the struggle and died; in consequence, the heaviest and most powerful cannon never arrived at all. The army arrived outside the city walls only on 27 September. Vast numbers of men were too sick or exhausted to function at all, far less to fight; but the Sultan, nothing daunted, pitched his camp and settled down to a siege.

He was soon to find that the Viennese defences were a good deal stronger than he had thought. Within the city, the defenders – who had been aware for some time of the coming danger – had brought in various regiments of European mercenaries, including a regiment of Spanish musketeers and another of German *Landsknecht* pikemen. Ferdinand himself was not present: he had preferred to remain in Linz, where he could organise further help if necessary and keep in some degree of contact with his brother the Emperor. Overall command was therefore given to the seventy-year-old German mercenary Count Nicholas of Salm, who had distinguished himself with extraordinary courage at Pavia. He now blocked the four gates to the city, strengthened the walls where necessary and constructed a huge inner rampart. He was, in fact, encouraging the Sultan to do his worst.

As was normal in Turkish siege warfare, the sappers set to work at once, digging a network of tunnels under the fortifications and laying mines at strategic points; but the defenders detected and detonated the mines almost as soon as they were laid. On 6 October Salm despatched a force of eight hundred men, which effectively put an end to sappers and tunnels alike but was then followed by a disastrous attempt at a sortie; that evening, five hundred Christian heads were piled up in celebration. Despite these minor triumphs, however, it gradually became clear to the Turks that the siege, if it continued, was going to be long and hard. Rain continued to fall, the wind grew colder, the sick soldiers grew sicker still and ammunition and supplies were running short. Finally the janissaries – the Sultan's crack regiment, on which he relied above all others – began to voice their impatience. In the middle of the month, unseasonably but inexorably, the rain turned to snow and the cold increased. Suleiman assembled all his available forces for one last desperate assault; and when that failed, he had no alternative but to lead his army home.

In Vienna the church bells rang and great celebratory salvoes were fired as the Ottoman army disappeared over the horizon; but its troubles were not yet over. It faced a long and terrible march back to the Bosphorus. Most of the artillery and much of the baggage was lost or abandoned, food was short and many of the prisoners were to die on the journey. For the Sultan personally, the campaign had been a disaster. It was to mark not only the limit of his westward advance but also — although he was not to know it — the turning of the tide, and the beginning of the steady decline of the Ottoman Empire over the next four centuries.

4

'Enough, my son!'

IN ITS EARLY years, Henry's marriage to Catherine of Aragon had been happy enough. It is perhaps unlikely that he felt the passion that was unquestionably – if briefly – aroused by Anne Boleyn, but he loved her none the less and was proud of her – proud of her youthful beauty, proud above all of her formidable intelligence, which he recognised to be far greater than his own. She had accompanied him everywhere; in the jousts he had called himself 'Sir Loyal Heart' and had worn her initials on his sleeve. On his return from his first campaign in France he had ridden straight to her side and laid the keys of Thérouanne and Tournai at her feet. But by 1527 all that was long ago: he was still young and virile; she was five years older, putting on weight (though nowhere near as much as he was) and deeply – perhaps a little tiresomely – pious. We know of Bessie Blount and the Duke of Richmond; we know too of Mary Boleyn, Anne's sister, who was also rumoured to have produced a son – though if she did, he was never acknowledged; on Anne's accession she was unsurprisingly dismissed from the court. And then there was Anne herself.

'Madame Anne', wrote one of the Venetian emissaries, 'is not one of the handsomest women in the world. She is of middling stature, swarthy complexion, long neck, wide mouth, bosom not much raised, and in fact has nothing but the King's great appetite – and her eyes, which are black and beautiful.' There was also the curious rudimentary sixth finger on her left hand, which induced many pious men and women surreptitiously to cross themselves to ward off the evil eye. But Anne also possessed enough intelligence to see that, if she simply gave herself to Henry, she would go the way of her sister and Mistress Blount, and vanish into obscurity. Fortunately there was an alternative. It was common knowledge that Henry was determined to dispense with Catherine, by whom he had now given up all hope of begetting a son.* Divorce – or annulment – was in the air. Anne knew that if she played her cards with care, the throne might well be hers. She played them very well indeed – with a skill that she would all too soon have cause to regret – refusing all his entreaties and staying firmly clear of his bed.

She was lucky, too, to have survived the 'sweating-sickness' which swept through London in the summer of 1528 – bringing, as the French ambassador remarked, more business to the priests than to the doctors. She was desperately ill for several days; had she died, the history of England over the last six centuries would have been radically different. Henry made no attempt to visit her; he had gone off like a shot to Hunsdon in Hertfordshire, hearing three Masses a day, making daily confessions and begging her, somewhat tactlessly, not to return to the court too soon. He also wrote to Wolsey, who had retreated only as far as Hampton Court, passing on medical advice and urging him to take care of himself.

The cardinal must have been reassured by his master's solici-

---

* She had tried hard enough. Apart from several miscarriages, there were two boys and a girl who were either still-born or lived for just a few hours, and another boy and girl who died after a week or two. Only Mary survived into adulthood.

tude. His last year had been one of increasing anxiety and fear. His worries had begun in 1527, when he had returned from France and found his admission to the King's chamber blocked, henceforth dependent on the will of Anne. In the following year, conscious now that he had lost much of the King's confidence and affection, he was still more uncertain where he stood. He had, however, one more important task to perform: to co-preside, with Lorenzo Campeggio, Bishop of Salisbury,* over a 'legatine court' summoned by papal commission to meet in the Parliament Chamber of the former Dominican priory at Blackfriars, with orders to settle the annulment problem once and for all. The court opened on 18 June 1529, and on the 21st Henry and Catherine both gave evidence.†

It must have been an extraordinary spectacle. The King was fully enthroned under a canopy, the two judges – in full cardinalian fig – beneath him, and then, just a little lower, the Queen. At their feet were the Archbishop of Canterbury, William Warham, and a whole bench of bishops. No one had ever seen anything like it before: a reigning king and queen appearing in their own land before a court summoned by an outside authority. In earlier years Henry would never have considered such an appearance for a moment; but if it were now required to achieve the long-awaited annulment, then so be it. As far as he was concerned, nothing else mattered.

Catherine spoke first. She had already appeared briefly three days before the court opened, protesting that it was hostile to her, the judges prejudiced. (They were too: Wolsey had been her enemy for years.) Anyway, was not her case *sub judice* in Rome? If so, what precisely was this court doing? This time she struck a very different note:

---

* A Milanese, he had been sent to England by Leo X in 1518 and had remained there ever since.

† See Shakespeare's *Henry VIII*, Act II, scene iv.

Sir, I beseech you for all the love that hath been between us, let me have justice and right, take of me some pity and compassion . . .

I take God and all the world to witness that I have been to you a true, humble and obedient wife, ever comfortable to your will and pleasure . . . I loved all those whom ye loved, only for your sake, whether I had cause or no, and whether they were my friends or my enemies. This twenty years or more I have been your true wife, and by me ye have had divers children, though it hath pleased God to call them from this world . . .

And when ye had me at the first, I take God to be my judge, I was a true maid, without touch of man. And whether this be true or no I put to your conscience . . .

Therefore I humbly require you to spare me the extremity of this new court . . . And if ye will not, to God I commit my cause.

Whereupon, having made a deep reverence to the King, she left the hall. An usher tried to call her back, but she refused to listen. She had said what she needed to say. The court was hostile; she would have no more truck with it.

In her absence, Bishop John Fisher of Rochester fought like a tiger on her behalf. All was reported straight back to Rome, where Pope Clement, realising that his court could achieve nothing, was bitterly regretting having authorised it in the first place. On 13 July he decided to bring it to an end. But already by this time proceedings at Blackfriars were in a hopeless state of confusion; a fortnight later, Wolsey reported that the hearing had deteriorated into a quagmire of insignificant disputes, and at the end of the month it fizzled out altogether. It was many weeks later that the papal instructions arrived calling for its abrogation – and summoning Henry to Rome.

Henry had, of course, no intention of obeying the papal summons; but a full year went by without any developments, and by the summer of 1532 he was growing seriously impatient.

It was now five years since he had revealed his intentions to Catherine; yet there she remained, still at his side, still the wife she had always been. He was also desperately regretting his treatment of Wolsey. The final blow had fallen in the autumn of 1529, only a few weeks after the Blackfriars fiasco. Wolsey had been arrested, charged, found guilty and ordered to surrender the Great Seal. Later the King had released him, but had replaced him as Chancellor by Sir Thomas More.* Wolsey was effectively banished to Esher – Henry had already appropriated Hampton Court – where he and his household were without 'beds, sheets, table cloths, cups and dishes', and where he had to beg money from his chaplains in order to pay his servants their wages. At this time he was informed that the King had also taken over his Westminster residence, York Place, despite the fact that it was technically not his property but that of the Archbishopric of York. His only consolation was that he was still an archbishop; and in the spring of 1530 he rode off to the north – it was, in fact, the first time in his life that he had done so – intending presumably to spend his enforced retirement in his own diocese. Alas, there proved to be little retirement to spend. That autumn saw the issue of another warrant, this time on a charge of treason; the cardinal was said to have 'intrigued . . . both in and out of the Kingdom', and to have been guilty of 'presumptuous sinister practices made to the court of Rome for reducing [the King] to his former estates and dignity'. On 4 November he was arrested while at dinner. Despairingly, he started back to London to face trial and most probably execution; but these, fortunately,

* More had accepted the office only reluctantly. He was steadfast in the old Catholic faith, from which the King was rapidly departing; moreover he deeply disapproved of the divorce, though he was careful not to say so. After little more than two years he resigned and retired from public life. Henry had promised not to 'molest' him, but after he had refused to attend the royal wedding he was arrested, found guilty of high treason and sent to the Tower. He was beheaded on 6 July 1535.

he was spared. He had got no further than Leicester when he was taken ill. He died there in the Abbey, quietly, on 29 November. He was fifty-seven.

Wolsey's downfall is generally attributed to his failure to secure the annulment of his master's marriage, but there were other reasons too. His relations with Anne Boleyn had been no better than they had been with Catherine, and in her conversations with the King Anne had doubtless taken every opportunity to blacken his character, to question his loyalty and to plant doubts in Henry's heart. Did the cardinal really care so much about the divorce? Was he really straining every sinew to obtain it? Nor was Anne his only enemy: behind her was the aristocratic party at court, where the Dukes of Norfolk and Suffolk had always resented the pomp and ceremony with which Wolsey surrounded himself and the arrogance with which the son of an Ipswich tradesman rode roughshod over the highest in the land. In pursuing his career, Wolsey had taken little trouble not to attract hostility; and Henry, always inclined to believe the last thing that was said to him and with his judgement now still further clouded by his love for his betrothed, was himself curiously lacking in the loyalty that he demanded from everyone else.

Seen in this light, Wolsey's fall was inevitable; and yet for Henry, after the dust had settled, he was a grievous loss. Among his many other strengths, for example, the cardinal had always known – nobody better – how to manage the Curia; in an attempt to strengthen his support in Rome, Henry had tried to obtain a few red hats for his friends, but without Wolsey's help he had failed miserably. His agents had meanwhile combed the universities and monasteries of England and the Continent for scholars and theologians, Greek and Hebrew, Christian and Jew, who would be willing to certify that his marriage to Catherine must indeed be annulled; but their countless testimonies had cut no ice in Rome. On the contrary, they had simply encouraged

Catherine's champions to rally to her defence.*The matter indeed seemed to have reached a stalemate; and the King had already decided, if the negotiations were to fail completely, to take the law into his own hands.

~

Fortunately for him, there was a rising star in the political firmament who was rapidly taking over Wolsey's role. The son of a Putney blacksmith, Thomas Cromwell was of origins humbler even than those of the cardinal. We know relatively little about his early life, except that he had somehow received a modicum of legal training and that he had sat for some time in the House of Commons before joining Wolsey's household. Early in 1530, when he was already forty-four, he entered the royal service; three years later he was Henry's chief minister. Having lost his wife and two daughters in the 'sweating-sickness' epidemic, he had no family life, so far as we know remarkably few friends and – unlike his magnificent predecessor – no extravagances; he had thus some fourteen or fifteen hours a day to devote to his sovereign's interests. He was in power for only seven years, compared with Wolsey's fifteen, but his achievement was far greater than the cardinal's. It was he who was to handle the eventual split from Rome, the establishment of the Royal Supremacy, the dissolution of the monasteries and much else

* Bishop Fisher wrote at least seven books and preached several sermons on her behalf. He was sent to the Tower in 1534, but in May 1535 Paul III made him a cardinal in the hope of securing his release. Alas, the Pope's gesture had the contrary effect: Henry forbade the cardinal's hat to be brought to England, declaring that he would send its owner's head to Rome instead. Fisher was executed on Tower Hill on 22 June.

besides. An administrator of genius, he was also a superb publicist, the first in England to recognise and to make use of the immense power of the printing press, which William Caxton had introduced a couple of generations before.

Cromwell was thus already in a position of considerable power when, in 1532, Henry decided that he must have another meeting with Francis. He was fully aware that behind the Pope's constant shilly-shallying over the annulment of his marriage to Catherine was the fear of offending her nephew the Emperor. Was it not just possible that the two kings together might succeed in persuading His Holiness to put aside this fear in the interests of keeping England in the Catholic fold? The idea was surely worth pursuing. In June 1532 the English and French governments signed a secret alliance whereby it was agreed that Henry should cross the Channel the following October. Rather dashingly, he decided to take Anne – now Marquess of Pembroke in her own right* – with him.

But there was a second reason for the visit, one that would have particular appeal for Francis: the Emperor's questionable position with regard to the Protestant princes in Germany. In January 1531 Charles's brother Ferdinand had been elected King of the Romans, and consequently heir to the Empire. Such an election during the lifetime of the reigning Emperor was unprecedented and, it was argued, unconstitutional; and those princes who had adopted Martin Luther's teachings were understandably alarmed by the election of a Catholic. In consequence they had appealed to Francis for help – the King's own Catholicism was outweighed by the fact that he remained the Emperor's principal enemy – and at the end of February in the same year six Protestant princes and ten cities had formed a league in the town hall of Schmalkalden in Thuringia to protect their political and religious interests. Two years earlier, at Cambrai, Francis had

---

* And therefore not Marchioness.

undertaken not to involve himself in German affairs, but the temptation to reply to the princes' appeal had been irresistible: he and Henry now needed to discuss what policy to follow in order to cause the Emperor maximum inconvenience.

The third reason Henry took some care not to mention. Francis fascinated him. It was, almost certainly, a fascination tinged with more than a little jealousy. His mind often returned to the Field of the Cloth of Gold, thirteen years before, when he had first been captivated by his fellow-monarch; since then he had never lost an opportunity of enquiring about him – his general appearance, his dress, his manner, his mistresses and any other information he could gather. But, he insisted, this next meeting should in no way be a repetition of its predecessor; there must be no 'precious apparel of gold, nor embroidery, nor any other sort of nonsense'. This would be an informal encounter between friends; his own retinue, he modestly added, would amount to no more than his personal household, plus six hundred men-at-arms – together, of course, with the royal bed. (The size and weight of this last item can well be imagined, but Henry never moved without it.) It was agreed that Queen Eleanor should not be present at the meeting; as the Emperor's sister and Catherine of Aragon's niece, she might have been something of an embarrassment. Francis asked his sister Margaret, Duchess of Alençon, to do the honours in her place, but she flatly refused to meet 'the King of England's whore'.

Henry and Anne boarded HMS *Swallow* in the early hours of Friday, 11 October 1532. The sea was mercifully calm, and they arrived at Calais in mid-morning. Deliberately or not, Francis kept them waiting, and for some considerable time: he arrived at Boulogne only on the 19th. The long-planned rendezvous thus finally took place on the morning of the 21st, at what the French called Saint-Inglevert; the English – whose territory it was – did their best with Sandyngfield. It was now twelve years since the two kings' last meeting – twelve years that had done neither of them any favours. Francis showed the effects of plenty of wine and women; but he was still only thirty-eight, and his passion for hunting kept him in moderately good physical shape. Henry, though only three years older, was already of formidable girth and looked nearer fifty than forty. Both, however, were fit enough to gallop across a broad meadow to the meeting-place, there to embrace each other while still in the saddle and to ride hand in hand into the French territory of Boulogne, where they were greeted by a salute of – we are told – a thousand guns.

In spite of Henry's plea to go easy on the pomp and ceremony, Francis was clearly determined that this second meeting should not be too much of an anti-climax after the first. It would be tedious again to spell out in detail the whole programme: the daily Masses, the banquets, the various sporting events (but no wrestling or jousting this time – the protagonists were too old for that sort of thing), and the endless exchanges of absurdly lavish presents that neither could afford. After four days the party moved on to Calais, where Henry took his turn to be host. It was here that Francis first met Anne, to whom – despite the fact that she was already dripping with Catherine of Aragon's jewels (which, it need hardly be said, Catherine had surrendered with the greatest reluctance) – on the first evening he sent a perfectly enormous diamond. The two seem to have got on remarkably well, dancing together and chatting for over an hour on a window-seat.

The festivities ended on Tuesday, 29th October, when Henry accompanied Francis on his seven-mile ride back to French soil. When in the past week the two had found time for serious discussions is not entirely clear; it had however been agreed that Francis would do everything he could to speed his friend's annulment; he professed himself to be very much in favour of the marriage to Anne. The two kings had pledged themselves to take up arms against the Turk – though in the years that followed neither of them was to show much inclination to do so. They had agreed too that something must be done about the Pope and the Emperor, who was known to be planning a return to Italy – which was bad news indeed for Francis. Finally – although at heart they probably disliked and certainly distrusted each other – they had shown the world, and especially the Pope and the Emperor, that they were brothers. There is no doubt that Henry felt the meeting to have been a success; it was only unfortunate that, just as he and Anne were about to re-embark, the weather closed in; only after twelve days of storms and dense fog in the Channel were they able to return to Dover.

Clement VII was by now seriously losing his grip. He seemed incapable of making any decisions about anything.* Francis and Henry had therefore resolved to make a formal approach to him by sending two high-powered French cardinals, bearing firmly worded letters – Henry's about his annulment and Francis's about Italy – that left no doubt of the two monarchs' dissatisfaction and displeasure. The Pope was at that time once again in Bologna, and when the cardinals arrived, in early January, they found the Emperor already there, busy discussing the possibility of holding a General Council of the Church – the only way, he felt, of settling once and for all the problems posed by the Reformation. The cardinals were nevertheless given a surprisingly warm reception, and by the end of the month were able to report two major successes; the Pope had agreed to a meeting with Francis and – more significant still – had given his consent to the marriage between his niece Catherine de' Medici and the King's second son, the Duke of Orleans.

* In March 1532 the French Ambassador reported that the Pope was so terrified of a Turkish invasion that he was seriously considering taking all the money he could lay hands on and bolting to Avignon, leaving Italy to look after itself.

~

Sultan Suleiman had felt a deep humiliation at his failure to capture Vienna. Determined on a second attempt, on 25 April 1532 he once again left Istanbul with his Grand Vizier Ibrahim Pasha for a new campaign along and around the Danube. Behind him were some 100,000 men, including 12,000 janissaries, dragging some 300 cannon. At Belgrade, another 15,000 were waiting – Crimean Tartars this time, put at his disposal by Giray, their Khan. The Sultan somehow seems to have assumed that the Christian army when he found it would be led by Charles in person, for when the army reached Niš in Serbia and Ferdinand's envoys offered him 100,000 ducats if he would recognise their master as King of Hungary, he dismissed them with the words:

> The King of Spain has long said that he wants to take on the Turks. By the grace of God I am now on my way to meet him with my army. If he is great of heart, let him await me on the field of battle and let the will of God be done. If he has no desire to meet me, let him send a tribute to my imperial majesty.

The army came to a halt on 5 August, when it reached Güns, a small fortress town some sixty miles from Vienna (it is now Köszeg, just over the Hungarian border). Suleiman had somehow been delayed on his march, and the army was temporarily under the command of Ibrahim. Put under siege, the Hungarian garrison of eight hundred men fought with enormous courage and determination, resisting nineteen major attacks in twenty-five days. On the sixth day the Grand Vizier called on its commander, Nicolas Jurisics, to surrender and to pay an annual tribute of 2,000 florins. Jurisics replied that he had no money; in any event, how could he be expected to surrender a castle that belonged not to him but to his master, the Archduke Ferdinand? So the fighting went on, and a contemporary reported:

> The janissaries rushed forward and had already planted eight standards on the walls. Protected only by the flimsiest defences and crushed against the walls, the inhabitants awaited their last hour; then the old people, women and children uttered a cry so pitiful and piercing that the attackers retreated in terror and even left two of their standards in the citizens' hands. This change of fortune occurred so suddenly and seemed so miraculous to both sides that the Turks believed they saw a heavenly knight brandishing a sword against them, and the Christians thought they recognised St Martin, the doughty patron of Stein on the river Anger.

An improbable account, to say the least; but so impressed was Ibrahim by the commander's courage that after a few more days he invited him under safe conduct to the Turkish camp – where Jurisics, who had by now lost half his men and was completely out of gunpowder, was only too pleased to accept the generous terms he was offered. The Grand Vizier treated him with elaborate courtesy, congratulated him and the entire garrison, and – though henceforth it would be in the Sultan's name – left him in command of the castle.

It is a pleasant enough story, but Güns was an unimportant little town, and its capture had cost a full month of fine campaigning weather. Was this why Suleiman, when he rejoined his army, decided to abandon his march on Vienna, and to march instead into the region of Styria in south-east Austria? Vienna had been, after all, the object of his entire expedition. But then, if the delay at Güns had indeed been responsible for the change of plan, would he not have shown at least some dissatisfaction with his Grand Vizier for wasting so much valuable time? There is no indication that he did anything of the kind. Another, much likelier, possibility, suggested by his words at Niš, is that he had somehow got it into his head that Charles was not far off, with the imperial army. In such an event he might quite probably have decided on the tactic that had served him so well in the Mohács campaign: first to meet the enemy in pitched battle and only after its destruction to advance on the capital. If so, he was disappointed. Charles was indeed on his way to Vienna; but he had no army with him. He certainly had no intention of meeting the Ottoman army in a battle that he might very probably lose.*

Suleiman spent the month of September plundering and sacking as many Styrian towns as he could; then he returned, via Belgrade, to his capital, which he reached on 18 November. The victory celebrations continued for five days, but must have rung a little hollow in his ears. This second expedition had been even less successful than the first. He had not even approached Vienna, far less attacked it. There would be no more attempts. The city – the one that he had longed more than any other to make his own – would remain in Christian hands.

~

Perhaps it was in part due to the encouragement that he had received from Francis, perhaps he had simply run out of patience: whatever the reason, Henry married Anne Boleyn in a secret marriage service almost immediately after their return to Dover. Within a few weeks she was pregnant, and a second – public – ceremony was held on 25 January 1533. On 23 May the Archbishop of Canterbury, Thomas Cranmer, sitting in

* In fact, the Emperor was to arrive in Vienna on 23 September – it was his first and only visit to the city – and was to stay there for only ten days before moving on to meet Pope Clement at Bologna.

judgement at a special court convened at the Priory of St Peter in Dunstable, declared the King's marriage to Catherine of Aragon null and void on the grounds that her former marriage to Arthur had indeed been consummated, and a few days later pronounced that of Henry and Anne – whose condition could no longer be concealed – to be valid. Catherine was formally stripped of her title as Queen; it was announced that as the widow of Prince Arthur she would in future be known as the Princess Dowager. Her daughter Mary was declared illegitimate, and thus placed outside the line of succession. The reaction of Pope Clement to this news may well be imagined. On 11 July he announced his formal condemnation of the King's marriage, threatening that, unless Henry took back Catherine by September, he would be excommunicated.

It is impossible not to feel sorry for poor Catherine. She had served both her native and her adopted countries well; the Venetian ambassador, Ludovico Falier, reported that 'she was more beloved by the islanders than any queen that had ever reigned'. Her appointment in 1507 as the official plenipotentiary of the Kingdom of Spain to England had made her the first female ambassador in European history. Henry had appointed her Regent, or Governor of England, during his absence on campaign in 1513, and when the Scots invaded in September, she had ridden as far as Buckingham before she heard of their defeat at Flodden, despite being heavily pregnant at the time. Only a month after the victory she had given birth to a still-born son; had she remained quietly in the palace, the whole of subsequent English history might have been different.

She had genuinely loved her husband, and was to remain loyal to him for the rest of her days, claiming always to be his lawful wedded wife and England's only rightful queen. For this reason she had categorically refused Wolsey's repeated suggestions – which later turned to entreaties – that she should renounce her marriage and retreat to a nunnery. No, she said, that she could never do. She had come to Henry a virgin; God had called her to matrimony, not to monastic retreat. After her rejection she went to live at The More – a palace in Hertfordshire* – from which she later moved, first to Buckden in Huntingdonshire and then to Kimbolton Castle in Cambridgeshire,† where she refused to leave her one small single room and where, on 7 January 1536, she died. She was buried, by royal command, in the choir aisle of Peterborough Abbey (now the Cathedral). She had suffered much: insults, humiliation and, worst of all, the absence of her daughter Mary, whom for the last five years she had been forbidden by Henry (or more likely by Anne Boleyn) to see – to say nothing of the ever-present possibility of the scaffold. But her spirit and her serenity had remained unbroken. Even her enemy Cromwell confessed his admiration. 'Nature wronged the Queen in not making her a man', he remarked to the Emperor's ambassador, Eustache Chapuys. 'But for her sex she would have surpassed all the heroes of history.' When the news of her death was brought to Henry, he characteristically dressed himself from head to foot in celebratory yellow with a white feather in his cap and celebrated with a ball and a banquet; but on the day of her funeral Anne miscarried a son.

It was Anne who now reigned supreme; few queens of England, however, have been more unpopular. On 29 May – just a week after her marriage had been pronounced valid – she came by river from Greenwich to the Tower, with an escort of over three hundred barges and smaller boats, all decorated with flags and banners; on the 31st she was carried on a litter through the City to Westminster; and on 1 June – it was Whit Sunday – she was crowned Queen of England by Archbishop Thomas Cranmer in

---

*   Not a trace remains. The French ambassador thought it more splendid than Hampton Court.
†   Now a school.

the Abbey.* On all three occasions, it was noted, there were far fewer crowds than had been expected; she received little acclamation, where Catherine would have been cheered to the echo. A little over three months later, on 7 September, she gave birth to a daughter – 'probably', writes Professor Scarisbrick, 'the most unwelcome royal daughter and most celebrated woman in English history'. Three days later that daughter was christened Elizabeth after Henry's mother, Elizabeth of York, with King Francis (naturally by proxy) and Cranmer standing as godfathers.† Until Henry should produce a son, it was now Elizabeth who was heir to the throne.

For Francis, too, 1533 was a memorable year – the year of the wedding of his own son to the Pope's niece, which Clement himself had promised to attend. On 11 October the papal fleet of sixty ships dropped anchor at Marseille as the shore batteries cannonaded their welcome. On the following morning the Pope entered the city in state, accompanied by fourteen of his cardinals, all riding their mules. Francis himself arrived on the 13th, and on the 28th, in the church of Saint-Ferréol les Augustins, Clement VII officiated at the marriage of his niece Catherine de' Medici to Francis's son Henry of Orleans. Both bride and groom were fourteen years old. The wedding Mass was interminable, and was followed by a sumptuous ball. Then at midnight, when both children must have been utterly exhausted, they were led to the bridal bedchamber – accompanied by Francis, who

---

* Cranmer had been a Fellow of Jesus College, Cambridge. He had been forced to resign on marriage, but after the death of his wife in childbirth he had been reinstated and ordained. In 1532 he went to Germany as ambassador to Charles V. While there he married again, without resigning the priesthood.

† Strangely enough, Henry himself, though present in the palace, does not seem to have attended the service. He is certainly not mentioned in Hall's very full account of it. Presumably he was reluctant to show his disappointment, which he would have been unable to conceal.

is said to have remained there until the marriage was properly consummated, afterwards reporting that 'each had shown valour in the joust'. The next morning, while they were still in bed, they were visited by the Pope, who added his congratulations and blessings. It was, one feels, all they needed.

Such a ceremony could have been interpreted only as a sign of a Franco–papal alliance; but since no written treaty followed it is impossible to say precisely what it was that Francis and Clement discussed during their many long conversations. The King would certainly have hammered away with his old obsession of Milan; Clement would have raised the time-honoured issue of Parma and Piacenza. Where Henry was concerned, we know that Francis asked for a further delay of six months before his threatened excommunication, but that Clement was prepared to concede only one. We also know that the Pope was left in no doubt as to Francis's feelings about the Turks, which he later reported to Charles. 'Not only will I not oppose the invasion of Christendom by the Turk', the King allegedly declared, 'but I will favour him as much as I can, in order the more easily to recover that which plainly belongs to me and my children, and has been usurped by the Emperor.' Clement may also have questioned the good taste of the present he received from Francis on his departure: a unicorn's horn with the magic quality that if it were placed on a dining table it would immediately signal the presence of poison in the food by breaking out into a sweat.

As for King Henry, he was in a bit of a sweat himself. His rupture with Rome had made him a good deal more dependent on Francis than he had been before. On the other hand, Francis was now effectively the Pope's kinsman: how far could he still be trusted? Francis, fully aware of Henry's doubts, played on them to the full, and in 1533 he sent a new and particularly high-powered ambassador to London – a personal friend since childhood, Admiral Philippe de Chabot, Seigneur de Brion. The admiral brought with him a proposal: for nothing less than the marriage of Henry's daughter Mary to Francis's third son, the Duc d'Angoulême. The idea had originally come from Mary's former betrothed, the Emperor Charles, presumably in an attempt to console her for her recently declared illegitimacy. She was still recognised by the Pope, however, as Henry's lawful heir, so Charles was fairly confident that Francis would leap at the opportunity.

Indeed, he almost certainly would have – had Henry been prepared to consider the possibility for a moment. He gave the ambassador a magnificent reception, lodging him in his own palace at Bridewell; but when Chabot told him of the proposal, his face clouded. The admiral, he said, must be joking. He would give Mary to Angoulême only on the condition that both he and she renounced all claims to the English throne. Failing that, he was prepared to offer the duke the hand of his daughter Elizabeth and renounce his own claim to the throne of France, if – but only if – Francis succeeded in persuading the Pope to lift the threat of excommunication that still lay upon him. Chabot, we are told, took no interest in either of these counter-proposals and returned to France 'much disgruntled'.*

When Pope Clement returned to Rome at the end of the year he was already a sick man, and on 25 September 1534 he died. As Supreme Pontiff he had not been a success. During the seemingly endless battle with Henry he had consistently underplayed his hand. He might have thundered out anathemas, imposed excommunications rather than merely threatening them, encouraged those faithful to him to stand up against Henry and promising them support; instead he had remained almost silent, terrified on the one hand of giving offence to the Emperor, on the other of taking too strong a line with the King, somehow always hoping that the whole thing would blow over. It was entirely typical of him that in 1532, when

* R. J. Knecht, *Francis I*, p. 235.

Anglo-papal relations could hardly have been worse, he should have written to Henry asking his permission to send a papal librarian to England, with the purpose of going through ecclesiastical and monastic libraries in search of books not yet in the Vatican collection. And yet, despite all his misfortunes – for many of which he had himself been responsible – he never forgot that he was a Medici and a Renaissance prince. He had been a patron of Cellini and Raphael, and it was he who commissioned Michelangelo to paint the Last Judgement on the east wall of the Sistine Chapel, as well as completing his work on the Medici tombs in the basilica of San Lorenzo in Florence. Nor was the marriage of his niece to the future King of France his only dynastic triumph; in that same last year of his life he also arranged for Alessandro de' Medici, at that time ruler of Florence, to marry Margaret of Austria, the natural daughter of Charles V.* His magnificently arrogant portrait by Sebastiano del Piombo (now in Naples) survives him.

At least Clement was spared the shame of his final defeat. It was only two months after his death that the English Parliament approved the Act of Supremacy, which declared the King to be 'the only supreme head on earth of the Church of England' and shook off for ever its subjection to Rome. The preposition was important: heretofore it had been the Church *in* England; the *of* made all the difference. Henry even went so far as to proclaim himself a Moses, delivering his chosen people from the bondage to which they had been condemned by the Papacy. Such a presumption was unprecedented; never before in Europe had a secular prince assumed such full spiritual authority over his

---

* Alessandro was generally recognised as the only son – possibly by a Caribbean servant girl – of Lorenzo II, grandson of Lorenzo the Magnificent; but there is a strong possibility that he was in fact the bastard son of Pope Clement himself. This second marriage was less successful. After only a year Alessandro was assassinated by his distant cousin Lorenzino.

subjects. The difficulty was to apprise those subjects of the fact. Decrees were promulgated the length and breadth of the kingdom: all those in authority were required to swear oaths, recognising Henry as Supreme Head of the Church and specifically renouncing Rome. The Pope's name was to be erased wherever it appeared in the liturgy; in the parish churches, sermons were to be preached every three months explaining what had occurred and congratulating the congregations on their escape from their former bondage. All this was supported by an endless succession of books and pamphlets, pageants and plays. Now, for the first time in England, the printing press showed what it could do.

The news of Pope Clement's death was, it need hardly be said, enthusiastically welcomed by Henry; to Francis, however, it came as a crippling blow. The new entente for which he had worked so hard was now in ruins. The magnificent marriage of which he had been so proud was henceforth a *mésalliance*; the Medici, for all their magnificence, had always been considered a fundamentally bourgeois family and always would be. Had Clement been succeeded by another member of his clan, all would have been well; but the election of Alessandro Farnese, who on 13 October was elected as Pope Paul III, meant a complete reappraisal of French policy towards the Holy See. And – as if that was not enough – only five days later came *l'affaire des placards*.

~

'*ARTICLES VÉRITABLES SUR LES HORRIBLES, GRANDS & IMPORTABLES ABUZ DE LA MESSE PAPALLE.*' Such were the opening words, in large Gothic type, of the *placards*, or broadsheets, that appeared all over Paris on the morning of

Sunday, 18 October 1534. The four long paragraphs following were purely theological in character and need not concern us; suffice it to say that they formed a violent attack on the Catholic Mass, expressed in a language that terrified their readers. The city was swept by a wave of hysteria as the rumours spread: all Catholic churches were to be burned to the ground, all the Catholic faithful were to be massacred in their places of worship. The panic increased further when it was learned that the *placards* had not been confined to Paris. They had also been found in Orleans, Tours, Blois and Rouen, and one, it was said, had even been discovered fixed to the door of the King's bedchamber at Amboise, where he was at that time in residence.

The search for those responsible began at once. Countless arrests were made; several innocent unfortunates were burned at the stake. And, sadly, Francis himself seemed to lose his head. What followed was nothing less than an inquisition. All new books were banned. In order, presumably, to defy the terrorists – for it was as such that they were seen – a 'general procession' was summoned for 21 January in Paris: the most sacred relics – they included the Crown of Thorns from the Sainte-Chapelle – were removed from the city's churches and paraded through the streets, from Saint-Germain-l'Auxerrois to Notre-Dame, the Blessed Sacrament being carried by the Bishop of Paris beneath a canopy borne by the King's three sons and the Duc de Vendôme. Immediately behind it walked Francis himself, dressed entirely in black, bare-headed and carrying a lighted torch. On arrival at the cathedral High Mass was celebrated, after which he and Queen Eleanor were entertained to lunch at the Bishop's palace. The King then addressed a large crowd, encouraging his subjects to denounce all heretics, even families and friends. The day ended with another six burnings.

And so the reign of terror continued. Why, one wonders, was there so wild an over-reaction to what had been in fact fairly slight provocation? The answer usually given is that Francis took the *placard* found at Amboise as a personal affront, but this is not easy to believe.* The truth, surely, is that he had no choice. The provocation was indeed slight; but it did not seem so at the time. The *placards*, couched as they were in violent and abusive language, attacked the Church, the Mass, the priesthood and, through them, every one of the King's god-fearing Catholic subjects. As the Most Christian King, Francis could not have ignored them, or even passed them over lightly. He may not have instigated the resulting persecutions, which were more probably ordered by the *Parlement*; but he could not possibly have withheld his approval.

What is undeniable is that after the *affaire des placards* France was never the same again. Between 1541 and 1544 six Parisian booksellers or printers were prosecuted – one was tortured and two were sent to the stake – and in 1542 the Sorbonne began to compile the first index of forbidden books. Henceforth, Protestantism was to be considered a dangerous threat. French Catholics felt themselves to be under siege, and the wars of religion began to cast their shadow.

~

When Henry and Francis had separated in October 1532 and had expressed their intention of joining forces against the Turk, the words 'one of these days' were almost audible; the two kings were speaking of a vague intent rather than of any specific plan. And this was perfectly easy to understand: the Ottoman Empire was a long way away and – to Henry at least – of little direct

---

* Less than two years earlier, in January 1533, three armed strangers had been found in Francis's chamber in the Louvre; his only reaction had been to ask the *Parlement* to show more vigilance at night.

concern. For Charles V, on the other hand, who had seen the Sultan at the gates of Vienna only three years before, it was a very real danger. Out of sheer necessity, he kept a close eye on his Turkish neighbour. And suddenly, in 1534, the alarm bells rang.

This new danger was not, as might have been expected, in eastern Europe; it was in the southernmost corner of his Empire, the island of Sicily. And it was represented not by the Sultan personally but by the most dangerous of his subjects, the pirates of the Barbary Coast. The expulsion of the Moors from Spain in the years following 1492 had led to a proliferation of rootless vagabonds, ruined, homeless, disaffected and longing for revenge; and many of them had joined their co-religionists in north Africa and adopted the life of buccaneers. Between Tangier and Tunis there were some 1,200 miles and, in what was for the most part still a moderately fertile and well-watered coastal strip, innumerable almost tideless natural harbours ideal for their purposes. And so the legend of the Barbary Coast was born.

In the early 1530s the leader of these corsairs was a certain Kheir-ed-Din Barbarossa. Born on the island of Mytilene (now Lesbos), he was the son of a retired Greek-born janissary and his wife, who was the widow of a Greek priest. (Since the janissaries were all forcibly converted Christians, Kheir-ed-Din possessed not one drop of Turkish blood.) He had inherited the leadership from his brother Aruj (known in Turkish as Oruç), who had wrought havoc along the coast among both Christian and Muslim shipping and who, in 1516, had strangled the Sultan of Algiers with his own turban. In the following year he had conquered much of what is now Algeria from Spain and had presented it to Suleiman's father, Selim I; in consequence the whole territory was now an integral part of the Ottoman Empire. Aruj had been killed during the Spanish siege of Tlemcen in 1518, but before the end of the year his brother had recognised the Sultan as his suzerain; and the subsequent exploits of Kheir-ed-Din Barbarossa along the coast over the next fifteen years had so impressed Suleiman that in 1533 he had appointed him *kapudan pasha* – chief admiral – of the Ottoman navy.

And so it was that in the early summer of 1534 Barbarossa sailed with a newly built fleet out of the Golden Horn, with the ultimate aim of an important new conquest – Tunisia, under its ruler Moulay Hassan, who was said to have murdered his forty-four brothers in order to obtain the throne, and then to have filled his harem with four hundred young boys of unusually exquisite appearance. Barbarossa began, characteristically, by ravaging the coastal cities and towns of Calabria. One night, so the story goes, he landed secretly at Fondi with the object of kidnapping Giulia di Gonzaga, the wife of a certain Vespasiano Colonna and one of the famous beauties of her day, in order to present her to the Sultan for his harem.* She, however, clad only in her nightdress, managed to escape on a horse, accompanied by a single knight whom – either because he had shown over-familiarity or because he had perhaps seen too much of her person – she subsequently ordered to be killed.

The capture of Tunis was not a difficult operation. Barbarossa arrived outside the harbour on 16 August and immediately began a bombardment, only to find that Moulay Hassan had already fled. All that winter he kept his men busy, reinforcing the harbour defences and building an impressive new fortress, big enough to accommodate a garrison five hundred strong. But he need not have bothered. This time he had overreached himself, having seriously underestimated the probable reaction of Charles V and his power to retaliate. A glance at the map will show that the two most prosperous ports in the extreme west of Sicily, Trapani and Marsala, are less than 150 miles from the Tunisian coast, and Palermo itself only very little more. The idle and pleasure-loving Moulay Hassan had constituted no appreciable danger, but now

* He is said to have been put up to this escapade by Ibrahim Pasha, who hoped that the lady might supplant Roxelana in Suleiman's affections.

that Barbarossa was supreme in Tunis, the Emperor's own hold on Sicily was seriously threatened.

As soon as he heard the news, Charles – mindful of his grandmother Isabella's dictum that the *Reconquista* would be complete only after the western Mediterranean had become a 'Spanish lake' – started to plan an immense expedition to recover Tunis. If, he reasoned, he did not act decisively and at once, there was a very real possibility that the whole coast would fall to the Turks; there would then be a serious threat to Sicily, and indeed to Spain itself. The invasion fleet that he collected would finally include ships from Spain, Naples, Sicily, Sardinia, Genoa and the Knights of St John on Malta. In effective command would be the celebrated Genoese Andrea Doria, a *condottiere* admiral – he might be described as a sailor of fortune – who had abandoned the French after a serious quarrel with King Francis only six years before. He had then transferred his allegiance to the Emperor, bringing Genoa with him and thus putting into Charles's hands an important naval base which would vastly facilitate his frequent journeys between Italy and Spain; but Charles himself, despite being tortured by gout, was determined to sail with the Spanish contingent in what was to be his first serious taste of naval battle.

The imperial fleet, estimated at over 400 ships and carrying an army of some 27,000, sailed from Barcelona at the end of May 1535 to the agreed rendezvous at Cagliari in Sardinia, where it arrived on 10 June to be joined by another 200 vessels of varying kinds. Then on the 13th it turned south, and on the following day hove to in the roadstead outside Tunis. Against such an armada Barbarossa, with only some 60 ships and a few thousand Turks, Arabs and Berbers, saw at once that there was little hope of retaining his hold on the city. Having no intention of losing more ships than necessary, he had already taken the precaution of sending 15 of his best along the coast to Bône, about half-way to Algiers, where they could be kept safely in reserve. He and his men fought valiantly, as they always did, through the African summer heat; but on 14 July – exactly a month after Charles's arrival – the fortress of La Goletta, which defended the inner harbour, was stormed by the Knights of St John, and a week later the many Christian captives who were being held in the city – the chroniclers say 12,000 but this seems unlikely – smashed their way to freedom and flung themselves on their erstwhile captors.* Now it was Barbarossa's turn to flee. In company with his two fellow captains and as many more of his men as were able to follow him, he slipped out of the city and made for Bône.

At this point Charles should have ordered his army to leave at once in pursuit and engage the old corsair in a pitched battle. Had he done so, he might have destroyed Kheir ed-Din Barbarossa for ever; the imperial fleet should have had no difficulty in preventing his escape by sea. But the soldiers – and probably the sailors too – were far too busy raping and plundering, as for three days and nights the rules of war allowed. Moulay Hassan, having agreed to pay the Emperor an annual tribute, was then formally reinstated in the empty shell of his city while the Spaniards, having repaired and refortified La Goletta, declared it Spanish territory and equipped it with a permanent garrison. The expedition, the victorious Christians all agreed, had been a huge success. Tunis was once again in friendly hands, Sicily was secure, hundreds if not thousands of their co-religionists had been freed from captivity and – best of all, perhaps – the previously invincible Barbarossa had been conclusively defeated. The Emperor had also clearly demonstrated that it was he, rather than the infidel-loving French, who was the true defender of Europe. Now he and his allies could all return to their various homelands, well satisfied with what they had achieved.

---

* La Goletta is now La Goulette. The Knights took possession of several cannon, which greatly to their surprise turned out to be French, having the *fleur-de-lys* clearly engraved on their barrels.

Or so they thought. Some days afterwards the Emperor actually did send Andrea Doria on an expedition westward along the coast to find the fugitive corsair and bring him to book. But he was far too late, and anyway he did not know his man. It was typical of Barbarossa that, instead of slinking back to Algiers as they had assumed he would, he had put in at Bône only to collect more ships and supplies before immediately heading north to the Balearic Islands. As his squadron approached, the islanders understandably assumed it to be part of the Emperor's fleet returning to Barcelona, an impression confirmed when the ships were seen to be flying the imperial colours; there was no resistance, therefore, when they glided soundlessly into the harbour of Mahon in the south-east corner of Minorca. A Portuguese merchantman, lying there at anchor, greeted them with a friendly salute; then, suddenly, the squadron opened fire. The Portuguese, taken by surprise, defended themselves as best they could; but their vessel was easily captured. It was only a matter of hours before the whole port, and indeed the whole city, was sacked and destroyed.

∼

On his return from Tunis, Charles had landed at Trapani in Sicily. He had then made his way first to Palermo and then along the coast to Messina, and was now travelling up through southern Italy on his way to visit the Pope in Rome. The recently elected Pope Paul III was so impressed by the Emperor's capture of a key north African port that he unwisely sent his reprobate son Pierluigi* to meet him in Naples. Pierluigi's

---

* Although a cardinal at twenty-five, Paul had since cheerfully fathered four sons.

instructions were made painfully clear. First, he was to show His Imperial Majesty every courtesy and make the most favourable impression possible; next, he was to do his best to discover his future intentions; and finally, his father emphasised, he must abstain so far as possible from sodomy while at the imperial court. The young man doubtless did his best on all three counts, but his mission was not a success. The Emperor seems to have taken an instant dislike to him, and he was almost immediately sent back to Rome.

The day before Charles landed in Calabria, on 1 November 1535, the Lord of Milan Francesco Sforza had died, leaving no male heir. For King Francis this was an opportunity and a challenge. The possession of Milan had been the keystone of his foreign policy since his accession; was the Duchess Valentina Visconti not his great-grandmother? Twice already, in Madrid in 1526 and again in 1529 at Cambrai, he had been obliged to renounce all rights to the duchy; but now, unhesitatingly, he reasserted his claim, proposing that it be bestowed on his second son Henry, Duke of Orleans. For Charles, however – who as suzerain of Milan had its investiture as his gift, but who twenty years later was to confess to his son that Milan had 'tormented him more than all the rest put together' and longed to shake off this most intractable problem once and for all – the proposal was out of the question. Henry was too close to the throne; as the husband of Catherine de' Medici, he had a claim to the Duchy of Urbino; if he were Duke of Milan, he would need only Naples to become effectively master of Italy. The Emperor agreed, however, to consider the investiture of Francis's third son, the Duke of Angoulême.

This was the position when, in the first weeks of 1536, it was reported to Charles that a French army had suddenly invaded the Duchy of Savoy and taken Turin. There was a quarrel of long standing between Francis and his uncle, Duke Charles III, whom he believed to be clinging on to territories that properly

belonged to his mother, Louise; and the outbreak of an insignificant little war between the Duchy and the Grand Council
of Geneva seemed to him the perfect opportunity to step in
and settle matters once and for all.* Overwhelmingly outnumbered, Savoy offered little resistance; Chambéry – then its capital
– fell on 29 February (1536 was a leap year), to be followed by
Turin a week or two later.

Francis claimed, as might have been expected, that his attack
was an act of self-defence, since he was only trying to recover
territories that were lawfully his; but this was transparently disin-
genuous. What he was really doing was providing himself with
a *quid pro quo* in any future negotiations with the Emperor over
the future of Milan, Turin being less than a hundred miles away.
Besides, if these negotiations were to fail, he would now have
the perfect springboard from which to invade the duchy. In any
case, it was clear that Milan was now once again under serious
threat. Charles was outraged. He must surely have discussed the
matter with the Pope the moment he reached Rome; but on
Easter Monday, 17 April 1536, to underline the gravity of the
situation, he made a formal set speech to Paul in Spanish – his
Italian was obviously inadequate to the occasion – on the subject
of his relations with France. He had, he declared, devoted many
years to attempts to win the goodwill of King Francis and to
gain his agreement to march with him against the infidel, but
all his efforts had been in vain. He now publicly offered Francis
a choice of three possibilities. The first was peace, in return for
which he was prepared to cede Milan to the Duke of Angoulême.
The second was war – a war that might so weaken Christendom
as practically to invite the Sultan to help himself to western
Europe. The third was the most surprising of all: single combat
between King and Emperor – the prize being Burgundy on the
one side and Milan on the other – after which the victor would

---

* Geneva was to proclaim itself a Protestant Republic in May of that year.

lead their combined forces against Constantinople. Would the
Pope support him or would he not? During this harangue Charles
– unusually for him – seems to have become overexcited and
perhaps somewhat hectoring; it is recorded, at any rate, that at
a given moment the Pope could not take it any more. Rising
from his chair, he laid a hand on the Emperor's shoulder,
murmuring, 'Enough, my son!'

No one took the idea of single combat very seriously, and in
the circumstances peace was out of the question; the result was
that Charles and Francis were once again at war – a war that
in the summer of 1536 brought the Emperor his first significant
defeat. His plan – originally suggested by Andrea Doria – had
been for a joint land and sea operation in Provence. He occupied
Aix without difficulty and reached the gates of Marseille; but
the scorched-earth tactics of Anne (that was indeed his name)
de Montmorency, Grand Marshal of France, proved too much
for him, Marseille was found to be impregnable and an outbreak
of dysentery in the army did the rest. He had no course but to
order a retreat to Genoa. By November he was back in Spain,
licking his wounds.

5

'Like a brother to the Sultan'

SVLIMANO IMPERATOR
DE TVRCHI

I T IS INTERESTING to speculate, as the Emperor Charles did battle off the north African coast with the navy of Suleiman the Magnificent, how much he knew of the Sultan's diplomatic activities, and particularly of his recent dealings with Francis. For the past decade – to the alarm, and frequently the disgust, of Christian Europe – King and Sultan had been in friendly contact. It was not altogether surprising: here, for Francis, was an invaluable ally prepared to fight his battles with the Emperor; for Suleiman there was an unrivalled chance of splitting the forces of Christendom more drastically than ever and even – to some degree at any rate – acquiring a Christian ally. For this purpose he offered Francis the services of the most powerful of his subjects, Kheir-ed-Din Barbarossa, who, from France in 1533, actually sent the King a number of French prisoners still in chains – so that he could have the huge pleasure of releasing them himself – and a quantity of magnificent presents, including a lion. This was shortly followed in 1534 by an embassy from Istanbul, requesting Francis on no account to make peace with the Emperor 'because the Sultan intended to force him to return everything that he had taken during the King's imprisonment'. 'The King of France is on terms of peace and concord with us', announced the Grand Vizier Ibrahim Pasha; 'He is like a brother to the Sultan.'

By 1535, however, fraternity was no longer enough. Francis needed Suleiman's active assistance against Charles. In February he despatched to Istanbul one of his most trusted diplomatists, Jean de La Forêt, a Knight of St John who spoke both Italian and Greek and carried with him detailed plans for a full-scale military campaign. The ambassador stopped first in Tunis to see Barbarossa – this was still several weeks before the Emperor's expedition against the city – to plan the year's campaigning. The general idea was that the corsair, with French assistance, would make a surprise attack on Genoa; meanwhile the main body of the French force would launch a campaign in Italy, while the Sultan would open another, by land and sea, against the Kingdom of Naples, which was at that time under a Spanish viceroy.

When La Forêt arrived on the Bosphorus he found that Suleiman was still away with his army in Persia, but the beginning of 1536 saw the Sultan and the Grand Vizier back in the capital, and it was there, on 18 February, that Ibrahim signed in the Sultan's name the Ottoman Empire's first formal agreement with France. No original text of this agreement has survived in Paris or in Istanbul, so the details remain uncertain; we know, however, from other sources a fair amount about it. Perhaps its most significant feature was that it was not only a military alliance; it included also a commercial treaty, by the terms of which the subjects of the Sultan and those of the French King were at full liberty to do business in each other's dominions. Frenchmen anywhere in the Ottoman Empire were answerable only to the French ambassador in Istanbul and to the French consuls in Damascus and Alexandria.* The agreement shifted the whole balance of power in the Mediterranean: western Europe was

---

* This was the origin of the 'capitulations' which allowed France to retain for several centuries her political and religious privileges in the Levant.

146

nearer to the east than ever before, and Turkey was now effectively a member of the concert of powers in Europe.

The signing of the treaty was the last important act of the
life of Ibrahim Pasha. On the morning of 15 March his dead
body was found in the huge palace that he had built for himself
on the north-west side of the old Byzantine Hippodrome. He
had clearly fought hard against the mutes who had been sent
to garrotte him; three years later, the bloodstains were still visible
on the walls. His corpse was taken to a dervish monastery behind
the arsenal and buried without any inscription or memorial.*
The motive for his assassination was never officially established;
but there was little doubt in palace circles that it was, at least
indirectly, the work of Roxelana, who had always detested him.
While he was alive, she was never able entirely to dominate her
husband. Besides, she wanted Ibrahim's post for her son-in-law
Rüstem Pasha, husband of her daughter Mihrimah; and what
Roxelana wanted she almost invariably got.

~

Despite the birth of Elizabeth, the marriage of Henry and Anne
was doomed almost before it began. The fault was mostly Anne's.
She was rude, irritable and possessed of a violent temper. Nobody liked her: by the time of her marriage, not even the King.
Already as early as the midsummer of 1534 he had started a
serious flirtation with Jane Seymour, one of Anne's maids of
honour; Anne now began to feel the bitter jealousy which, thanks
to her, had for so long filled the heart of Catherine of Aragon;

---

* His name is now chiefly remembered because his old palace on the
Hippodrome still bears his name. It is now the home of the Turkish and
Islamic Arts Museum.

it was her great misfortune that she utterly lacked the mental and spiritual resources that had enabled Catherine to endure her sufferings. The result was a series of tempestuous rows with her husband, each of which – had she but known it – hammered another nail into her coffin.

For Henry the situation soon became intolerable. By 1535 he was keeping his contacts with his wife to the absolute minimum, on their increasingly rare meetings barely addressing to her a civil word. He would probably still have forgiven her everything if she had only borne him a son, but there followed only the all-too-familiar succession of false pregnancies and still-births. In his heart he probably still saw his inability to engender a male heir as God's punishment for his marriage – even though it had now finally been annulled – to Catherine; and his continued failure with Anne strongly suggested that he had not yet been forgiven. But reflections of this kind could not save his unfortunate wife. If she could not deliver what he wanted, he must find someone who could. For Anne, the writing was on the wall. While Catherine lived, she had been safe; her death would have involved Henry in too many complications. But Catherine was dead; and her death sealed the fate of Anne.

On 24 April 1536 Henry set up a commission under the chairmanship of Thomas Cromwell and the Duke of Norfolk to find suitable grounds for divorce. Its work was soon done. There were none of the difficulties that had beset the King's separation from Catherine. In less than a week Anne had been charged with adultery with several members of the court; and once each of these men had been found guilty of treason the King had all the evidence, true or false, that he required. On 2 May he sent his wife to the Tower of London, charged not only with adultery but with incest and witchcraft, there to be tried before a jury of her peers – which included her uncle Thomas Howard and Henry Percy, son of the Earl of Northumberland, to whom, at the age of twenty-two, she had been secretly betrothed. The verdict was, of course, a foregone conclusion. A special swordsman was brought over from Calais – the normal executioner's axe was considered too crude – and on the morning of Friday, 19 May 1536, the Queen of England was beheaded in an open courtyard of the Tower.

Whether or not Anne had committed adultery with any or all of the half-dozen men now accused – they included George Boleyn, her own brother – we shall never know for certain. It seems unlikely, though doubtless anything was better than sex with Henry. She had certainly flirted with Mark Smeaton, one of the court musicians, with the Groom of the Stool, Sir Henry Norreys (or Norris), and quite possibly with Sir Francis Weston, a Gentleman of the Privy Chamber; and it may well be that she slept with one or more of them simply in the hopes of having the son that she felt she could no longer expect from her husband. But the risks would have been great. And there was another consideration: in the Tudor court the Queen was never alone. How could these clandestine meetings – if they ever occurred – possibly have been arranged? It is worth recording, too, that all the accused categorically denied any misconduct – with the single exception of Smeaton, who finally made a confession only after Cromwell had threatened him with torture.

With Catherine of Aragon and Anne Boleyn both dead, was there any good reason why Henry should not now return to the Roman Catholic fold? The Pope was certainly ready to welcome him back, allowing him the same degree of authority in his lands as Charles and Francis enjoyed in theirs. But Henry had long passed the point of no return. He would have liked to have the threat of excommunication lifted, but Protestantism was rapidly gaining ground in Germany and he preferred to keep his options open; besides, he had already embarked upon the project that was to occupy him – and Thomas Cromwell – over the next five years: the dissolution of all the monasteries,

priories, convents and friaries in England and the confiscation
of their assets.*

~

Less than three months after Anne's execution, on 10 August 1536,
Francis's eldest son and namesake, the Dauphin, then eighteen,
called for a cooling drink after a strenuous game of *jeu de paume*
(an early form of tennis). One of his equerries, the Italian Count
Sebastiano Montecuculli, obliged with a glass of iced water. The
Dauphin drank it – and promptly collapsed, dying a few days
later. Foul play was inevitably suspected, and Montecuculli was
first put to the torture and then, with extreme brutality, executed.
This did not however prevent the French government from also
accusing the Emperor and the Governor of Milan, both of whom
angrily denied the charges, accusing in their turn the dead man's
brother Henry – now himself the Dauphin – and his wife,
Catherine de' Medici. In fact there is no reason to believe that
the young prince's death was due to anything but perfectly natural
causes – he had never entirely recovered from the tuberculosis
he had contracted while imprisoned in Spain – but its conse-
quences provide a good illustration of the state of Franco–
imperial relations, which they did little to improve.

---

* From the cultural point of view, the resultant loss was appalling, especially
where the libraries were concerned: of the 646 books possessed by the Abbey
of the Augustinian Friars at York at the time of the dissolution, only three
have survived. On the other hand it must be admitted that there were far
too many religious houses – altogether nearly nine thousand – and that the
monks enjoyed far too much of the Church's wealth for the good of the
country, or indeed of themselves.

~

Meanwhile, in the ports and harbours as well as on the high seas of the Mediterranean, both Christian and Muslim fleets were busy. In Istanbul, Suleiman took personal charge of an immense shipbuilding programme, 'visiting the arsenal and the cannon-foundries twice a day', noted La Forêt, 'to hasten and encourage the work'. In 1536, while a Turkish naval squadron wintered in the harbour of Marseille, an imperial fleet under Andrea Doria captured ten Turkish merchantmen off Messina, following up its victory with an intrepid raid on a squadron of the Ottoman fleet off the island of Paxos. The Sultan, determined that these two insults should be properly avenged, left Istanbul on 17 May 1537 for Valona on the Albanian coast, the closest Ottoman port to Italy. With him he took La Forêt, showing clearly enough that he saw this as a joint operation with France. The ambassador was much impressed by what he saw; 'I went to the camp of the *Grand Signor*', he wrote,

> as he arrived in his pavilion, built like a huge castle and beau-tifully enriched with hangings, embroidery and rich cloths in figured gold. And afterwards he led me to a high place, where he could show me the great expanse of the country, covered by the marvellous and infinite number of their pavilions.

Suleiman's strategy was simple enough: it was to join Francis in a pincer movement across Italy. He would first capture the vital port of Brindisi, and would then work his way up and across the peninsula to Naples and Rome; Francis had meanwhile promised to invade from the north; his chief targets would be Genoa and Milan. Unfortunately for the Sultan, however, at the last moment the King – not uncharacteristically – changed his mind. Ignoring the plans he had agreed with Suleiman, he headed north instead of south, for Picardy and Flanders. By the time the Ottoman fleet reached Valona, the French navy was still riding at anchor in the harbour of Marseille, totally unprepared for any sort of action. With both his army and his navy already in the Adriatic, a furious Suleiman had to decide quickly on an alternative. While he was deliberating, Barbarossa staged a series of lightning raids along the coast of Apulia, returning – with the usual shiploads of treasure and slaves – to learn that his master had decided to attack the island of Corfu.

The largest of the Ionian islands, Corfu had been a Venetian colony for well over three hundred years, since the Fourth Crusade. To the Sultan with his enormous army it must have seemed an easy prey. He landed some twenty-five thousand men and all his ordnance – some thirty cannon, including a gigantic fifty-pounder, the largest in the world at that time* – surrounded the chief citadel of the town and began bombarding it into submission. But Corfu's defences were strong. The town, half-way up the east coast of the island, lay behind and below the high citadel crowning the rocky peninsula that juts out towards the shores of Albania, commanding the approaches from both land and sea. Within this citadel was a garrison of some two thousand Italians and roughly the same number of Corfiots, together with the crews of such Venetian vessels as happened to be in port at the time. Food and ammunition were in plentiful supply; morale was excellent. It needed to be, for the defenders were faced not just with an attack from the sea but with a combined naval and military operation, carefully – if hurriedly – planned and on a considerable scale. The devastation suffered by the local peasantry, as well as by the ordinary citizens, was appalling; but the citadel, despite constant

---

* It was not a great success. In five days it fired nineteen cannonballs, but only five of them had any effect; the rest flew straight over the town and splashed into the sea.

battering from Turkish cannon and several attempts to take it by storm, somehow stood firm. Then, mercifully, came the rain. Corfu has always been famous for the ferocity of its storms, and those which burst upon it in the early days of September 1537 seem to have been exceptional even by local standards. The cannon became immovable in the mud; dysentery and malaria spread through the Turkish camp. After barely three weeks' siege, the Ottoman army re-embarked on the 15th, leaving a triumphant if still somewhat incredulous garrison to celebrate its victory.

But the war was not over. Barbarossa's fleet was still active, and the other Mediterranean harbours and islands that remained in Venetian hands were not as well defended as Corfu. One by one they fell: Nauplia and Malvasia (now Monemvasia) on the east coast of the Peloponnese, then the islands – Skyros, Aegina, Ios, Patmos, Astipalaia – all of them considerably nearer to the Turkish mainland than to Venice, whose fleet was now blocked by the throng of Ottoman ships in the Adriatic narrows. With some twenty-five of its islands devastated and thousands of young Christians carried off into slavery, the Most Serene Republic had been brought to its knees; and it was Kheir-ed-Din Barbarossa who was responsible for its humiliation. No wonder that when he returned to Istanbul it was to a hero's welcome such had never been known. And the old pirate gave as good as he got: 400,000 gold pieces, 1,000 young women and 1,500 youths. There was also a personal present for the Sultan: 400 more youths, dressed in scarlet and carrying vessels of gold and silver, bales of precious silks and embroidered purses overflowing with gold coins.

The victory of Corfu had already gone sour; every week was now bringing reports of new defeats, new losses. The Sultan was again on the offensive; and the Christian princes, for all their plans and promises, seemed incapable of forming alliances that existed otherwise than on paper or that were not poisoned by mutual suspicions and petty bickering before they even took shape. In the summer of 1538 one such attempt, embarked upon by Venice, the Pope and the Emperor with all the fervour of a Crusade and a degree of wild optimism such that the participants actually made advance plans for the division of the Ottoman Empire between them, ended not as they had imagined, with the capture of Constantinople, but with a further miserable defeat off Preveza, a Turkish stronghold on the coast of Epirus, opposite the spot where the Battle of Actium had been fought 1,569 years before. It was here that Andrea Doria, reluctantly persuaded to return to the theatre of war, delayed and prevaricated until the battle was as good as lost. He had some 160 ships, Barbarossa 22. The result should have been a walkover, but after a few initial exchanges Doria simply refused to fight. He was neither a coward nor a fool, and treachery or deliberate malice is surely improbable. Perhaps the most likely explanation is that he had received secret orders from his Emperor, who saw the Barbary corsairs as a more immediate threat and was anxious to preserve his fleet intact. In any event, Doria was indirectly responsible for the seven Venetian galleys that were sunk. The Turks, by contrast, sustained no damage of any kind.

It was by now clear that Venice must negotiate a peace with the Sultan on whatever terms she could. Of all her recent losses, those which crippled her most were Nauplia and Monemvasia, her last trading posts in the Peloponnese, and her ambassador, Tommaso Contarini, was authorised to offer a stiff ransom: 150,000 ducats in the first instance, rising to 300,000 should the Sultan prove particularly intractable. This last sum was by any standards enormous, and it was thought that Suleiman – who had new preoccupations in the east and was known to be not averse to the idea of at least a truce in western waters – would be only to happy to accept it. Alas, he proved to be nothing of the kind, and Venice found herself obliged to agree to a treaty on terms far harsher than she had ever contemplated. The 300,000 ducats that she had offered were exacted from her as general reparations; there was to be no question of the return of the two Peloponnesian ports, or indeed of any of the other territories lost to her in the past three years. In future, too, Venetian ships might no longer enter *or leave* Turkish ports without permission. There were also several minor items that seemed calculated to cause the maximum of inconvenience and humiliation, but Venice had no choice but to accept, and she knew it.

~

The spring of 1538 saw Charles and Francis still at daggers drawn. In March, Francis had invaded Italy and advanced as far as Rivoli in Piedmont before Pope Paul managed to arrange a truce, but his heart had not really been in it. The fact was that the Provençal campaign had exhausted both rulers; neither was in any condition to continue serious fighting for the present. But they remained bitterly divided on any number of issues, of which the most pressing was – as always – Milan. Charles was now willing to invest the King's third and youngest son, Charles, Duke of Orleans, with the Duchy, but only after Francis had joined him in a Crusade against the Turk. Francis claimed that he was quite prepared to go on the Crusade, but only after Orleans had been invested with Milan. At length they both accepted an invitation to attend a meeting to be held under papal auspices at Nice in May and June 1538.

While there, the two never met; each negotiated separately with the Pope. Somehow, however, they managed to agree on a ten-year truce, which they signed on 18 June. Their careful avoidance of each other seemed mildly ridiculous; but their mutual relations greatly improved shortly thereafter, when in July, as the Emperor was on his way back to Spain, the two met at Aigues-Mortes. Ostensibly, their purpose was to discuss the

projected Crusade against the Turks and the stamping out of
Protestant heresies. Francis – who had no intention of going to
war with his friend the Sultan – is reported as having spent
most of the time making long and noisy protestations of eternal
friendship; Charles, we may imagine, was more inclined to hold
his peace. But for some time after this the two brothers-in-law
remained surprisingly friendly. They became friendlier still in
the following year, after the death of the Empress Isabella on
1 May 1539. To Charles it came as a crushing blow; despite his
frequent though necessary absences from Spain, he had loved
his wife to distraction, and he now made no secret of his sorrow.

It was perhaps as a gesture of sympathy as much as anything
else that, when a rebellion broke out in Ghent that autumn,
Francis invited him to travel from Spain to the Low Countries
by land through France. Charles gratefully accepted, keeping
Christmas with the King at Fontainebleau and paying his first
and only visit to Paris – which, on New Year's Day 1540, the
two of them entered together. Throughout the Emperor's
two-month stay, we are told, Francis could not have been more
friendly and considerate – though some felt that his gentle pressure on the recent widower to marry his own daughter Margaret
was perhaps a trifle premature. As for Charles, rumour had it that
he had even offered Francis the imperial crown of Byzantium,
once Suleiman had been eliminated after their joint Crusade.

All this, as may be imagined, caused considerable problems to
Antonio Rincón, the portly Spaniard who had succeeded La
Forêt as Francis's ambassador to the Porte and whose duty it
was to keep the Sultan happy at all costs. Astonishingly, he
managed to do so, assuring Suleiman that his master had signed
the Peace of Cambrai – by which France and the Empire were
effectively reconciled – only to secure the release of his children.
In September 1539 the Sultan even invited Francis to Istanbul
to celebrate his son's circumcision; and soon enough, after relations between Charles and Francis had returned to their normal

level of hostility, Rincón returned to Paris with concrete proposals for a joint attack by King and Sultan on the Emperor. Before doing so, he proudly reported, he had been accorded an exceptionally long audience with Suleiman, lasting for two hours or more – 'an honour which he had granted to no one else, either Christian or of his own religion'.

Alas, poor Rincón was never again to see the Bosphorus. In the early summer of 1541 he set off from Paris on his way back to Istanbul, but while sailing down the River Po with a companion he was set upon and killed by a party of men in the service of the Marquis del Vasto, who was then governing Milan in the Emperor's name. Not till September was the truth discovered, when the French ambassador in Venice tracked down one of the watermen who had been forced to transport the murderers and, later, to help carry the corpses ashore. This flagrant violation of the conventions of diplomacy caused a storm of protest, not only among the subjects of Francis and Suleiman – both of whom held the Emperor personally responsible – but even in the imperial territories. Pope Paul condemned it in the harshest terms, while the Sultan spoke grimly of impalement.

~

As soon as King Henry heard the news of his wife's execution, he summoned his barge and went straight to Jane Seymour. Next day the two were betrothed; and on 30 May 1536, just eleven days after Anne's death, he married Jane in the Palace of Whitehall. The new queen – who had been a lady-in-waiting to both her predecessors – was nowhere near as highly educated as Catherine, or even as Anne. She could probably read and write a bit, but by far her greatest skill, we are told, was with her needle: her embroidery was reported to be a wonder to behold. What most recommended her, however, was her character. Sir John Russell, who was later to serve Henry as his Lord High Admiral, described her as being 'as gentle a lady as ever I knew'; in this respect she must certainly have been a welcome contrast to her predecessor. It soon became clear, on the other hand, that life under Jane was going to be a lot less fun than it had been under Anne. The extravagant entertainments and banquets that had been such a feature of life during the previous regime were replaced by shorter, simpler meals, and it was not long before the new Queen had formally banned the elaborate French fashions that Anne had introduced. There must have been many at court who soon found themselves dreaming fondly of the bad old days.

In her dealings with her increasingly difficult husband, however, Jane could boast one important success. It concerned her step-daughter Princess Mary. Mary's recent life had been little short of a nightmare. For over three years she never once saw her father. She was, first of all, held to be illegitimate, with all the shame that such a condition entailed; thus she was invariably obliged to give precedence to her three-year-old half-sister and was even prevented from showing herself in public lest she should be acclaimed or cheered – for despite all Henry's efforts, the people as a whole remained determinedly loyal to her mother and herself. Constantly shunted from one great house to another, she was barred from the only place where she wished to be – at her mother's side. Why, one wonders, why did Henry so adamantly refuse the entreaties of his former wife and daughter to be allowed to see each other, even when Catherine lay on her deathbed? It has been suggested that he was simply afraid – afraid of the secret links that he always believed them to maintain with the Emperor (who was nephew to the one and first cousin to the other) and through him to the Pope.

Perhaps he was – though we may be sure that Anne Boleyn had worked on his fears and exaggerated them; as the mother of Elizabeth, she had, after all, every reason to see that Mary was kept at arm's length. But Anne and Catherine were now both in their graves; the situation had changed. And Jane it was who first herself befriended Mary and then, thanks to her own gentleness and sweetness of character, managed finally to bring the sad princess back into relative favour. She failed to restore her to the succession as she had hoped – that was to be the work of Henry's sixth and last wife, Catherine Parr – but she did at least ensure that relatively cordial relations between father and daughter were eventually re-established.

With Jane Seymour – the first of his wives who caused him no trouble – Henry was probably as happy as he had ever been; but away in the north serious trouble was brewing. It had many causes: the breach with Rome, the incipient attack on the monasteries and abbeys, the King's ignoble treatment of his previous two wives and two daughters, the insecurity of the succession, the continual executions – all these played their part, and in October 1536 the dissatisfaction burst out into open rebellion. It began in Lincolnshire, but it was only when it spread to Yorkshire that it assumed serious proportions and became known as the Pilgrimage of Grace. It was headed by a barrister named Robert Aske, who led a body of some nine thousand followers to York and occupied the city. Within a week or two their number had increased to about forty thousand; and it was now that Thomas Howard, Duke of Norfolk, and George Talbot, Earl of Shrewsbury, opened negotiations with the rebels.

Norfolk promised, in the name of the King, a general pardon and a parliament to be held at York within a year, as well as a reprieve for the religious houses until after the parliament had met. He had in fact no authority to make any promises of this kind, although the mood of the 'pilgrims' was such that, had he not done so, he and Shrewsbury might not have escaped alive. Aske dismissed his men – a decision that he was later to regret – and then travelled to London, where he had an audience with the King. Henry received him with every courtesy and made him further promises, including safe conduct back to Yorkshire. But just as he was beginning his journey back to the north, fighting broke out again. It was all Henry needed to make him change his mind. He immediately had Aske arrested and taken to the Tower. He was charged and convicted of high treason at Westminster and was then sent back to York, where, on a special scaffold erected at Clifford's Tower (which still stands), he was hanged in chains. And that was only the beginning of the King's revenge. Over the next two years a total of 216 were executed: some hanged, drawn and quartered, others beheaded or burned at the stake.

It was while these executions were at their height, some time during the early spring of 1537, that Jane Seymour murmured to her husband that she was pregnant. She developed a craving for quails, which Henry in his excitement ordered in vast quantities from Flanders. During the following summer she cancelled all engagements and remained in the care of the best doctors and most experienced midwives that could be found in the kingdom; and finally, at two o'clock in the morning of Friday, 12 October, at the Palace of Hampton Court, she gave birth by Caesarean section to the King's only legitimate male child. The father was not present – he had hurried off to Esher to escape the plague – but the good news quickly brought him back to London, where he ordered a whole series of celebrations and ceremonial banquets. Three days later the baby was baptised with the name of Edward. This time it was his mother who was absent – baptisms in Tudor times, for obvious reasons, tended to follow very shortly after births, and mothers were normally excused them – but there was another reason too: she was far from well. Why we shall never know; most likely it was a puerperal fever due to some bacterial infection. Whatever the reason, Jane died on the 24th, less than a fortnight after the birth of her child.

Her husband mourned her, but not excessively. He now had

Henry VIII of England, aged forty-five when painted by Holbein in 1536.

Sultan Suleiman the Magnificent and, to his own people, 'the Lawgiver'.

'The personification of the French Renaissance': Francis I of France in 1530 when he was thirty-six, painted by Jean Clouet.

The Emperor Charles V aged about thirty – the Habsburg chin perhaps a little exaggerated?

The children of Philip the Handsome: on the left, his sons Ferdinand and Charles (aged seven); on the right, his daughters, all of whom became queens – Eleanor (of France), Isabella (of Denmark, Norway and Sweden), Mary (of Hungary and Bohemia) and Catherine (of Portugal).

Isabella of Portugal, wife of Charles V, painted by Titian, 1543. After her death Charles never remarried, and dressed in black for the rest of his life.

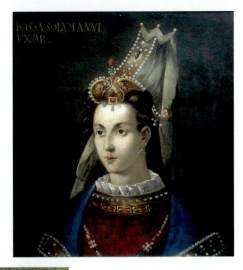

Roxelana, wife of Suleiman the Magnificent. The highly imaginative painter is unknown.

Sultan Suleiman and his court, from the *Süleymanname* by Arif Celebi, 1558.

The arrival of Henry VIII at the Field of the Cloth of Gold in 1520,
where he was to meet Francis for the first time.

Francis I with Queen
Eleanor, only too clearly
the sister of Charles V.

Francis's emblem, the
crowned salamander,
from his château at Blois.

Anne de Pisseleu,
Duchesse d'Etampes:
*'la plus belle des savants,
la plus savante des belles'.*

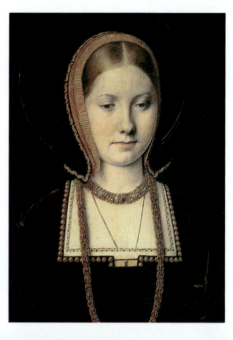

Portrait of a Princess by the Estonian painter Michiel Sittow, *c.*1510, traditionally believed to be a portrait of Queen Catherine of Aragon.

Henry VIII playing the harp in the company of his jester William Sommers. Illustration from the King's own psalter.

Nonsuch Palace, Surrey, commissioned by Henry in 1538, and intended
as a proclamation of Tudor wealth and power – a rival, he hoped,
to Francis's Chambord; not a trace remains.

The Château de Chambord, begun by Francis in 1519 as a hunting lodge
and still unfinished at the time of his death.

Francis at the Battle of Marignano, 13–14 September 1515.

Suleiman at the siege of Belgrade, 1521. Note the row of cannon.

The Battle of Pavia, 24 February 1525. The capture of Francis
is shown in the foreground, right.

The towers of the Alcázar, Madrid, in one of which Francis was imprisoned, 1525–6.

'But no matter; more was lost on Mohács field'. Suleiman at the Battle of Mohács, 29 August 1526.

Suleiman at the siege of Vienna, 27 September–mid-October 1529: the weather already turning nasty.

On 24 February 1530, in Bologna, Charles V was crowned
Holy Roman Emperor by Pope Clement VII.

Anne Boleyn, *c.*1533: 'rude, irritable
and possessed of a violent temper'.

Thomas Cromwell, 'perhaps the most
accomplished servant any English monarch
has enjoyed', was approaching fifty when
painted by Holbein in 1532–4.

Kheir-ed-Din Barbarossa, the Barbary pirate who later became commander of the Ottoman navy.

The battle for Tunis, 1535, its capture a triumphant victory for Charles V.

Alessandro Farnese, Pope Paul III, leader of the Counter-Reformation and convener of the Council of Trent, in a portrait by Titian.

The ceremonial entrance of Francis I and Charles V into Paris on New Year's Day, 1540. (The weather seems to have been surprisingly clement for the time of year.) Fresco by Taddeo Zuccaro in the Villa Farnese, Caprarola.

The siege of Malta, 1565: the Turkish assault on Fort St Elmo, 27 May.

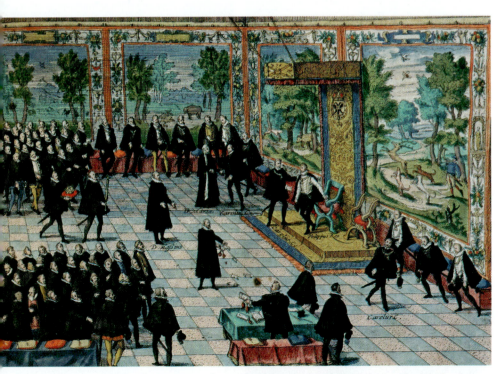

The abdication of Charles V, Brussels, 25 October 1556. Philip II ascends the throne, while Charles walks out (he was in fact on crutches). Engraving by Franz Hogenberg.

Suleiman the Magnificent: the tenth and greatest of the Ottoman Sultans.

The Emperor Charles V, aged forty-eight, painted by Titian, 1548. 'No Emperor strove harder to do his duty, nor was any so important to Christendom.'

a son – that was the important thing. He wore black for the required three months, but long before even this short period had expired he was actively seeking a new wife. His first choice had been the sixteen-year-old Christina, daughter of the deposed Christian II of Denmark and the Emperor's niece.* At thirteen she had married the Duke of Milan, but had been widowed within a year. Alas, the girl herself was far from enthusiastic about the match, 'for her Council suspecteth that her great aunt was poisoned, that the second was put to death and the third lost for lack of keeping her child-bed'. Unsurprisingly, she had no desire to be wife number four. Henry now turned his attention to France. There were no fewer than five suitable French princesses in whom he was interested, and he now proposed that all five should be gathered at Calais so that he could make his choice; but at this point it was made clear to him that he had gone too far. Francis replied icily that in France it was not the custom to send noble ladies to be paraded in review as at a horse sale. He would agree to any one of the girls being sent to Calais, but no more.

It was not only his renewed hopes of matrimony that caused the King concern. He was becoming increasingly anxious over the behaviour of his fellow-monarchs. He had been informed of the ten-year truce of Nice, and also of the meeting of Charles and Francis at Aigues-Mortes. In recent years he had been sincerely thankful that, thanks to his difficulties with the Reformation and his campaign in north Africa, the Emperor had been too busy to launch a Catholic Crusade against him, as he might very well have done. But it could still happen. At Aigues-Mortes he and Francis had signed a treaty in which Henry, King of England, had been completely ignored. And a new serious danger was now looming, from Paul III himself. Henry's continued despoliation of the monasteries, his open

---

* King Christian had married Charles's sister Isabella.

negotiations with the Lutherans and his destruction of sacred shrines – including that of Saint Thomas Becket at Canterbury – had convinced the Pope that he could no longer be tolerated as King and must be removed. On 17 December 1538 he signed a bull by which Henry was not only excommunicated but formally deposed, his subjects absolved from all obedience. Ten days later he secretly sent the English cardinal Reginald Pole to rally the Catholic powers and to persuade them to take the necessary action. The first step would be to break off diplomatic relations and impose a trade embargo, and it was clearly envisaged that an armed invasion of England would follow. Less than a month later, Charles and Francis concluded yet another pact, this time at Toledo, in which each promised not to enter any agreement with Henry without the other's consent, while various further marriages were planned between the Houses of Habsburg and Valois.

Some years before, Henry had shouted at the papal nuncio that he cared not a fig for excommunications, which was probably true at the time. Nevertheless, by early 1539 he was in a state of near-panic. Rumours were rife: there was talk of imminent invasion, of fleets gathering at Antwerp and Boulogne. The English defences were reinforced, not only along the south and east coasts but also along the Scottish border, since the Scots too were in a threatening mood. The King himself was galvanised into action – inspecting palisades and ramparts, bulwarks and barricades and blockhouses, visiting ships in London and Portsmouth, reviewing troops in half a dozen different counties. He was right to be worried: were the invasions that he feared actually to take place, and were revolution simultaneously to break out at home as it had in 1536, his position would have been serious indeed.

He was saved by the situation in Germany, where the ideas of the Reformation were spreading like wildfire across the whole of the north. Protestant princes had taken over in Saxony

and Brandenburg; only Brunswick still held out. Charles – whose dreams of a Crusade against Suleiman were now retreating further and further into the distance – had more than enough on his plate without getting involved with Henry, and when Cardinal Pole arrived at Toledo he told him so in no uncertain terms. Pole was so disappointed by his reception that he decided against his projected visit to Francis, retiring instead to the papal city of Carpentras to await further instructions from his master. It was, as it turned out, a wise decision. Francis showed himself no keener to receive him than Charles had been; he made it perfectly clear that he had no intention of breaking with England just to please the Pope, or of taking any action against its King without the agreement of the Emperor. In May, to Henry's surprise and considerable relief, a French ambassador arrived in London and assured him that his master had no hostile intentions. The panic was over.

And the King's mind returned to the question of marriage. Jane Seymour had been eighteen months in her grave; he himself was forty-eight, not getting any younger but now putting on weight with alarming speed; his infant son was weak and sickly and he urgently needed another. He was also anxious to ally himself with the Protestant princes of Germany. Prompted as always by Cromwell, he now opened negotiations with the German Duke of Cleves – whose sister Anne, as his ambassador Christopher Mont reported, was said to be incomparable 'as well for the face as for the whole body', excelling the beauty of the Duchess of Milan 'as the golden sun excelleth the silver moon'. Henry was interested, but it was only after he had sent Hans Holbein to Cleves and had studied the portrait with which Holbein returned that he was ready to propose.*

---

* A local painter who was considered for the commission was Lucas Cranach the elder, but he was ill at the time. It is interesting to speculate, if he had indeed produced a portrait, how Henry would have reacted.

Was Holbein to blame for what followed? Surely not. There are two versions of his portrait: one in the Louvre, the other in the Victoria and Albert Museum. In both of them Anne looks perfectly presentable, though perhaps not much more than that. One of the envoys to Cleves, a certain Nicholas Wotton, described the portrait as 'a very lively [i.e., lifelike] image', warning the King at the same time that the lady spent most of the time with her needle, that she was scarcely cultivated and was quite unable to sing or play 'for they take it here in Germany for a rebuke and an occasion of lightness that great ladies should be learned or have any knowledge of music'. Meanwhile, since it was the dead of winter, the young princess travelled from her home at Düsseldorf via Antwerp to Calais in order to give her the shortest possible sea journey – 'for the good', it was said, 'of her complexion'. She arrived at Deal on 27 December and rode from there to Rochester, where she arrived on New Year's Day 1540. The King, understandably impatient to see his bride, rode down with some trepidation for a secret glimpse – and was horrified. 'I am ashamed', he declared, 'that men have so praised her as they have done, and I like her not.' The New Year gifts he had brought her were withheld, and he was at his wits' end as she travelled to Greenwich. The marriage was delayed for two days while he tried in vain to find a way out. At last, finding none, he resolved to go through with it, but the union with 'the Flanders mare' was never consummated; the very sight of his new wife, he claimed, induced instant impotence. As he himself put it, 'he left her as good a maid as he found her'.*

---

* After a month of marriage, Anne praised the King to the Countess of Rutland. 'When he comes to bed,' she said, 'he kisseth me, and he taketh me by the hand and biddeth me "Goodnight, sweetheart", and in the morning kisseth me and biddeth "Farewell, darling".' 'There must be more than this', Lady Rutland remarked, 'or it will be long ere we have a Duke of York.'

The marriage was annulled – in the circumstances, without much difficulty – on 10 July. Anne made no trouble. She did all that was expected of her and somewhat surprisingly, in spite of her brother's entreaties, decided to stay on in England. She then retired, to enjoy Richmond Palace and Hever Castle – formerly the property of the Boleyns – both of which magnificent residences Henry had settled on her, together with an income of £500 a year. As time went on, the two became surprisingly good friends, and Anne was always referred to as 'the King's beloved sister'. She was the last of his wives to die, and the only one to be buried in Westminster Abbey.

~

When Francis returned from Aigues-Mortes to Paris, it was to find to his satisfaction that the persecution of the Protestants – frequently accompanied by hideous tortures – was continuing as relentlessly as ever. By now several hundred had been burned at the stake, many thousands rendered homeless. On 1 June 1540 he issued what was to become known as the Edict of Fontainebleau, which declared that Protestantism was 'high treason against God and mankind', and so deserved the appropriate punishments of torture, loss of property, public humiliation and death. And as if that were not enough, several other edicts of a similar kind were to be published in the reigns of his successors. Meanwhile, the reign of terror continued; often, if Protestants formed the majority of the population, whole villages were destroyed.

The worst of these atrocities occurred during the summer of 1545 in the little town of Mérindol in the Vaucluse. The victims on this occasion were not Huguenots but Waldensians, a Christian sect of ancient origin – still existing today – which, despite a number of doctrinal differences, had embraced the Protestant Reformation. Somehow they came under the scrutiny of the authorities in Paris, as a result of which on 18 November 1541 the *parlement* of Provence issued the so-called *Arrêt de Mérindol,* which proved effectively to be the town's death warrant. There was a pause for four years, during which successive appeals were made on its behalf, all of them unsuccessful; then, in 1545, there arrived an army of two thousand men returning from the Italian wars. They showed no mercy, destroying not only the town itself but some two dozen neighbouring Waldensian villages. Thousands were killed, thousands more lost their homes, while hundreds of able-bodied men were sent off to be galley slaves. When it was over, both Francis and Pope Paul announced their enthusiastic approval, the Pope going so far as to decorate the man principally responsible, Jean Maynier d'Oppède, who happened to be President of the *parlement* of Provence.

~

At three o'clock in the afternoon of Saturday, 10 June 1540, just a month before the annulment of Anne of Cleves's marriage, Thomas Cromwell was arrested by the Captain of the Guard as he sat, surrounded by his ministers, at the council table. Then and there the Duke of Norfolk and the Earl of Southampton tore off his Order of the Garter with the words 'A traitor must not wear it.' 'This then is my reward for faithful service', he murmured in reply. He was then led through a postern to a boat waiting in the river and rowed down to the Tower.

Cromwell had long faced formidable enemies: ambitious rivals such as Stephen Gardiner and aristocrats like Norfolk whom he had elbowed aside, all of whom were determined to regain royal favour but knew that they could never do so while this plebeian upstart remained in power. His fall was remarkably like that of Wolsey, ten years before – engineered by Norfolk, assisted by Gardiner and hinging on a failed marriage. The failure of Henry's proposed union with Anne of Cleves, which Cromwell had been the first to suggest and had enthusiastically supported, had given the conspirators precisely the opportunity they had been waiting for. Having sought an audience with the King, they accused his chief minister not only of having been responsible for the débâcle but also of other, far more serious charges, including treason and heresy. He had, they continued, supported the Anabaptists,* protected Protestants accused of heresy and even plotted to marry Princess Mary himself. The bill of attainder has been described as 'a tissue of half-truths and lies', and it may have been for that reason that Cromwell was never brought to trial. He was simply beheaded on Tower Hill, after which his head was set on a spike on London Bridge. The contemporary chronicler Edward Hall records that he spoke briefly on the scaffold, protesting that, though many had slandered him, he was dying 'in the traditional faith'. After that he 'patiently suffered the stroke of the axe, by a ragged and Boocherly miser, whiche very ungodly perfourmed the Office'. Why Henry had allowed himself to be persuaded to execute his greatest and most faithful counsellor is hard to understand; he was to regret his action bitterly before the year was out. But by then the damage was done, and, in the words of his principal biographer, 'he had lost for ever a genius, perhaps the most accomplished servant any English monarch has enjoyed, a royal minister who cut a deeper mark on the history of England than have many of her monarchs'.†

When he first fell in love with Anne Boleyn's cousin Catherine

---

* A Christian sect which believed in delaying baptism until the candidate confessed his or her faith. It was heavily persecuted during the sixteenth century.

† J. J. Scarisbrick, *Henry VIII*.

Howard, Henry would describe her as 'a rose without a thorn', but he did not do so for long. Catherine had been introduced to the court at the end of 1539 – a short, rather plump girl, nineteen years old at the most – by her uncle the Duke of Norfolk. Her family praised her 'for her pure and honest condition', but this was not strictly true: she already had at least two affairs to look back on, one with her music teacher Henry Mannox, the other with the dashing young courtier Francis Dereham. Even after her marriage to Henry – which took place on the day Thomas Cromwell was beheaded – she remained incurably flirtatious. Henry, on the other hand, as everyone around him knew, was by now a deeply unsatisfactory lover. For him sex had long been a means of propagation and little else: once the job was done, he had no further interest in the matter. It was thus perhaps not entirely surprising that by the late summer of 1541 Catherine had got herself seriously involved with one of the gentlemen of the Privy Chamber, Thomas Culpeper – an association which, when it was discovered by Archbishop Cranmer, proved fatal to both of them – and to Dereham as well. Culpeper's sentence was for some reason commuted to one of simple beheading; Dereham, less fortunate, was hanged, drawn and quartered. Both executions took place at Tyburn on 10 December.

Henry had loved the vapid little Catherine in his fashion. Such had been his reaction when he received proof of her behaviour that the French ambassador thought that he had been driven insane. He had even called for a sword with which to kill her himself, and had spent Christmas wandering from palace to palace, from room to room, in abject misery – though how much this was due to bereavement, how much to jealousy and how much to wounded pride is hard to assess. Catherine lived a little longer than her two lovers. It was not until Monday, 13 February 1542, that she was taken by boat to the Tower – passing under the bridge where their heads were still to be seen, impaled on those all-too-familiar stakes – and there, on the Hill, that she was beheaded by a single stroke of the axe.* Eustache Chapuys, who had been the Emperor's ambassador for the past thirteen years and knew him better than most, describes in a letter how the monstrous old King, already giving premature signs of senility, was struck helpless and blind with tears in the middle of a court ball when the cannon from the Tower told him that his fifth wife had suffered the same fate as his second.

Then suddenly, after her death – and how typical it was of him – Henry's mood changed. He gave a great banquet with twenty-six ladies around him, and within a week of the beginning of Lent he celebrated the carnival with still further feasting. It was even rumoured that he was ready to take Anne of Cleves – with whom he had exchanged sumptuous New Year presents – back to his bed. But no: for the moment he had had enough of Venus. It was time, once again, for Mars.

---

* Many people believe that her ghost still frequents the Haunted Gallery at Hampton Court, where her shrieks have occasionally been heard.

6

'Noisome to our realm'

PAVLVS·III·PONT·OPT·MAX·
fu fatto del 15 24 vise ani 15 mesi e giorni 15

WHEN, ON 29 August 1526, the forces of Suleiman the Magnificent smashed the Hungarians at Mohács and shortly afterwards sacked their capital at Buda, rule over the defeated country was disputed by the Sultan's vassal John Zápolya and Charles V's brother Ferdinand. In 1538 the two had come to an agreement, according to which each might reign in peace over his own territory, but on the death of Zápolya – who was at the time a bachelor of fifty-one – all Hungary should go to the Habsburgs. In the following year, however, a complication arose: Zápolya married Isabella, the daughter of King Sigismund of Poland, who shortly afterwards bore him a son, John Sigismund. This made the situation difficult enough; and when the proud father died two weeks later, it became trickier still. Ferdinand lost no time in claiming that the baby was not Isabella's at all, at the same time sending an embassy to Istanbul insisting that the kingdom should be immediately made over to him.

Now Suleiman obviously had no intention of agreeing to a further expansion of the already vast Habsburg domains, but he decided first of all to establish the identity of this problem child. An emissary was at once sent off to Isabella. On his arrival, we are told, the queen took her infant in her arms and presented it to the Turkish ambassador as an orphan, with no support except the protection of the Great Lord; then, with a completely maternal grace, she bared her breast of alabaster and nursed the baby in the presence of the Turk, who kneeled, kissed the feet of the new-born and, putting his hand on the chest of the Porte's tiny *protégé*, swore that the son of King John, to the exclusion of all others, should rule over Hungary.

The ambassador's oath, when it was reported to Ferdinand, was by no means what he wished to hear; he immediately laid siege to Buda, whereupon Isabella appealed to the Sultan for help. For Suleiman there was only one option. Ferdinand was on the march; Isabella was clearly powerless against the turbulent Hungarian nobility; John Sigismund was still a baby. He must quickly annex the entire country. And so he did. As a Turkish flotilla sailed up the Danube, the Austrian opposition seemed to melt away, and on 2 September 1541 the Sultan, accompanied by his son Bayezit, made his formal entry into Buda. He did not, however, keep the whole of Hungary under direct Ottoman control; after long and difficult diplomatic negotiations the country was split once again, this time into three separate parts. The central and southern provinces – including Buda itself – were retained by the Sultan and subjected to his direct rule; the north-western region – 'Royal Hungary', as it was known – was to remain under the Habsburgs; the eastern part was the subject of a diploma 'written in characters of gold and azure', in which the Sultan promised 'by the Prophet, his sabre and his ancestors' to surrender it to John Sigismund as soon as he attained his majority.

～

Just three weeks after Suleiman marched into Buda, Charles V set sail for Algiers. Six years earlier, his capture of Tunis had been a triumph; this time he was heading for disaster. Algiers was by now the most powerful of all the Turkish corsair bases that lay along the Barbary Coast; Charles, who had obviously enjoyed his previous north African adventure, was determined that the city should be destroyed. His admirals strongly advised him against any such attempt so late in the year – and he would have done well to follow their advice. It was late October by the time he landed, and the weather had broken. Several ships had been lost in a storm – some of them carrying sections of the imperial archives; torrential rain made organised disembarkation impossible; furious winds tore the anchors from their moorings and smashed the ships against each other. A day or two later the Emperor himself narrowly escaped capture. He had no choice but to beat an immediate – and fairly ignominious – retreat. Abandoning both his horses and his guns, he returned via the Balearic Islands to Spain.

Fortunately for Charles, Barbarossa had not been in the neighbourhood at the time. Now about sixty but obviously feeling a good deal younger, he was deeply engaged in the planning of a further campaign, this time against southern Italy. In 1542 the Sultan, who was himself preparing to lead another of his immense expeditions into central Europe and had no need of his fleet, had offered it to Francis for the following summer; this, consequently, would be a joint operation with France. Some 120 vessels left Istanbul in April and ravaged the coasts of Italy and Sicily – although, allegedly at the King's insistence, they carefully avoided the Papal States. (At Gaeta the old pirate, almost unbelievably, married the Governor's eighteen-year-old daughter – a girl, we are told, of quite startling beauty; his passion for her was said to have hastened his death.) After several weeks of successful looting, the fleet at last arrived at Marseille, where a tremendous welcome awaited it. Barbarossa, himself superbly dressed and encrusted with jewels, was received by the twenty-three-year-old François de Bourbon, Count of Enghien, who presented him with a plethora of priceless gifts, including a silver sword of honour. In return the Duke received, on behalf of the Sultan, a small stable of magnificent Arab horses, superbly accoutred.

Here – if indeed one was needed – was an impressive illustration of the importance that France attached to her friendship with the Turks; but the celebrations ended badly. Barbarossa had expected to discuss plans for the forthcoming campaign against the Emperor; but he soon discovered that the French, for all their promises and solemn undertakings, had made virtually no serious preparations at all. Their ships were completely unprepared for war; they had not even been provisioned. Suddenly, protocol was forgotten; Barbarossa lost his temper. 'He became scarlet with anger', wrote an eyewitness, 'and tore at his beard, furious to have made such a long voyage with such a large fleet and to be condemned in advance to inaction.' The news was reported to Francis, who did his best to pacify him, ordering the immediate provisioning of several of the Turkish vessels as well as his own; but even then there was serious disagreement as to their joint plan of action. Barbarossa had hoped for a direct attack on the Emperor in Spain, but for Francis such an operation was clearly impossible; the reproaches of all Christendom would rain down upon his head. He proposed instead an attack on Nice, which was at that time ruled by the staunchly imperialist Duke of Savoy. This was not by any means the sort of campaign that Barbarossa had had in mind; but he was forced to accept, though with considerable reluctance, that in the circumstances it was the best that could be hoped for.

If the siege of Nice in August 1543 is remembered at all in the city today, it is because of the courage of its local heroine. Early in the morning of the 15th, heavy bombardment by Barbarossa's galleys had opened a breach in the walls near one of the principal towers. The French and Turks poured through it, and a Turkish standard-bearer was about to plant his flag on the tower when a local washerwoman – her name was Catherine Ségurane, and it has passed into history – seized it from his hands and, with a few brave men whom she had summoned to support her, led a furious counter-attack. The invaders were beaten back, leaving three hundred dead behind them. Nice was temporarily saved, but for all her heroism Catherine had only delayed the inevitable.* Just a week later, on the 22nd, the Governor of the city formally surrendered. In doing so, he was entitled – and doubtless expected – to be offered honourable terms, but within two days Nice was sacked and put to the torch. Inevitably, the Turks were blamed; in fact, it was almost certainly the French who were responsible. Such was the opinion of the Maréchal de Vieilleville, dictating his memoirs shortly before his death in 1571:

> The city of Nice was plundered and burned, for which neither Barbarossa not the Saracens can be blamed, for when it occurred they were already far away . . . Responsibility for the outrage was thrown at poor Barbarossa to protect the honour and reputation of France, and indeed of Christianity itself.

The siege and capture of Nice was the first and last joint operation of the Franco–Turkish alliance. The sight of Christians fighting Christians with the help of infidels left many deeply shocked; but that was only the beginning. Barbarossa now demanded that his entire fleet should be refitted and revictualled,

---

* According to another version of the story, Catherine showed her heroism by standing in front of the invading forces and exposing her bare bottom, the sight of which is said to have so shocked the Muslim sensibilities of the Turkish infantry that they turned tail and fled. A memorial plaque, with an illustration in bas-relief, was erected in 1923 near the supposed location of her action; perhaps unfortunately, it illustrates the first version of the story, not the second.

and Francis was obliged to invite him to occupy Toulon for the winter. Many of the town's inhabitants – brought up on hideous tales of Turkish atrocities – left the town in terror; to the astonishment of those who remained, however, Barbarossa imposed an iron discipline and, in the words of a French diplomat, 'never did an army live more strictly or in better order'. Presents, as always, were exchanged: the commander of the French galleys Virgilio Orsini was delighted to receive a beautiful box of ivory and ebony with pictures of the eleven Ottoman sultans painted around the rim. The only drawback was the expense. Francis was obliged to pay Barbarossa 30,000 ducats a month, and Provence and the whole surrounding area was heavily taxed in consequence. To make matters worse, the old ruffian did not seem in any hurry to leave; nor indeed did his men, for most of whom it was their first experience of the Côte d'Azur and they were predictably enchanted by it. Finally, however, it was made clear to them that they were outstaying their welcome, and in April 1544 Barbarossa (having at the last moment completed his revictualling operations by ransacking five French ships in the harbour) returned to a hero's welcome in Istanbul – ravaging *en route* Elba, Procida, Ischia and Lipari with its fellow Aeolian islands, all of which were imperial territory. Two years later he was dead.

~

Just a month before the siege of Nice, at Hampton Court on 12 July 1543, King Henry married for the last time. Catherine Parr was his sixth wife; she herself had been twice widowed, so he was her third husband. (After his death she was to marry a fourth.) The daughter of a Northamptonshire squire, she was worth a dozen of her four immediate predecessors in the King's bed – though even she could not have held a candle to Catherine of Aragon. She was a moderate Protestant, intelligent and highly educated; and she took Henry firmly in hand. It was thanks to her, for example, that his three children were brought together for the first time in their lives, and that Mary and Elizabeth were both restored to the line of succession. At her urging, too, they both undertook translations of Erasmus.* Her own book, *Prayers Stirring the Mind unto Heavenly Meditations*, was the first work ever published by an English queen under her own name – though these have admittedly been few. Thus it was that although Henry's declining years could only have been a martyrdom, in his last marriage at least he was perhaps almost as happy as in the early years of his first.

Meanwhile the somewhat desultory war between Charles and Francis dragged on. Henry had originally planned to intervene with a major invasion of France in 1543, but it had had to be postponed owing to serious trouble with the Scots. There had been problems too with his new alliance with Charles: the Emperor was deeply embarrassed at the prospect of concluding any alliance with an excommunicated schismatic, and refused absolutely to sign any document according the King his full style, which included the title of Supreme Head of the Church. Nor, by the terms of Henry's excommunication, could he undertake to defend England against attack if the Pope were to decide to turn the war into a Crusade. Henry pointed out that Charles had not always been so respectful of Rome; his destruction of the city and imprisonment of the Pope in 1527 were still fresh in the minds of all Romans. A Crusade was in fact extremely unlikely, owing to Francis's friendship with Suleiman; none the less, Europe was now faced with what would – and should – have seemed an unlikely situation indeed: that of an alliance

---

* Elizabeth also translated *The Mirror of Glass of the Sinful Soul*, by Marguerite of Navarre.

between an emperor and a schismatic king against the Most Christian King and the infidel Turk.

Matters were eventually settled when Henry agreed to be described as 'Defender of the Faith' rather than 'Supreme Head of the Church', but now a new embarrassment arose: he announced that he himself would be in command of both the forthcoming English invasion of France and its projected advance on Paris. This decision caused a degree of consternation, both in England and in the Empire. The King was now fifty-three, in poor health and suffering constant pain from his ulcerated leg; the rigours of the campaign might well prove too much for him. Moreover the royal armourers would have a hard time accommodating his prodigious bulk, and by the time they had done so it would be hard to find any horse mighty enough to carry him. Even if nothing worse befell, his presence could not fail to slow the entire army down. The difficulty was that no one except the Emperor dared to tell him so, and the Emperor's words fell on deaf ears.

Fortunately, as the time for departure drew on, Henry himself began to lose his nerve. He now proposed that neither ruler should take the field in person, but that each should entrust his army to the best commanders available. This proposal, however, was at once rejected by the Emperor. He was, he pointed out, nearly ten years younger than Henry, and – apart from his gout – in much better physical shape. Had he not travelled all the way from Spain to Germany with the express purpose of leading his army into France? How then, possibly, could he pull out at the last moment? To do so would involve serious loss of face, and might even invite accusations of cowardice. He was implacably resolved to march with his men.

To Henry that settled the matter: if Charles was determined to march, he would march too. His armourers would simply have to use their ingenuity, and a suitable horse must somehow be found. But was he himself capable of riding all the way from the coast to Paris? Alas, almost certainly not. But then the Emperor must not do so either. He sent a further message to Charles: was it really wise at this early stage to make directly for the capital, leaving the army's flanks exposed to hostile action? Would it not be better first to concentrate on the towns along the coast and the frontier, before plunging deep into the French heartland? Once again he was snubbed. The plans had already been agreed; Charles saw no point in changing them. The argument was still continuing when, early in June, the English army crossed the Channel to Calais, under the joint command of the King and of those two hoary veterans, the Dukes of Suffolk and of Norfolk. It then moved eastward into French territory, but still without any orders informing it of its ultimate destination or of what it was to do when it got there. This indecision was to continue for well over a fortnight. The month was nearing its end when the Duke of Norfolk, sitting disconsolately in a field somewhere in France with a large, bewildered and increasingly hungry army, pointed out somewhat tersely to the Privy Council that most generals, before they were despatched abroad, were given orders as to where they were meant to be going. Such incompetence would never have occurred, he rather ill-advisedly pointed out, in Wolsey's day or in Cromwell's.

At last the King made up his mind. Norfolk was to lay siege to Montreuil, while he himself and Suffolk would concentrate on Boulogne. Charles protested indignantly once again that the plan had been to advance against Paris, to which Henry retorted – without a shred of justification – that without possession of the two towns under siege there would be no means of adequately provisioning an advancing army. And that, so far as he was concerned, was that. He marched with Suffolk to Boulogne and in early August settled down to the siege. Charles meanwhile continued his advance through Champagne until Paris itself was seriously threatened; Francis, back in the Louvre, declared his resolution to live and die there.

It soon became clear that Norfolk's attempt on Montreuil was doomed to failure. His best efforts seemed to have no appreciable effect on the fortifications. The Boulogne operation, on the other hand, proved a remarkable success. Henry enjoyed himself enormously, trotting from station to station, giving and countermanding orders; all those around him remarked on how much better he was in health and spirits. On 11 September, to his great delight, his men managed to blow up the castle, and on the 18th he entered the town in triumph. Once the excitement was over, however, and he had begun to weigh up the achievements of the campaign in comparison with its immense cost, his ebullience deserted him. He had not taken Paris, or even attempted to; his alliance with the Emperor was in shreds. Worse, he now learned that Charles had now abandoned his march on Paris, and that on the very day the English had taken Boulogne he and Francis had made peace at Crépy-en-Laonnois,* agreeing, *inter alia*, to abandon their conflicting claims and, later, to wage a joint campaign against the Turks. This peace was disastrous news indeed; Henry, left in the lurch, now had the whole weight of the French army against him. Worse still, a considerable force led by the Dauphin was already on the march to relieve Montreuil. Not that Montreuil needed much relieving. It was, so far as the miserable Duke of Norfolk could see, totally impregnable and well supplied with provisions of all kinds. His men, on the other hand, were frustrated and half-starved, and he was only too pleased to receive the King's orders to raise the siege and – avoiding the Dauphin's army as best he could – to withdraw to Boulogne.

Not, however, for long. Leaving his army in the newly captured town, Henry returned to England at the end of the month; but he had not even reached London when still more disastrous

---

* In Picardy. Not to be confused with Crépy-en-Valois, some forty miles north of Paris.

news was brought to him. The Dukes of Norfolk and of Suffolk, in flagrant defiance of his own clearly expressed orders, had led almost the entire army out of Boulogne and had returned with it to Calais. Their excuse was that the King's plans for building new defences for Boulogne were impracticable, and that it was Calais that needed help and support against the advancing Dauphin; but Henry did not believe them for a moment. He knew perfectly well that with the approach of the French army the two had simply lost their heads and fled back for safety on English soil. Furious, he ordered them to return to their posts, but this was no longer possible; the army was now near mutiny, and the Dauphin had Calais surrounded.

There was nothing for it but to do their best to come to terms with the French, and in mid-October talks began at Calais. They failed completely. Henry insisted that he must keep Boulogne, and also that Francis should abandon his alliance with Scotland, with which he had recently renewed all his country's former treaties. Neither of these demands was acceptable to the French, who early in November returned angrily to Paris. Henry had earned himself a little breathing space with the approach of winter, but he and Francis were still in a state of war, and now his relations with Charles were very little better. He had complained bitterly of the Emperor's defection, but Charles had indignantly replied that it was the English who had been guilty of betrayal. It was they, not he, who had refused to undertake the planned march on Paris, while their so-called siege of Montreuil had been pure pretence: they had merely sat outside the town doing nothing. The attack on Boulogne had been their sole intention from the very beginning. If Henry had not insisted so ridiculously on participating in the campaign himself, then he – the Emperor – would never have acted as he did. And anyway, had not Henry specifically agreed that Charles should be free to make peace unilaterally? No, replied Henry: their agreement at Calais had been that each might negotiate independently, but that neither would conclude a treaty without further consultation between them.

And it got worse. Henry now began accusing Charles of allowing Spanish troops to fight for the French, and of turning a blind eye when the Inquisition dared to mistreat innocent English merchants in Spain. Charles – who had been seriously delayed by the siege of Saint-Dizier, where the French garrison had held out heroically for forty-one days – countered with complaints that the English had laid hands on imperial ships and cargoes, that seven hundred Spanish arquebusiers had been lured to the Scottish borders (where another war was in progress) and that Henry had been secretly negotiating with the German Lutherans. By midsummer 1545 relations between the two rulers were once again near breaking point. And meanwhile the French were closing in; French ships were blockading Boulogne, and a French invasion became once again a serious danger. Money also was a problem. The campaign of 1544 had cost nearly three times what had been expected. Already for the past three years Henry had been subsisting largely on what he called 'benevolencies' – forced loans, or more accurately false gifts, from donors who for the most part were very far from benevolent – and on the sales of formerly monastic lands. The currency meanwhile had been debased on a dramatic scale, by re-minting coins with increasing proportions of base metal; and Henry even conceived a project of 'borrowing' church plate, a practice much approved of by the Earl of Hertford, whose influence with the King was by this time considerable. 'God's service,' he assured his master, 'which consisteth not in jewels, plate or ornaments of gold and silver, cannot thereby be anything diminished, and those things better employed for the weal and defence of the realm.'

Henry may well have been desperate for money; but, as he knew in his heart, it was all his own fault. His passion for campaigning – which for the last five years of his life was to cost him well over two million pounds – had yielded him remarkably little; and now, thanks entirely to him, England was in greater danger than she had been even in 1539 – and perhaps for generations. He had also quite unnecessarily antagonised his most important fellow-rulers, from one of whom he now confidently expected an invasion. And he was right to do so. On the evening of Sunday, 19 July 1545, a French fleet of over two hundred ships entered the Solent; Henry, who chanced to be dining that night on board the *Henry Grâce à Dieu* – better known as the *Great Harry* – hastened ashore, while the English fleet moved against the invaders.* A recently prepared chain of beacons was lit to carry warnings across the country, and on the following day the French landed on the Isle of Wight. After only twenty-four hours, rather surprisingly, they re-embarked, only to land again at Seaford shortly afterwards; but this landing too proved temporary, and after a quick and inconclusive skirmish with the English fleet off Beachy Head they set sail for home.

It was all rather an anti-climax; the danger was, however, that these short raids might well have been simply exploratory, preparing the way for something a good deal more ambitious. Henry certainly feared as much, and on 10 August he ordered the Church authorities to stage religious processions throughout the kingdom, together with public prayers for victory.† In fact, there were to be no more invasions; but the situation remained desperate. Stephen Gardiner, now Bishop of Winchester, wrote:

We are at war with France and Scotland, we have enmity with the Bishop of Rome; we have no assured friendship here with

---

* It was on this occasion that the English flagship, the *Mary Rose*, suddenly keeled over and sank. The wreck was rediscovered in 1971 and is now on show in its own museum in Portsmouth.

† It would have been more suitable, notes Professor Scarisbrick, if they had prayed for survival.

the Emperor and we have received from the Landgrave, chief
captain of the Protestants, such displeasure that he has cause to
think us angry with him . . . Our war is noisome to our realm
and to all our merchants that traffic through the Narrow Seas
. . .We are in a world where reason and learning prevail not and
covenants are little regarded.

He spoke no more than the truth. By the end of 1545 England
was as near bankruptcy as she had ever been.

~

But the Emperor Charles had his worries too; and among his
principal ones was Sultan Suleiman, whose operations in
Hungary were becoming an increasingly dangerous threat to
his Empire. Early in 1544, at the Diet of Speyer, in return for
the promise of generous financial support, Charles had undertaken to lead a campaign in person against the Turks, but had
been prevented from doing so by the subsequent fighting in
France. His brother Ferdinand had accordingly attempted to
negotiate a truce to buy a little more time. This, however, had
been bitterly resented by his Hungarian subjects, who had
accused him of going back on his word, and of agreeing to a
shoddy peace when he had promised to make war. By this time
Charles had become convinced that Francis, despite the promises that he had made at Crépy, had no intention of marching
against Suleiman, with whom his surprisingly friendly relations
were well known across Europe. He and Ferdinand accordingly
entrusted Francis with the task of renegotiating a truce, one
that the Hungarians would be readier to accept. Both they and
the French sent special envoys to Istanbul. The Empire was to
be represented by a certain Gerhard Veltwyck, a converted Jew

and an eminent Hebrew scholar, France by an experienced diplomat, Jean de Montluc.

The trouble was that Charles and Francis had not given their respective ambassadors similar briefs. Thus, from the very beginning, confusion reigned. Montluc had instructions to explain to the Sultan that the Emperor was coming as a supplicant, on Francis's insistence; Veltwyck, on the other hand, had been briefed to claim that the Emperor had been assured by Francis that the Turks longed for peace, and had guaranteed the success of the mission. If, in other words, the negotiations were to fail, it would be the fault of the French. All this was unfortunate enough, but there was worse to come. Veltwyck now discovered that yet another ambassador, a Dr Secco, was already in Istanbul, having been despatched by Archduke Ferdinand. He wrote at once to Secco instructing him to suspend all negotiations until his arrival, but his letter was intercepted by the Turks, who concluded – correctly – that Charles and his brother must be at cross purposes. Almost incredibly, there was another French representative there too, one Gabriel d'Aramon, who deeply resented the arrival of Montluc and managed to prevent any further instructions being sent to him.

All this could have ended in disaster. Suleiman had still not forgiven Francis for what he considered was a betrayal at Crépy, after which he had very nearly impaled the luckless French ambassador; but he was fully occupied with his preparations for a new campaign in Persia, and had no wish to fight on two fronts simultaneously. He was happy to agree to a limited pause in hostilities, its precise duration to be settled later. Veltwyck and Montluc then returned to their respective courts, with d'Aramon returning separately. The following summer – 1545 – Veltwyck and d'Aramon were back in Istanbul, Montluc having presumably had enough of his fellow-ambassadors' intrigues. D'Aramon arrived this time with a magnificent entourage and sumptuous presents for the Sultan, including a vast clock made in Lyon with a fountain, which worked for twelve hours once the water had been poured in.* His purpose was to persuade Suleiman to launch an immediate attack on the Emperor in Hungary, but the Sultan remained firm. He gratefully accepted the clock, but refused any suggestion of an attack. On 13 June he agreed with Veltwyck on a five-year truce, by the terms of which Charles and Ferdinand gave their full recognition to Ottoman Hungary and undertook to pay an annual tribute of 30,000 gold florins in respect of their Habsburg possessions in the north and west of the country. He in return gave his assurance that peace would be maintained along his borders. He then wrote Francis a cordial letter of explanation, in which he promised to maintain the 'friendship and fidelity' that the two had enjoyed in the past.

The agreement was eventually signed at Adrianople – the modern Edirne – in November 1545, and was replaced by a full peace treaty two years later; Charles was at last free to turn to his problems in Germany; he was, however, bitterly criticised throughout Europe. For all good God-fearing Catholics, the Sultan was Antichrist, the Beast of the Apocalypse; to treat him as an equal – arguably even as a superior – was a sin not to be forgiven. It had been bad enough when Francis, the Most Christian King, had allied himself with the infidel; but for the Emperor himself to do so, and to undertake furthermore to make an annual payment of a very considerable sum in return for the relatively small part of Hungary under Habsburg control – a payment that implied recognition of Turkish sovereignty over the whole country and which the Turks unhesitatingly described

---

*   One member of d'Aramon's following, Pierre Belon, left a full account of his travels – noting, *inter alia*, that the Turks had no understanding of the pleasures of the table. They served nothing but cucumbers and raw greens, without oil or vinegar; the main course tended to be porridge. '*Ne font jamais délices*', he moans.

as a tribute — that was far, far worse. What was it indeed but a betrayal, a betrayal not only of Christendom but of Jesus Christ himself? Patriotic Hungarians now spat at the very mention of the Emperor's name. They had looked to him to help them regain their ancient kingdom, but this last action had proved that he was no longer to be trusted, that he had feet of clay.

As for the German Protestants, their hatred for the Sultan was every bit as heartfelt, but — whether they confessed it or not — they owed him a considerable debt. As the Bishop of Montpellier pointed out to Francis, had it not been for the Turks the Reformation might easily have suffered the same fate as had the Albigensians.* The fact was that Charles needed the German Protestants to help him to resist Ottoman pressure on Central Europe; thus he had had no choice but in 1532 to sign the Peace of Nuremberg — which was finally to lead to the Peace of Augsburg in 1555, officially recognising the existence of Protestantism in Germany. The Turks were fully aware of all this. They had always favoured the Protestants more than the Catholics because of their disapproval of the worship of idols; and they were probably every bit as quietly grateful to the Protestants as the Protestants were to them.

~

But if Charles was at least in part reconciled to the Protestants, the Pope was not. Reared in the court of Lorenzo the Magnificent, Alessandro Farnese was a child of the Renaissance: although a cardinal at twenty-five, he had since cheerfully fathered four

---

* The Albigensians, or Cathars, were a medieval Christian sect based in south-west France which was brutally stamped out by a Crusade under Louis VIII and by the Inquisition.

children. As Pope Paul III he was equally shameless in his nepotism, raising two of his grandsons to the Sacred College at the ages of sixteen and fourteen respectively. He revived the Carnival in 1536; Rome resounded to the cheers of bullfights, horse races and firework displays, the Vatican to the music of balls and banquets. And yet – and this is what makes him one of the most interesting popes of the sixteenth century – he turned out to be a man of strong moral conscience and one of the most effective reformers of the Roman Catholic Church.

The more Pope Paul considered how best to contain the surge, the more convinced he became that the prime necessity was for a General Council – and one, he accepted, that would have to include a strong contingent of Lutherans. Objections, inevitably, were raised on all sides. The cardinals saw any reform as a threat to their own comfortable lifestyles; the Emperor, terrified that the proposed Council might take so rigid a stand on doctrine as to make a compromise with his Protestant subjects impossible, preferred that it should leave aside all theological questions and confine itself to measures of reform; the Lutherans demanded a totally uncommitted meeting of all Christians, and steadfastly refused to attend any assembly held on Italian soil, or one presided over by the Pope.

Charles himself, who never felt particularly strongly about doctrine, would happily have accepted any compromise proposed or agreed to by Rome; all he wanted was unity. As for the King of France, he was only too pleased to see the Emperor enmeshed in his religious problems, and had no wish at all to have them resolved. But Pope Paul persisted, and meanwhile summoned a special commission; this was instructed to report on all the ills of the Church and to recommend measures that should be taken to remedy them. In due course the commissioners submitted their report. They did not pull their punches. They listed the current abuses and laid the blame for all of them – the sale of indulgences and Church benefices, the sinecures, the stockpiling of bishoprics and countless others – squarely on the Papacy. The result of all this, they pointed out, had been the Protestant Reformation, and no wonder: had the Church kept its house in order, the Reformation would never have occurred. The horrified Curia – which had been deliberately banned from the commission – did all it could to sweep the report under the carpet; but a copy was leaked, and before long a German translation was going the rounds of the jubilant Lutheran churches.

Now, at last, reform – serious reform – was in the air, and Pope Paul did everything he could to encourage it. He gave an enthusiastic reception to the young Filippo Neri, whose mission was concentrated on the seedy inns and whorehouses of the Roman underworld; and a year or two later he accorded a similar welcome to the rather older Ignatius Loyola, a Basque who had arrived with half a dozen like-minded colleagues from Spain, grouped together in what they called the Society of Jesus. In 1540 the Pope issued a Bull giving the Society his official approval. The Jesuits, with no distinctive dress for their Order, no fixed headquarters and no choral prayer, were bound together by two things only: strict discipline and unconditional obedience. They were to have a chequered history, but they were the spearhead of the Counter-Reformation.

Finally, on 13 December 1545, the long-delayed Council opened at Trent, a city recommended by the Emperor because it lay safely in imperial territory. It got off to a shaky start, its first sessions being attended by only a single cardinal, four arch-bishops and thirty-one bishops; but it was gradually to gain momentum and to continue at intervals, in Trent and later in Bologna, for the next eighteen years. It was overwhelmingly weighted in favour of the Italians; even when best attended, with more than 270 bishops, the Germans never numbered more than thirteen. But the important thing about the Council was that – in the teeth of all opposition to it – it actually happened;

moreover, it showed itself ready to defy the Emperor and fearlessly to debate the hoary old questions of doctrine: justification by faith, transubstantiation, purgatory and many more.

It was never more than a partial success. When it was at last dissolved, the Protestants, who understandably saw it as little more than a Roman puppet-show, naturally remained unsatisfied; even for the Catholics its reforms were less radical and comprehensive than many had hoped for. Not a word was said, for example, about the reform of the Papacy itself, which was far more necessary than anything else. Owing largely to the undiminished hostility of the Emperor and the King of France the Council sat only intermittently, often without the French contingent. It never came near to being the ecumenical council of union for the whole of western Christendom that had been so long hoped and prayed for; it was simply the confessional council of the Counter-Reformation, formed for the purpose of re-catholicising the continent, if necessary by force. The results were to be all too evident: in France no fewer than eight civil wars against the Huguenots (more than three thousand of whom perished in the Massacre of Saint Bartholomew in Paris during the late summer of 1572); a war between Spain and the Netherlands that lasted for more than eighty years; and the nightmare Thirty Years War (1618–48), which was to cause untold devastation through northern Europe.

But the Council of Trent nevertheless established a solid basis for the renewal of discipline and spiritual life in the Church, which emerged a good deal stronger and more focused than before. It led to the codification of the Tridentine Creed and the Tridentine Mass (from *Tridentum*, the Latin name for Trent), which remained in use for the next four centuries; and it finally succeeded in stemming the Protestant tide. And for all that, the lion's share of the credit must go to that epicure, nepotist and adulterer Pope Paul III.

~

By the end of 1545 King Henry's health was deteriorating fast. He was more enormous than ever, and with his festering legs was almost completely immobile; he could be moved about only on trolleys, with huge winches to take him up and down stairs. On the other hand, he remained as determined as ever to continue the endless diplomatic struggle with his fellow-monarchs. No longer did he have a Wolsey or a Cromwell to take decisions for him; no matter: he was quite prepared to take his own. Nor, come to that, did he have a Pope to argue with; but the situation was quite complicated enough without the Papacy. At least he knew what he wanted; and what he now wanted above all was to retain his hold on Boulogne. Again and again his Council pressed him to give it up; until he did so, they pointed out, there could be no peace with France, and the country simply could not afford to continue the war. But Henry would hear none of it. The conquest of the town had cost him dear; it had become a symbol, and he intended to hang on to it come what might. Unfortunately he was unlikely to succeed in doing so without the help of the Emperor – whom he was now vehemently urging to renounce the peace he had so inexcusably agreed at Crépy and return to the Anglo-imperial alliance he had made the year before.

Charles, however, was not really interested. He was prepared to accept Henry's suggestion for a meeting, on condition that the King first reached an agreement with Francis; but any such agreement, he knew, would have to hinge on the surrender of Boulogne, which Henry refused to contemplate. The fact was that the Emperor was bored with both the squabbling monarchs and would happily have wished a plague on both their houses. His overriding purpose now was to root out Protestantism from Germany. For the moment, so far as he was concerned, nothing else mattered.

The German Protestants knew, for their part, that if they hoped to survive at all, they would need all the help they could get. In September 1545 Hesse, Saxony and Württemberg actually sent a joint delegation to England – not to ask directly for aid, but with an offer to mediate between Henry and Francis in order that the two kings, once again on friendly terms, might then join them in an alliance to resist imperial attack. Henry agreed to their proposal, but their attempts failed; they had not begun to understand the complexity of the problems involved, and the French were not in a giving mood. The war therefore continued. There had been intermittent skirmishing around Boulogne and Calais for some months past, culminating in an unfortunate incident when a smallish force under the Duke of Norfolk's son, the swashbuckling young Earl of Surrey,* had been badly mauled near the fortress of Saint-Etienne; and in January 1546 Henry decided to assert his position. He sent Edward Seymour, Earl of Hertford, to France with some 25,000 men and 4,000 horses, supported by a fleet of 45 sail.

Hertford and his army duly landed at Calais in March, but they did not get very far – not because of French resistance, but because the King suddenly changed his mind. Why he did so we do not know; perhaps his agents had failed to find enough food, arms or munitions; perhaps it was Charles's refusal to help him; perhaps there was simply not enough money. At any rate, he decided to make peace. Talks began towards the end of April. Both the English and the French were hard bargainers, and they were still arguing at the beginning of June; but on the 6th the

---

* Surrey was a far better poet than he was a soldier. He and his friend Sir Thomas Wyatt were the first English poets to write in the sonnet form that Shakespeare was to make famous, and he was the first to publish blank verse – unrhymed iambic pentameters – in his translation of Books II and IV of the *Aeneid*. He is buried in a spectacular tomb of painted alabaster in the church of St Michael the Archangel at Framlingham in Suffolk.

details were finally agreed, and on the 7th, in a tent between Ardres and Guînes – virtually on the site of the Field of the Cloth of Gold – the peace treaty was signed. Boulogne would be returned to France in 1554, on payment of two million crowns. A week later the imperial ambassador remarked to Henry that at such a price the town would remain English for ever. The King, we are told, 'smiled knowingly'.

Good relations were, however, restored. At much the same time Henry stood godfather – by proxy – to Francis's grandson. And when, at Fontainebleau on 1 August 1546, Francis ratified the treaty, the Most Christian King had no hesitation in designating Henry as he wished to be designated: as Supreme Head of the Church of England and Ireland.

~

But by this time it was clear to all around him that King Henry had little time left. Despite his by now prodigious girth, that superb constitution with which he had been born had until recently preserved him remarkably well. He had survived an early attack of smallpox in 1514, and had never shown the faintest sign of the consumption that had accounted for his father, his elder brother and his bastard son, and which was soon to carry off his legitimate son, King Edward VI. Unfortunately he was not proof against accidents, particularly in the tiltyard. There had been a particularly serious one at Greenwich in 1536, when his armoured horse had fallen on top of him and he had lain unconscious for two hours. At that time he was already forty-four years old and dangerously overweight; to those who knew him well, he was never quite the same again. And then there was the ulcer on his thigh; it had already plagued him for years, certainly since 1528. Inevitably it had led to suspicions of syphilis, but these were almost certainly groundless; more likely is that it was the result of varicose veins, or even perhaps osteo-myelitis. Whatever the cause, it had spread to the other leg; both were by now badly ulcerated, giving him constant pain; and yet, as late as 1544, we find him not only still in the saddle but fighting in France.

The final decline seems to have begun in the autumn of 1546. It was then, too, that the King began behaving strangely, notably by turning with unprecedented savagery on the Duke of Norfolk and the Earl of Surrey, his son. Surrey had admittedly failed to distinguish himself while on campaign in the previous year, but he was certainly not plotting to seize the throne, as Henry seemed to think. Nevertheless he was beheaded – at the age of twenty-nine or thirty – on 19 January 1547 on a charge of treason. The Duke himself, despite his almost universal unpopularity, had served his country well; but he too was charged, and subsequently condemned to suffer the same fate as his son. Fortunately he was to be saved by the King's death; the Council had no wish to inaugurate the new reign of Edward VI with bloodshed. He remained, however, in the Tower throughout Edward's reign, to be finally released and pardoned by Queen Mary in 1553.

On 26 December 1546 Henry sent for his will, with which he pronounced himself deeply unsatisfied. The last month of his life was taken up with endless arguments and changes of mind, all of which probably stimulated him and kept him alive a little longer. Among a number of other provisions, he confirmed the legitimacy of his daughters, Mary and Elizabeth, and restored them both to the line of succession. But the end was near, and he knew it. He died in the early hours of Friday 28 January 1547, aged fifty-five, having reigned for the best part of thirty-eight years. On 14 February his embalmed body was carried to Windsor in a procession four miles long and buried in St George's Chapel, next to the coffin of Jane Seymour, as he had directed.

And that should have been the end of the story of King

Henry VIII. Alas, it was not. All through the five-year reign of his sad and sickly son the work continued on his magnificent tomb; but on the succession of Queen Mary it suddenly stopped.*
A certain Sir Francis Englefield, one of Mary's privy councillors, later revealed that he had been present at Windsor when Henry's grave had been opened, and what was left of his body pulled out and ceremonially consigned to the flames. He may have been the Queen's father, but he was an unrepentant heretic and schismatic; in the eyes of his daughter, no other fate was possible.

But, when the smoke had cleared away, one fact remained undisputed: of all the kings since the Norman Conquest, King Henry VIII had been by no means the best, but none had been more radiant of kingship, nor had any done more to change the face of England. Henry had defied both Emperor and Pope; he had shaken off the grip of Rome, although – and this should be emphasised – he had not embraced Protestantism, which was to come only in the reign of his son Edward. To the day of his death he would certainly not have changed a word of his book against Luther, for which Leo X had granted him the title of Defender of the Faith – except to make it clear that it was no longer to the Pope but to the King that Englishmen owed obedience. All the other essentials of Catholic worship, including the liturgy, remained unaltered. With the help of Thomas Cromwell he had given the country a superb administrative organisation, far more efficient than it had ever possessed before; he had transformed the English navy, building for the first time ships that fired broadsides and thus revolutionising naval warfare; he had brought to his subjects the splendour of the English Bible; and he had broken the power of the monasteries – raising, it should be noted, no issues of doctrine. On the debit side he

---

* As much of the tomb as had already been built was demolished by Parliament in 1646 during the Civil War; the empty sarcophagus and its base were eventually used in 1806 for the tomb of Lord Nelson in St Paul's.

had been responsible for the destruction of literally hundreds of glorious buildings and thousands of the priceless treasures they contained. As a child of the Renaissance and a professed lover of the arts, did he ever regret what he had done? He showed no sign of doing so. Nor, despite countless undertakings and promises, did he make proper use of the immense wealth that he gained from the dissolution. He could have built hospitals and schools, universities and almshouses, and perhaps even a road or two, but no. A considerable sum probably went on the building of Nonsuch Palace, which by November 1545 had already cost £24,000 and was to be demolished a hundred and fifty years later, while two military expeditions to France in swift succession accounted for much of the rest.

Sadly, too, he had shown little interest in exploration. During his lifetime the known world had more than trebled in size: Spain, which played the leading role in the discovery of the Americas, reaped benefits almost beyond computation; Portugal opened up first the coast of Africa and then the Indies – another bottomless source of wealth. France too played her part (see pp. 11–12 above). But for Henry the New World was of little interest – less even than it had been to his father and infinitely less than it was to be to his daughter Elizabeth, who encouraged her faithful sea dogs for all she was worth and hugely enjoyed giving the Spaniards a run for their money. Had he lavished on South America half the attention that he paid to his grotesquely outdated ambitions in France, it is quite possible that parts of that continent might be speaking English today.

~

As his ambassador to Paris had written to Henry in 1543, King Francis was as active and restless as he had ever been – 'never sojourning two nights in one place, disposing himself as the report of great harts [stags] is made to him, and continually removing at an hour's warning so that no man can tell where to find the Court'. But by the time Charles and Suleiman set their seals to the Treaty of Adrianople in 1545, the King lay desperately ill. Already in January of that year he was suffering an agonisingly painful abscess 'in his lower parts'. It was opened and drained repeatedly, and in early February he was sufficiently recovered to leave Paris in a litter for the Loire valley. He was, he told the imperial ambassador, quite restored to health, 'albeit dead in respect of the ladies'. But there was more trouble with the abscess in March, and as the year went on he grew steadily weaker.

Not for a moment did he relax his grip on government, and foreign ambassadors seldom failed to comment on his knowledge and understanding of international affairs. But by the summer of 1546, although he continued to hunt when he felt strong enough, it was clear that he had not long to live. At the end of January 1547 came the news that Henry VIII had died in the Palace of Whitehall. The English embassy was informed of Francis's grief over the loss of 'his good and true friend'; and although on that same evening he was seen 'laughing much and enjoying himself with his ladies', within days he had fallen into a feverish depression, from which he never properly recovered.*
He tried to return to Paris, where he had planned a memorial service for Henry at Notre-Dame; but when he reached Rambouillet, he found that he could go no further. He died there, between 1 and 2 p.m. on Thursday, 31 March, aged just fifty-two.

The funeral ceremonies lasted almost two months. Perhaps

---

* Rumour had it that the depression was brought on by a letter he had received from the dying Henry, reminding him that he too was mortal; but for a number of reasons this seems unlikely. Henry was a reluctant correspondent at the best of times.

the most curious feature was the continued serving, for eleven days from the end of April, of meals to the dead King. While his remarkably lifelike effigy – by François Clouet – lay on a bed of state in the great hall of Saint-Cloud, these were served as if he were still alive: the table was laid, the courses brought in one by one, the wine poured out twice at each meal. At the end, grace was said by a cardinal. Not till 11 May was the King's coffin taken on a wagon to Notre-Dame and thence, after a short service, to its final resting place in the Abbey of Saint-Denis, where all but three of the kings of France are buried. There the new King, Henry II – whose filial conscientiousness was exemplary, though Francis had never liked him much – commissioned an exquisite tomb from the architect Philibert de l'Orme: Francis and Queen Claude lie together, as it were in state, on the pedestal, while their naked and worm-eaten bodies can be seen below.

What – the question continues to be asked – was the cause of the King's death? Traditionally, he was said to have died of syphilis. He had certainly been treated for the disease, but the symptoms described by those who attended him on his deathbed, together with the fact that he was mentally in full possession of his faculties, make the theory that it killed him most unlikely. There can be no doubt that the problem was urological; more than that – given the state of sixteenth-century medicine – we shall never know.

7

'A reasonable regret'

A ND SO IT was that the first three months of 1547 saw the deaths of two of the four princes who form the subject of this book. Their somewhat pathetic successors cannot constitute anything but an anti-climax, nor will their fortunes be followed with the degree of detail afforded to their fathers; on the other hand, since they reigned at the same time as our other two princes – who remained very much alive, and on whom we shall be concentrating from now on – they cannot entirely be ignored.

King Edward VI of England was a boy of nine when he came to the throne, and never reached his majority. The son of Henry and Jane Seymour, he was the first English monarch to be raised as a Protestant. Of his early youth, the generally accepted opinion is that he was a sickly child, unlikely to outlive his father; more recently, however, historians have challenged this view. He certainly seems to have been a healthy baby: in May 1538 Henry was seen 'dallying with him in his arms . . . and so holding him to a window to the sight and comfort of the people', and a few months later Thomas, Lord Audley, the Lord Chancellor, reported his rapid growth and vigour. At the age of four he fell ill with quartan fever, a form of malaria causing fevers that recur every fourth day; but he recovered, and it now appears that he may have enjoyed a few years of reasonable health until he contracted the tuberculosis that killed him. His formal education began in his seventh year, when he began learning Latin, French, Spanish and Italian, and took additional lessons on the lute and virginals. Meanwhile his spiritual development was guided by Archbishop Thomas Cranmer, whose Book of Common Prayer is still in use today. By 1549 he had written a treatise on the Pope as Antichrist, so he must have been an apt pupil – and heading in the right direction.

From his babyhood, inevitably, Edward was a pawn in the eternal diplomatic chess game. As early as 1 July 1543 his father signed the Treaty of Greenwich with Scotland, whereby his five-year-old son was betrothed to Mary, Queen of Scots, then aged seven months.* When the Scots repudiated the treaty in December, such was the King's anger that he ordered his son's uncle – Edward Seymour, Earl of Hertford – to invade Scotland and 'put all to fire and sword, burn Edinburgh town, so razed and defaced when you have sacked and gotten what ye can of it, as there may remain forever a perpetual memory of the vengeance of God lightened upon them for their falsehood and disloyalty'. Seymour took him at his word; the campaign that followed showed no mercy and took no prisoners. Of all the campaigns in history launched by the English against the Scots, this was the most pitiless and most savage. Mary, meanwhile, was hastily removed to France, where she was betrothed to the Dauphin – the later Francis II – and was to reign as Queen of France for seventeen months, from July 1559 until his death.

Edward was crowned in Westminster Abbey four days after his father's burial. The ceremonies were shortened, firstly because of the 'tedious length of the same which should weary and be hurtsome peradventure to the King's majesty, being yet of tender

---

* Born in December 1542, Mary was only six days old when her father, James V of Scotland, died and she succeeded him on the throne.

age', but also because the Reformation had rendered some of them inappropriate. There was, however, time for Cranmer to reaffirm the Royal Supremacy – the fact that the King was now head of the Church of England – and to urge the young prince to continue his father's work on it, in order that 'the tyranny of the Bishops of Rome [should be] banished from your subjects, and images removed'. In the years to follow, religious images were not just removed, they were smashed to bits. Edward's reign was to see orgies of iconoclasm unparalleled until the days of the Commonwealth, a century in the future. And indeed, after his accession the swing towards Protestantism moved at a quite remarkable speed. Hardly had the old King been laid in his grave before the liturgy was changed, and the old traditional Catholic vestments were replaced by Geneva gowns and bands. Now, too – Cranmer having set the fashion – priests began to marry in their hundreds.

But the reign did not last long. In January 1553 the young King fell sick of a fever. He partially recovered, and was well enough to move to Greenwich, but he worsened again and his legs became so swollen that he could no longer walk. He died at Greenwich, aged fifteen, at eight o'clock in the evening of 6 July, and was buried in his grandfather Henry VII's Chapel in Westminster Abbey, after a reformed funeral service led, it need hardly be said, by Cranmer. As almost always in the sixteenth century, the cause of his death was uncertain; there were, inevitably, rumours of poisoning by Catholics anxious to bring his sister Mary to the throne, but these were almost certainly unfounded. The most likely answer is that he died of a tubercular consumption, but the point is largely immaterial. It was not the cause that mattered, it was the result; and the result was the accession of his thirty-one-year-old half-sister Mary – whose reign was even shorter than his but amounted to a genuine reign of terror: in little over five years she was to burn over 280 Protestant dissenters at the stake.

~

King Henry II of France was the fourth child and second son of Francis I. His elder brother having died, unmarried and childless, in 1536, he succeeded his father on his twenty-eighth birthday. Catherine de' Medici, with whom he had suffered so excruciating a wedding night, was to bear him no fewer than ten children – there were three illegitimate ones as well – but the love of his life, of whom he made absolutely no secret, was the lovely Diane de Poitiers, twenty years his senior, who wielded very considerable political power throughout his reign, during which she was by far the most powerful woman in France.* Like Queen Mary across the Channel, Henry was as bigoted as any Catholic of the time could be; the religious policy he followed was very much the same as his father's. Persecution of Protestants – the Huguenots – continued, more savagely than ever. If found guilty, they risked being burned at the stake or, at the very least, having their tongues cut out.

Henry's own life ended prematurely at the age of forty, after an accident. On 1 July 1559 he was jousting in the Place des Vosges in Paris during a tournament to celebrate the Peace of Cateau-Cambrésis, which had effectively put an end some two months before to the eight-year war between himself and Philip of Spain. His opponent was Gabriel, Comte de Montgomery, a French nobleman who happened to be captain of the King's Scots Guard. Montgomery's lance shattered, and – by a one-in-a-million chance – a splinter from it slipped under the King's visor, ran through his eye and penetrated deep into his brain. Henry died ten days later, to be succeeded by his son Francis, husband of Mary, Queen of Scots. When in 1560 Francis

---

* A fact that did not prevent her agreeing to be painted by François Clouet, naked in the bath.

contracted a high fever — the result of an ear infection — and followed him to the grave, the throne passed in turn to his two younger brothers, Charles IX and Henry III, both of whom died without legitimate children. By this time France was deeply enmeshed in the hideous wars of religion. Only after Henry's death in 1589 was the way clear for the accession of Henry IV of Navarre, after which the country had once again a king worthy of the name.

~

Apart from his countless concubines, there were three women in the life of Suleiman the Magnificent. The first was Gülfem Hatun. Having borne him a son, Murad, who died shortly after birth, she was soon afterwards set aside and can safely be ignored. The second, Mahidevran Sultan, he called Gülbehar, 'Rose of Spring'. Historians are still arguing over her origins: she seems to have been either Albanian or Circassian. Between 1512 and 1525 she bore Suleiman five children, but by 1520 she in her turn was facing a serious rival: Haseki Hürrem Sultan, whom we know as Roxelana, 'the Russian woman' — and Roxelana was very dangerous indeed.*

By the 1550s, Roxelana herself was beginning to worry. She had borne Suleiman five strapping sons; but the Sultan's eldest was not one of them, being the child of Gülbehar. Mustafa was now in the prime of life, thirty-seven or thirty-eight, highly cultured and of immense charm, a fearless soldier who promised in the fullness of time to be in every respect a worthy successor to his father. The problem from Roxelana's point of view was that, if he were to assume the throne, the first thing he would

* She is described more fully in Chapter 1 (page 32).

almost certainly do, in the age-old Ottoman tradition, would be to have all his half-brothers – *her* children – strangled. Her own life would probably be spared, but she would be sent to the deeply unpleasant Old Seraglio, to which all the elderly concubines now surplus to requirements – they probably included Gülbehar – were consigned to moulder their lives away. Clearly, therefore, there was only one solution: Mustafa must be eliminated. In matters of this kind, Roxelana was not without experience; if the palace rumours were true – which they almost certainly were – it was she who had engineered the assassination of Ibrahim Pasha in 1536. Mustafa might prove a slightly more formidable challenge; but she now had on her side Ibrahim's successor, her small, swarthy, crafty and faintly sinister son-in-law the Grand Vizier Rüstem Pasha,* who she knew would be only too pleased to give her all the help she needed.

Now Rüstem had recently been appointed commander-in-chief of the army on the new campaign against Persia, which had begun in the spring of 1552; and the following winter the army, in which Prince Mustafa was serving, was encamped at Karaman, in southern Anatolia. The Sultan, however, had returned to the capital for the winter. In the course of that winter Rüstem despatched to Istanbul his chief of cavalry – a man known as Şemsi, whom he knew that Suleiman respected and trusted – with a report on the campaign to date but also a warning: that since he was not with his army the soldiers were murmuring that their Sultan was getting old – he was indeed fifty-nine – and were discussing the possibility of putting someone younger on the throne. The report went on to say that Mustafa was interested in this proposal and had even been in secret contact with the Persians to seek their assistance. Suleiman, not surprisingly, flew into a towering rage, showering curses on his eldest

---

* The small, exquisitely tiled mosque that he founded and which bears his name is one of the loveliest in Istanbul.

son. He immediately recalled Rüstem and made arrangements personally to take over the supreme command in the spring.

We may imagine that, after Roxelana, Rüstem and their friends had worked on the Sultan all winter; by the time he reached Karaman, his mind was made up. On arrival he immediately sent a message to his son, summoning him to appear at once before him 'in order to clear himself of the crimes of which he was accused', adding reassuringly that if he were able to do so he had nothing to fear. Mustafa knew perfectly well that he was on a knife-edge, but being sure of his innocence had no choice but to obey his father's command. Ghislain de Busbecq, Archduke Ferdinand's ambassador, received an account of what followed from an eyewitness; he reports it thus:

Mustafa entered. The drama commenced, and he was seized on every side. But the prince, in the moment he believed would be his last, regained his strength and was inspired with heroic courage. He knew that if he triumphed, he would gain the throne; he imagined the disorder, where the heat of battle would arouse pity in the janissaries; he saw them already armed to defend him against Suleiman's barbarity; he believed he could hear himself proclaimed Sultan by the whole army. This was indeed exactly what Suleiman had feared, and he had taken the precaution of hanging up curtains behind his tent, where the tragedy took place, so that nobody could see anything or even suspect anything and no noise could be heard.

Yet Mustafa's ardent desire to live and reign made him invincible, although alone against them all; the result of the combat was still uncertain but Suleiman, on the other side and impatient for success, raised his head above the hangings and saw that his mutes were ready to succumb; his fears were greatly increased and he looked menacingly at them, his eyes full of anger and filled with cruelty at their lack of courage. What was the effect of this look on the mutes? I cannot describe it: the fury he

excited in them was without parallel. They instantly threw themselves on Mustafa for a second time, knocked him straight down
and snatched his life from him. They then exposed the body of
the unfortunate prince on a carpet in front of Suleiman's tent,
so that the janissaries should understand his power and authority
from the fate which had just been inflicted on the man they
wanted to have as Sultan.

Mustafa had been enormously popular with his men, and his
cold-blooded murder sent a wave of indignation and disgust
through the whole army. They insulted Suleiman to his face –
something that had never before occurred – and pronounced
curses on Roxelana and Rüstem, whom they accused of having
extinguished 'the most brilliant sun, whose brightness would have
increased the glory of the imperial house'. To calm them down,
the Sultan put all the blame on Rüstem, taking his seals of office
from him and appointing a replacement, but the old Vizier was
too valuable to lose: within two years he was back at his post.

Alas, Mustafa's murder was not quite enough. He had a son,
Murad, still in his teens and living quietly at Bursa. Now Murad
had done no harm to anyone; but Roxelana was taking no
chances. A week or two later, he too came to an unpleasant end.
The news of the two atrocities, when it eventually leaked out,
shocked all Europe; but it also came as something of a relief.
Mustafa, it was known, had been intelligent, ambitious and
courageous. Had he lived and duly succeeded Suleiman, how
much further would he have pushed the boundaries of his
Empire? As it happened, the princes of Europe knew next to
nothing about the Sultan's other sons, or which of them was
eventually to succeed. Had they done so, their relief would have
given place to jubilation.

~

The Emperor Charles was fully aware of the changes that were taking place in England, and was much distressed. Particularly concerned as he was for his first cousin the Princess Mary – who, it seemed almost certain, would be obliged to obey the new Protestant laws – he demanded, through an English envoy, guarantees that she would be allowed to continue to pursue her religion as she always had. His fears were, as might have been imagined, fully justified: the Council of Regency was already threatening Mary's chaplain with dire punishments if he continued to ignore its ordinances. The poor man could only reply that, whereas everywhere else he would unfailingly adopt Cranmer's recently published Book of Common Prayer, in his mistress's own house he had no choice but to comply with her instructions.

For Mary herself, this was a serious crisis. The Mass was her only comfort, her only hope of salvation; rather than renounce it, she was determined to leave the country. This was not at all what Charles wanted, since to do so would greatly reduce her chances of succession; moreover her presence would be a most unwelcome embarrassment if she were to end up at his court. Eventually, however, he was persuaded that her only hope lay in escape to somewhere, and actually approved an elaborate cloak-and-dagger scheme to spirit her out of England. The plan was for two imperial agents disguised as corn merchants to sail up the Blackwater river to Maldon in Essex with a cargo of wheat. They would then take Mary on board under cover of darkness and smuggle her out to a Spanish man-of-war which would be waiting off the coast. The plan never materialised, but proved in any case unnecessary. Mary stayed where she was, and continued – in private – to hear Mass as she wished.

With the death of Edward, however, in the summer of 1553 a new set of problems arose. By the terms of her father's Act of Succession, confirmed by his will, Mary was Queen. On the other hand, England was by now a thoroughly Protestant nation; were she to succeed to the throne, the Catholics would be once again in control and all the work of the past few years would be undone. It was with this thought in his mind that the young King had on his deathbed nominated as his successor not his half-sister but the irreproachably Protestant Lady Jane Grey. Lady Jane was the great-granddaughter of Henry VII through his younger daughter Mary, and consequently Edward's first cousin once removed – not, it must be admitted, a particularly close relative; but in the absence of any grandchildren of Henry VIII she represented the only hope of escaping the renewed grip of Rome. She also enjoyed the additional advantage of having married, just two months previously, the son of the Duke of Northumberland, who, as leader of the Council of Regency, was the most powerful man in England. On 10 July she was formally proclaimed Queen.

At once there were murmurings of discontent. Despite her Catholicism, there were many for whom Mary's lawful claim to the throne as Henry's eldest surviving child overrode any religious considerations; because of it, all those who had refused to accept the Protestant faith were ready to welcome her with open arms. Immediately after her half-brother's death she had hurried to her estates in Norfolk, where she was popular and knew that she could rally support. From there she sent a message to the Council asserting her right and title to the throne and demanding that she be proclaimed England's legitimate sovereign, as indeed she had already proclaimed herself.

Northumberland realised that he had made a disastrous mistake. He should never have allowed Mary her liberty; the moment the King was seen to be dying he should have put her under arrest. On 14 July, with a body of some three thousand men, he marched off to East Anglia, hoping that he might still be able to do so. He reached Cambridge the following day, only to find that he was too late. Mary was already rallying her forces at Framlingham Castle in Suffolk, where in less than a week she had managed to accumulate an army of nearly twenty thousand.

Back in London, the Council saw that it could no longer stand against her. On 19 July – perhaps a little sheepishly – it proclaimed Mary as Queen. Lady Jane's nine-day reign was at an end. The announcement was greeted with wild rejoicing in London. Away in Cambridge, Northumberland was ordered to make a similar proclamation; he did, but it did him no good. He was arrested on 24 July and beheaded on 22 August. Poor Jane Grey was imprisoned in the Tower, and in November was convicted of high treason.

In Rome, meanwhile, the news of Mary's accession had also caused a considerable stir. The current Pope, Julius III, sent Cardinal Pole – who could easily have been pope himself had he bestirred himself a little more during the conclave, having missed election by only two votes – post-haste to London as Legate, with full powers to encourage the intended restoration of Catholicism and to help it to succeed. Unfortunately His Holiness was at the time giving rather more of his attention to a seventeen-year-old boy, somewhat inappropriately named Innocenzo, whom he had picked up in the streets of Parma and whom on his accession he had instantly made a cardinal. He doubtless rejoiced when England returned to the Catholic fold; but there can be no doubt that his principal object in life was the pursuit of pleasure. In February 1555 an envoy was despatched from England to inform him of the country's formal submission, but by the time he reached Rome the Pope was dead. For a man notorious, *inter alia*, for his gluttony, there was a certain poetic justice in his end: his digestive system ceased to function and he died effectively of starvation.

Julius's successor was Pope Marcellus II, but after only twenty-two days in office he suffered a fatal stroke.* He was succeeded in turn by Pope Paul IV – the oldest pope of the sixteenth century and by a long way the most unpleasant. The Emperor

---

* Palestrina's *Missa Papae Marcelli* is his only lasting memorial.

had done everything within his power to block his election, but his efforts had been counter-productive. Gian Pietro Carafa was already seventy-nine years old, and with his intolerance, his bigotry, his refusal to compromise or even to listen to any opinions other than his own he was a throwback to the Middle Ages. Such was his austerity and the fear that he inspired that when he strode through the Vatican sparks were said to fly from his feet. He suspended the Council of Trent; he introduced the Index of Forbidden Books, including in it the complete works of Erasmus; he took a special delight in the Inquisition, never missing its weekly meetings; finally, he opened the most savage campaign in papal history against the Jews – to the point where, in the five short years of his pontificate, the Jewish population of Rome was halved. It was under him that they were rounded up into a ghetto, forbidden to trade in any commodity except food and second-hand clothing, permitted only a single synagogue in each city (in Rome seven synagogues had to be demolished), compelled to speak only Italian or Latin and obliged to wear yellow hats in the street.

Next to the Jews, Paul IV hated the Habsburgs. He never forgave the Emperor Charles for concluding the Peace of Augsburg, which in 1555 pacified Germany by conceding to the Lutherans those areas that had Lutheran rulers. Two years later, abandoning the neutrality of his immediate predecessors and ignoring the fact that Charles was now the principal champion of the Catholic Reformation, he allied himself with Henry II of France and declared war on Spain. He even instructed the Inquisition to institute proceedings for the excommunications of both Charles and his son Philip – who, hearing of this, sent orders to Spain that, if any such instrument arrived there, the Papal Nuncio was to be thrown out of the country. In August 1557 the town of Saint-Quentin in Picardy was besieged by a Spanish army, looted, plundered and deserted for the next two years. When the Pope heard of the French collapse, he is said to have nearly died of rage. He even managed to quarrel with Mary, who had, after all, restored her country to the Catholic faith. He deprived the estimable Cardinal Pole of his legateship, summoning him back to Rome to answer charges of heresy, and generally made himself so disagreeable as greatly to facilitate the efforts of Queen Elizabeth in returning the country to Protestantism. He died in 1559 a broken man, the most generally detested pope of the sixteenth century. As the news of his death spread through Rome, the populace exploded with joy. They first attacked the headquarters of the Inquisition, smashing the building to pieces and releasing all its prisoners; then they marched to the Pope's statue on the Capitol, tore it down, knocked its head off and threw it into the Tiber.*

~

Charles, on learning in July 1553 of his cousin Mary's triumph, now fixed his attention on a new objective. Here was a chance to ally England with the old Burgundian lands, forming something like a pincer movement threatening France and thus immeasurably strengthening his own position vis-à-vis King Henry. The first step was, clearly, the marriage of Mary to his son Philip. One thing only worried him: the new Queen's almost insane fanaticism. Time and again he advised her not to go too fast in her determination to re-establish the old religion; excessive zeal, he believed, might easily antagonise her subjects and increase anti-Catholic feeling. Mary, however, refused to listen. Her devotion to the Church of Rome was indeed fanatical; she

---

* It was subsequently retrieved and can now be seen in the Castel Sant'Angelo.

would not rest until her country was once more firmly under its sway. There were other difficulties too in the way of the marriage: for one thing, Philip at twenty-seven was eleven years younger than his intended bride; for another, he had been married once already – to the Infanta of Portugal, who had died giving birth to a son, Don Carlos, now nine years old and generally believed to be insane. Everything, in fact, depended on Mary herself: would she or would she not take Philip for her husband? The Emperor's brilliant young ambassador, Simon Renard, had instructions to seek an audience as soon as possible; he managed to speak to her in secret on the day of her proclamation as Queen, and reminded her that her duty to her people made it necessary that she should marry; the important thing, he reported, was 'to put her in a marrying mood'.

There was no point, on the other hand, of her being in a marrying mood if she did not marry the right man; and there were several possibilities other than Philip. Mary had once confessed to Renard's predecessor that her preferred husband would have been the Emperor himself – to whom she had actually been betrothed from 1522 to 1525 – but Charles had let it be known that he was too old and infirm, and would never take another wife. Failing him, she was known to fancy Edward Courtenay, whom she had released on her accession from a fifteen-year imprisonment in the Tower and created the Earl of Devon. Renard continued to press the case for Philip as strongly as he dared, but Mary now confessed that she had made a number of enquiries and did not much like the sound of him.

And so the weeks dragged on, with the Queen tormented by indecision. It was one of the leading members of the Privy Council, Lord Paget, who eventually made up her mind. This great step that Her Majesty must now take, he told her – she must not look upon it as a marriage. Rather was it a 'solemn alliance which might be of the greatest advantage to her kingdom and her subjects'. By this argument she seems to have been persuaded. There remained one more obstacle: the determined opposition of the Chancellor, Bishop Stephen Gardiner, who argued passionately for Courtenay, claiming that the people would simply not tolerate their Queen's marrying a foreigner, least of all a Spaniard; it was only when Mary turned on him, declaring that rather than marry an Englishman she would remain single all her life, that he admitted defeat. At a parliamentary enquiry a week later he made one last hopeless attempt, confessing tearfully that his fondness for Courtenay stemmed from the years that they had spent together in prison. Was that, scornfully demanded the Queen, the reason why she should marry him?

The necessary treaty was signed on 12 January 1554, and Renard reported to his master that, if Philip could reach England in time for the marriage to be celebrated before the beginning of Lent, there should be no further problems. A week later he was less optimistic. There was apparently much anxiety in the City of London, on the grounds that the marriage would be bad for business; it was also rumoured that Philip intended, on the strength of his descent from John of Gaunt,* to claim the crown of England for himself. Then on 27 January the balloon went up. The son of the poet and ambassador Sir Thomas Wyatt – also named Thomas – with the active encouragement of Edward Courtenay (now Earl of Devon), rose in revolt, calling on his compatriots to join him in the sacred task of keeping the Spaniards out of the country. As a rebellion, it did not last long; by 8 February Wyatt was under arrest. But Mary and her Council had for a few days been thoroughly frightened. Devon was returned to the Tower, where the Princess Elizabeth soon afterwards joined him. Poor Jane Grey had not been remotely

---

* John of Gaunt's daughter Philippa had married King John the Good of Portugal, ancestor of Philip's mother Isabella.

implicated in the rising, but it made no difference: on 12 February 1554 she and her husband were accused of complicity and separately beheaded – he publicly on Tower Hill, she inside the Tower, on the Green.

By this time Renard had informed the Queen that there could be no question of her intended husband's setting foot in England until 'those two great persons' – Devon and Elizabeth – had been executed or otherwise rendered harmless. Try as they might, however, the authorities could find absolutely no evidence to suggest that either was in any way implicated in the Wyatt rebellion.* Renard was obliged to report ruefully to his master that the laws of England were so unsatisfactory that it was impossible to have people executed unless they had previously been proved guilty. Elizabeth was moved from the Tower to Woodstock – crowds cheering her along the way – where she was to spend a year under house arrest in the charge of Sir Henry Bedingfeld. Devon was soon released, but was sent into exile. He settled in Venice, where he very wisely spent the rest of his life.

And so at last the doubly royal wedding took place, in Winchester Cathedral on 25 July 1554, just two days after the happy couple's first meeting. Philip – to whom his father had granted the Kingdom of Naples, lest he should be outranked by his bride – was to enjoy all Mary's titles and honours for as long as their marriage should last. All Acts of Parliament were to be issued under both their names; coins should show the heads of both. As the new King of England could understand not a word of English or even French, it was decreed that notes of all state affairs should additionally be made in Latin and Spanish. If the marriage were to be blessed with issue, their heir was to succeed

---

* Wyatt had in fact incriminated both of them in his declarations to the Privy Council, but on the scaffold he had retracted this and cleared them of all complicity.

both in England and in the Burgundian possessions, Philip's son Don Carlos – insane or not – succeeding in Spain and Italy. If it were childless, then Philip's entire connection with England would cease on Mary's death. There was to be *no* Spanish interference in English affairs, and – as a final blow to Philip's ambitions – on 26 December Parliament refused to sanction his coronation as King of England.

~

Unlike his father, Philip was a Spaniard born and bred. When he came to England to marry Queen Mary, it was only the second time he had left the Iberian. peninsula, the first being when he had visited the Low Countries and the Empire in 1549. He had had to stay nearly two years, and had hated northern Europe – hated the cold, hated the beer, hated the Protestantism, hated the barbaric languages he could not understand, hated the habitual drunkenness of almost everyone around him. England threatened to be even worse, with all those disadvantages plus a not very attractive elderly lady by whom he was expected to beget children. The task, he believed, would be neither easy nor pleasant: his great friend Ruy Gómez de Silva wrote that, although the Queen was a very good thing (*'muy buena cosa'*), 'it takes a great god to drain this chalice' (*'Mucho diós es menester para tragar este cáliz'*). Nor was the situation improved by the fact that he had brought over a complete Spanish household to look after him, only to find an equally comprehensive English one ready and waiting. It was several weeks before a mutually satisfactory compromise was reached.

But Philip made the best of it, and to many of the English, despite his ignorance of their language, he came as a pleasant surprise. He was not by any account good-looking – although in that respect there was no doubt that he was a great improvement on his father – but he was capable, when he chose to turn it on, of considerable charm. The situation was improved still further when, towards the end of September 1554, Mary stopped menstruating, gained weight and was regularly sick in the mornings. Virtually everyone at court, including her doctors, jumped to the obvious conclusion. In the last week of April 1555 Elizabeth was released from house arrest and called to attend on her halfsister and to witness the coming happy event.

Philip was standing by – according to the Venetian ambassador Giovanni Michiel all ready, in the event of his wife's death in childbirth, to marry Elizabeth instead. He himself on the other hand, writing to his cousin (and brother-in-law) Maximilian of Austria, expressed doubts as to whether his wife was pregnant at all; and, as we all now know, he was right. In July 1555 the bulge began to recede; it was the classic example of a false pregnancy, probably brought on by Mary's overwhelming desire to have a child. Characteristically, she herself saw it as 'God's punishment' for her having tolerated heretics in her realm. Heartbroken and humiliated, she stepped up the burnings and fell into a deep depression; and now, to cap it all, Philip broke the news to her that he was leaving to see his father, who had made it clear to him that he needed him back in the Netherlands. He had known that she would take it badly; according once again to Michiel, she was by now 'extraordinarily in love' with him. 'Let me know', he wrote to Ruy Gómez, 'what you think I had better say, and what line I am to take with the Queen about leaving her . . . I see I must say something; but God help me!' What he actually did say is not, alas, recorded; but on 4 September 1555, some fourteen months after his arrival in England, Philip crossed the Channel and headed for Brussels.

A year and a half later, in March 1557, he was back – though this time his visit was to be shorter still. He was now thirty years old and, after an unusually sedentary life for a European prince, he was perhaps looking forward to a bit of adventure; he may have been anxious too to acquire some experience of battle, of which he had seen practically none. The French were the only possible enemy; and fortunately, very soon after his return, they provided perfect provocation, by materially supporting the rebel Thomas Stafford when, in April 1557, he seized Scarborough Castle and called upon his countrymen to join him in driving the Spaniards out of England. Stafford was captured within a day or two and beheaded soon afterwards, together with thirty-two of his companions; but the Queen, furious, declared war on France. On 4 July Philip landed with an army largely composed of German mercenaries, but which also included a not very impressive English contingent commanded by the Earl of Pembroke. The expedition was a hopeless failure. Its principal achievement was the loss in January 1558 of the port of Calais, which had been English for over two hundred years. Every English schoolboy knows – or used to know – the Queen's reaction when the news was brought to her;* rather less well known is the fact that she had recently suffered her second false pregnancy and had little strength left to sustain this second blow.

She was in fact sicker than she knew. As always in the sixteenth century, it is hard to be sure of an accurate diagnosis; but from what evidence there is, the probable cause seems to have been uterine cancer, in which case the disease would already have taken hold. She died on 17 November 1558. Her specific instructions that she should be buried next to her mother in Peterborough Cathedral were ignored; instead she was interred in Westminster Abbey, in a tomb that she would one day share with her half-sister Elizabeth. Her husband, who was at the time

---

* 'You shall find', she said, 'when I am dead and opened, *Philip* and *Calais* lying in my heart.'

in Brussels, wrote to his sister Joanna of Austria that he felt 'a reasonable regret' for her death.*

Not many other people did. With burnings at the stake averaging nearly one a week during her five-year reign, it is hard indeed to argue that Bloody Mary did not richly deserve her nickname. Not only Protestants but also the majority of her Catholic subjects were revolted by her ferocity. Simon Renard warned that such 'cruel enforcement' might easily cause a revolt; Philip's chief ecclesiastical adviser, Alfonso de Castro, condemned the Queen's conduct out of hand. It was not surprising that her unpopularity steadily grew; it was increased further by her marriage to Philip, by his loss of Calais and – most unfairly – by appalling weather and consequently a series of abysmally bad harvests.

But perhaps we can pity her too: surrounded by priests and monks as fanatical as she was herself; suffering appalling loneliness in the absences of her husband – whom she loved, but who during a marriage of fifty-two months spent only seventeen at her side; humiliated at her inability to have children, made more painful still by the false pregnancies that raised her hopes and then dashed them again. She was only forty-two when she died, but her life had brought her virtually no real happiness, and she was probably ready enough to go.

---

* A very short time afterwards, he was shamelessly angling for the hand of Elizabeth. Thank God she refused him.

8

Fray Carlos and 'the drum of conquest'

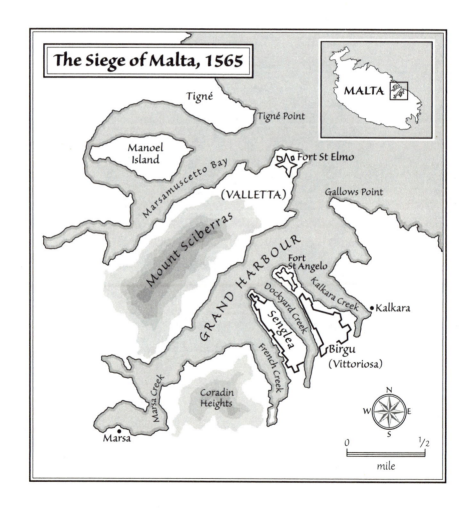

The Siege of Malta, 1565

MALTA

Tigné

Tigné Point

Manoel
Island

Marsamuscetto Bay

Fort St Elmo

(VALLETTA)

Gallows Point

Mount Sciberras

GRAND HARBOUR

Fort
St Angelo

Kalkara Creek

Kalkara

Dockyard Creek

Senglea

Birgu
(Vittoriosa)

French Creek

Marsa Creek

Coradin
Heights

Marsa

N
W · E
S

0   1/2
mile

THE EMPEROR HAD long been dreaming of abdication. He had first had the idea in 1535, after the capture of Tunis, when he noticed his first few grey hairs; by then he had already reigned for twenty years, which he maintained – probably rightly – were like forty in any other occupation. But he could not abdicate yet; Philip, his son and heir, was only eight years old. He was obliged to stick it out for another twenty, though this figure might have been reduced to fifteen if Philip had shown a little more aptitude, energy or enthusiasm for the task that lay before him. There was no doubt about it: Charles's only legitimate son had been something of a disappointment. The time of his departure was therefore still uncertain. From the very first germination of his idea, however, the Emperor had known, when the moment of release should come at last, exactly where he was going: to the monastery of Yuste in Extremadura, founded by the Gerolamite Order in 1402 to mark the spot where fourteen bishops had been murdered by the Moors.

Mentally and physically exhausted and tortured by gout, he was anxious to leave just as soon as he could arrange for Philip to replace him adequately in Flanders and Spain. But by the summer of 1555 it was four and a half years since the two had met, and in 1551 he had been far from certain that Philip would ever be capable of doing so. What he had to discover was, in short, whether the boy was by now up to the job. And so, the moment Philip arrived in the Netherlands from England, he was carried off to the castle of Le Roeulx, near Mons, where he and his father spent several days entirely alone together. Philip seems to have passed the test. Charles formally passed on to him the sovereignty of the Low Countries and, in January 1556, the crown of Spain and its dependencies – which included, of course, the New World. Since Germany, together with the old Empire, was already safely in the hands of his brother Ferdinand, there was now nothing left to him but his title as Emperor.

The great abdication ceremony was held on 25 October in Brussels, where all the Estates of the Netherlands were assembled in the Great Hall of the Palace. At precisely three o'clock in the afternoon the Emperor arrived, leaning heavily on the shoulder of the young Prince William of Orange.* They were immediately followed by Philip II and, after him, the Governor of the Low Countries Mary of Hungary, the Archduke Maximilian, Duke Emmanuel Philibert of Savoy and a crowd of other dignitaries. The historian J. L. Motley, in *The Rise of the Dutch Republic*, gives a superb description of Charles and his son:

> Charles the Fifth was then fifty-five years and eight months old, but he was already decrepit with premature old age. He was of about middle height, and had been athletic and well proportioned. Broad in the shoulders, deep in the chest, thin in the flank, very muscular in the arms and legs, he had been able to match himself with all competitors in the tourney and the ring, and to vanquish the bull with his own hand ... He had been able in the field

---

* Better known as William the Silent, at the age of twenty-two he was already commanding one of the Emperor's armies. Later he was to lead the Dutch revolt against the Habsburgs. He was assassinated in 1584.

to do the duty of captain and soldier, to endure fatigue and exposure, and every privation except fasting. These personal advantages were now departed. Crippled in hands, knees and legs, he supported himself with difficulty upon a crutch, with the aid of an attendant's shoulder. In face he had always been extremely ugly . . . His hair, once of a light colour, was now white with age, close-clipped and bristling: his beard was grey, coarse and shaggy. His forehead was spacious and commanding; the eye was dark-blue, with an expression both majestic and benignant. His nose was acquiline but crooked. The lower part of his face was famous for its deformity. The under lip, a Burgundian inheritance . . . was heavy and hanging; the lower jaw protruding so far above the upper that it was impossible for him to bring together the few fragments of teeth which still remained, or to speak a whole sentence in an intelligible voice. Eating and talking, occupations to which he was always much addicted, were becoming daily more arduous . . .

The son, Philip the Second, was a small, meagre man, much below the middle height, with thin legs, a narrow chest, and the shrinking, timid air of a habitual invalid . . . In face he was the living image of his father; having the same broad forehead and blue eye, with the same aquiline but better proportioned nose. In the lower part of the countenance the remarkable Burgundian deformity was likewise reproduced: he had the same heavy, hanging lip, with a vast mouth and monstrously protruding lower jaw. His complexion was fair, his hair light and thin, his beard yellow, short and pointed. He had the aspect of a Fleming, but the loftiness of a Spaniard. His demeanour in public was still, silent, almost sepulchral. He looked habitually on the ground when he conversed, was chary of speech, embarrassed and even suffering in manner. This was ascribed partly to a natural haughtiness, which he had occasionally endeavoured to overcome, and partly to habitual pains in the stomach, occasioned by his inordinate fondness for pastry.

Charles, we are told, made a moving speech, quickly reviewing his record as Emperor. If God had granted him continuing good health, he said, he would never have contemplated the step he was now taking; but now that his life was ebbing away his affection for his subjects required his departure. When he finished, according to Motley, 'he sank almost fainting in his chair and wept like a child', as did all those who had heard him. Then it was Philip's turn. In a few barely audible words of Spanish he expressed his regret that he was unable to address the gathering in either French or Flemish, and asked the Bishop of Arras to speak on his behalf. His audience was not impressed.

It was nearly another year before the Emperor sailed for Spain. Not, heaven knows, that he had the faintest wish to cling on to power; all the evidence points to the contrary – that he could hardly wait for his retirement. The truth was that, while he was perfectly happy to entrust Philip with the government of Spain – indeed, he had already done so for some time – he was still far from confident of his son's ability to handle the Low Countries. Not only was Philip of rather less than average intelligence; he was a Spaniard through and through and, as he had so recently and embarrassingly demonstrated, conspicuously lacking in any gift for languages. After well over a year in England he had failed utterly to learn English; his French, German and Flemish – in all of which his father was fluent – were very little better. Never in a thousand years could he have dealt with the Protestant princes of Germany as Charles had done – though the strain had very nearly proved fatal. Moreover, even if he had been able to communicate with them, he would have been utterly incapable of treating them as equals: he claimed that even speaking to a heretic gave him acute physical pain. The Low Countries, on the other hand, might be just about within his powers once he had gained a little more experience. For the past quarter of a century they had been admirably governed by Charles's sister Mary of Hungary, widow of King Louis; but Mary had made it clear that, when her brother went, she was going too. Meanwhile for Charles there was nothing for it but to cling on until such time as it seemed safe to leave Philip in control. At least his son would not be succeeding to the Empire: when, in the autumn of 1555, Ferdinand and Maximilian were officially informed that Philip had no wish to follow his father as Emperor and would support Maximilian in the next imperial election, Charles can have felt nothing but relief.

~

At last, on 13 September 1556, the Emperor – he was to retain the title for another two years, resigning it only just before his death – boarded his ship, *La Bertandona*, at Flushing and headed for Spain. The picture is indubitably romantic: the old, exhausted monarch divesting himself of all that he possessed and taking refuge as an anonymous member of a remote and distant monastery. With the final act of Verdi's *Don Carlos*, when the aged monk – in fact a ghost – emerges from the Emperor's moonlit tomb, the illusion is complete; but illusion it is. In the spring of 1556, in Brussels, a list was drawn up of the household that was to accompany Charles into his retreat. It amounted to a total of 762, which he eventually managed to reduce to 150. Even then it included not only secretaries and doctors but also cooks and musicians, barbers and valets, even brewers. Nor, it need hardly be said, was there any austere monastic cell awaiting him; instead he moved into a large and extremely comfortable south-facing building on a hillside and prepared for his use some years before, surrounded by gardens and running streams and enjoying a spectacular view.* It was decorated with priceless tapestries and superb pictures – among them a Titian or two – together with magnificent furniture and works of art. For Charles it was little less than a terrestrial paradise – or would have been, had it not been for the gout which plagued him more and more insistently, so that when the pain came upon him he had to be carried round the monastery on a litter or in a sedan chair. On these occasions he would remind those in attendance of a Spanish proverb, *la gota se cura tapando la boca* – 'the cure for gout is to keep the mouth covered' – in other words, to avoid food and drink – but then do precisely the reverse. The days of his youthful austerity were gone: he had now become, so far as one can see, both a gourmet and a glutton – and a copious drinker too, with a head like a horse. The letters of Don Luis Méndez Quijada, who had served him faithfully for thirty-four years without once taking any leave, constantly complain of the difficulties suffered by his staff in keeping him supplied with the delicacies he demanded – for he insisted not only on quantity but on quality too: oysters, anchovies, eels, partridges, *chorizos*, all of them almost calculated to bring on his gout, or the piles from which he also suffered untold agonies.

Most of his court absolutely hated the monastery: Quijada declared that the place was so lonely that no one but a man determined to leave the world behind him could endure it at all. But Charles loved it. He was happier there than he had been for years; his only regret was that he had not managed to get there sooner. What he now longed to do more than anything was to cast off the title of Emperor, which continued to weigh

---

* So I understand, though I confess I have not been there myself. The main monastery buildings were burned to a cinder during the Peninsular War, but the Emperor's apartments have survived. The Pauline monks – whose Order takes its name from the earliest Christian hermit, St Paul of Thebes, and not, thank God, from Pope Paul IV – are said to welcome visitors.

all too heavily on his shoulders. He could not do so voluntarily; he had been chosen by the seven imperial Electors, and they only could release him. There were attendant dangers too – notably Pope Paul, who, with his loathing of all Habsburgs on principle, might at any moment violently denounce his brother Ferdinand – who was all set to succeed him – on the grounds that Ferdinand's son Maximilian was to all intents and purposes a Protestant (which happened to be true). But deliverance was on the way. On 27 April 1558 Charles was informed that the Electors had freed him from his last shackle; Ferdinand was now Emperor in his place.* Instantly Charles ordered new seals to be struck, bearing only his name and the arms of Spain and Burgundy. He is said even to have asked to be addressed as *fray Carlos*, brother Charles, though it is far from certain that many of his court dared avail themselves of the invitation.

Brother Charles or no, after so many years at the centre of power he could not suppress a lively interest in the outside world. He had not been two months at Yuste when his friend Ruy Gómez arrived,† with news of his son's plans for a major offensive against France the following summer and bearing a message from Philip imploring his father to come and join him. Naturally Charles refused; the idea of travelling to the Low Countries – particularly if he had to do so by litter – was more than he could even contemplate. When, however, in February 1558, he heard of the loss of Calais, Quijada tells us that 'he never felt anything more bitterly'. And there were other shocks too. He had always believed that his beloved Spain was free from any Protestant taint, but on the very day after he heard of his

---

* Ferdinand needed no election, having been elected King of the Romans (the Emperor's legitimate successor) in 1531.
† 'A man of meridional aspect, with coal-black hair and beard, gleaming eyes, a face pallid with intense application, and slender but handsome figure' (Motley).

release from the Empire he was told that a Lutheran cell had been discovered in Valladolid. A biographer describes this as being 'one of the cruellest blows he ever received', which seems a little hard to believe – a tendency to overstatement seems to have been prevalent at the imperial court – but he certainly flew into a fury, and gave orders to his daughter Joanna, who was acting as Regent during her brother Philip's absence in Flanders, that heresy must be ruthlessly exterminated throughout the kingdom, whatever the cost might be.

In September 1557, on the other hand, there came a series of happier events: regular visits by his sisters Eleanor – widow of King Francis I – and Mary of Hungary, who were now living at Jarandilla, not far away. Eleanor died – to the great distress of Charles and Mary, who had genuinely loved their plain and somewhat colourless sister – in February 1558; but five months later there came a new interest. For the past four years Charles's bastard son, now eleven years old and at that time known as Jeroním, had been brought up by Quijada's childless wife, Doña Magdalena, and in July 1558 she brought him to Yuste. He was never officially recognised by his father, but Charles wrote a special codicil to his will in Jeroním's favour. He had encouraged the boy to enter the Church; he would have been overjoyed, had he lived another thirteen years, to see him, as Don John of Austria, commanding the navy of the Holy League and, in one of the great naval battles of history, utterly destroying the Turkish fleet at Lepanto. But those thirteen years were not granted to him. After three weeks of what we are told was intense suffering, Charles died at two o'clock in the morning of Sunday, 21 September 1558, in his fifty-ninth year, not of the gout which had plagued him since his early middle age but of a fever contracted during the scorching Spanish summer.

In the thousand-year history of the Holy Roman Empire, no Emperor strove harder to do his duty than did Charles V, nor was any so important to Christendom. His values were not ours: for him

Christianity was the most important thing in the world, and to see the Church he loved split down the middle, first by Martin Luther and his followers and later by King Henry VIII, caused him bitter sorrow. He tried, quite desperately hard, to reunite it in the only way it could be reunited, under the Pope of Rome. Rome, he knew, was in urgent need of reform, a fact that he had never ceased to emphasise both in his conversations and his correspondence with the seven successive pontiffs with whom he had had to deal. All of them put up a determined resistance to the idea; but then all of them, he also knew, fell far short of what they should have been. Clement VII had been a nightmare, Paul IV even worse; from his point of view the only tolerable ones – though neither had shown much aptitude for his task – had been Adrian, who had reigned for a year, and Marcellus, who had lasted for just three weeks. But if the popes were incompetent, that only meant that others must redouble their efforts; and if that in turn meant that a few heretics had to go to the stake, then to the stake they must go.

One of Charles's many biographers describes him as a military genius. There seems little evidence for this; on the other hand, he possessed two supreme qualities for a general: immense personal courage and infinite consideration for his men. The courage was shown not only in actual fighting but also in the sheer determination that enabled him to ride day after day while in agonies of gout – and no one who has not suffered personally from that affliction can have any idea of what those agonies are like* – with never a word of complaint, even when he had

---

* Philibert de Bruxelles, a member of the Netherlands Privy Council, described it in his speech at the abdication ceremony: 'A most truculent executioner, it invades the whole body, from the crown of the head to the soles of the feet, leaving nothing untouched. It contracts the nerves with intolerable anguish, it enters the bones, it freezes the marrow, it converts the lubricating fluids of the joints into chalk; it pauses not until, having exhausted and debilitated the whole body, it has rendered all its necessary instruments useless, and conquered the mind by immense torture.'

to ride with his leg resting in a sling attached to his saddle. His soldiers loved and admired him – as indeed did almost all of those with whom he came into contact. They loved him for his personal charm, his kindness and – a rare quality, perhaps, in his day – his sense of humour. There was also his appreciation of the finer things in life: of painting, for example (are children still told the famous story of how he immediately stooped to pick up Titian's paintbrush when the master dropped it?) or of music, for which he had a genuine passion. Even his gluttony evokes sympathy in many of us. He died a disappointed man, all too conscious of how much he had had to leave undone; but he understood, far more than most people realised, just how much that is beautiful and pleasurable life has to offer. And whenever he had the chance, he enjoyed it.

The face of western Europe was changing fast. Just eight weeks after Charles's death, Queen Mary of England followed him to the grave, to be succeeded on the throne by her half-sister Elizabeth. The year 1559 saw in July the fatal wounding of King Henry II (see p. 206); in August the death of the odious Pope Paul IV, regretted by none; and, on Christmas Day, the election of Giovanni Medici* as Pius IV. In 1560 Henry's heir, Francis II – husband of Mary, Queen of Scots – died in his turn a month before his seventeenth birthday, leaving the throne to his brother Charles IX.

Apart from the death of the Pope, there had been one other item of good news in 1559: the conclusion in April of the Peace of Cateau-Cambrésis. Spain had beaten France on points, thanks

---

* To his shame, sorrow and considerable embarrassment, no relation.

in large measure to the assistance given by the house of Savoy. This was one of the oldest ruling families of Europe, having been founded in the year 1003;* by the middle of the sixteenth century it covered the area of the present Italian region of Piedmont, together with the French departments of Savoie and Haute-Savoie, with its capital at Chambéry.† All had been well until Francis I had invaded and occupied it in 1536; Duke Charles III ('the Good') and his son Emmanuel Philibert – who succeeded his father in 1553 – were then effectively exiled, and had thus become enthusiastic allies of Charles V.‡ The Peace, which was signed by Henry II and Philip – both by proxy – restored to the House of Savoy all its former territories, and Henry renounced any further claims in Italy. This meant that Philip kept direct control of Milan, Naples, Sicily and Sardinia; it also meant that the only truly independent states in Italy were Savoy and the Republic of Venice. France, on the other hand, regained the plundered town of Saint-Quentin and kept Calais. The English were predictably furious about this latter provision, but there was nothing they could do. Meanwhile the agreement was sealed with the gift, by Henry to Emmanuel Philibert, of the hand of his sister Margaret, Duchess of Berry, now aged thirty-six and described by a contemporary as 'a spinster lady of excellent breeding and lively intellect'.

The wedding celebrations were tragically clouded by King Henry's jousting accident and death a few days later. Just before he lost consciousness, obviously fearful lest Emmanuel Philbert

---

*   Its members have at various times held the titles of King of Sicily, King of Sardinia, King of Croatia, King of Spain, King of Cyprus, King of Armenia, King of Jerusalem and Emperor of Ethiopia. They were also to provide the four kings of Italy from the country's unification in March 1861 to June 1946, when it became a republic.

†   The capital was to be moved to Turin in 1563.

‡   Charles III and Charles V were brothers-in-law, having respectively married the two sisters Beatrix and Isabella of Portugal.

should take advantage of his death to renege on the alliance, he ordered that his sister's wedding should take place immediately. Plans for an elaborate service at Notre-Dame were scrapped; the two were married at a midnight ceremony in a small church near the place where the King lay dying. Queen Catherine de' Medici, the bride's sister-in-law, sat apart from the rest, making no effort to restrain her tears.

With peace now concluded – at least temporarily – in Europe, Philip decided in the summer of 1559 that the time had come for him to tackle the Turks. His target would be Tripoli, the most formidable centre of corsair activity along the whole Barbary Coast. He consulted with the Viceroy of Sicily, the Duke of Medinaceli – whom he appointed commander-in-chief of the coming expedition – and also with Jean de la Valette, Grand Master of the Knights of St John, obviously hoping to regain the city which his Order had lost to the Turks only eight years before. Over the next six months Philip gathered a fleet of about a hundred ships, including fifty-three galleys, together with troops from Italy, Spain and Germany. The idea was a surprise attack; but, as he should have known from his father's disaster at Algiers in 1541, large-scale offensives during the winter in the Mediterranean were never a good idea. Five times the fleet put out to sea from its base in Malta; five times it was blown back to port. Six precious weeks were lost; two thousand men succumbed to illness of one kind or another.

Spring came, bringing with it more reasonable weather, and the fleet – supplemented now with papal and, perhaps surprisingly, French contingents – set sail, not directly for Tripoli but for the island of Djerba, off the Tunisian coast, which Medinaceli had chosen as a base for his operations. This was occupied without difficulty; but then, on 11 May, a Turkish fleet of eighty-six vessels under the young admiral Piale Pasha appeared on the horizon. Piale had been alerted by one of the leading corsairs, Kiliç Ali, and had broken all records by completing the journey from Istanbul in just twenty days. The Christians, taken completely by surprise and overwhelmingly outnumbered, had little option but flight. Wholesale panic followed, as the Turks moved in for the kill. Twenty galleys and twenty-seven transport vessels were sunk, eighteen thousand soldiers killed or drowned. Piale returned in triumph to Istanbul with five thousand prisoners, his ships towing the captured enemy hulks, now rudderless and shorn of their masts. There then took place a magnificent victory parade through the city, the streets lined by cheering crowds, the captured admirals and commanders bringing up the rear. The Sultan appeared on a magnificently decorated platform to take the salute. According to the ambassador Busbecq, his expression was so severe and sad that 'one would have thought that the victory did not concern him, and that nothing new or unexpected had occurred'; he was, however, appreciative enough to grant to Piale, as a reward, the hand of one of his granddaughters in marriage.

Suleiman was now in his sixty-sixth year, and had been forty years on the throne. He was still in fine physical condition, but inevitably he had aged, and he was now worrying increasingly about the succession. Mustafa had been safely despatched, but now the Sultan's two surviving sons, Bayezit and Selim, were at each others' throats and – Roxelana having died in 1558 – no longer had a mother to control them. Soon their quarrel turned into open warfare, and on 31 May 1559 Selim met his brother in a battle outside Konya and soundly defeated him. Bayezit escaped to Persia with his five sons and a small army, fully prepared to continue the fight. Shah Tahmasp I gave him a friendly welcome; but all too soon Suleiman, convinced by Selim that his brother was a traitor busy plotting his overthrow, sent envoys to the Shah requesting him to make arrangements for the young prince's execution. Finally it was a Turkish executioner who did the job, on 25 September 1561. Selim was now the sole remaining heir to the Ottoman Empire.

How, one wonders, could the Sultan, normally so far-sighted and so shrewd, have twice allowed himself to be persuaded – the first time by his wife, the second time by one of his children – to destroy the two ablest of his sons, and indeed the only two who might have shown themselves to be worthy successors to himself? Perhaps all absolute monarchs are to some degree paranoid, given to imagining plots and conspiracies where none exists; perhaps too – and this seems particularly true of dictators, who have no obvious heirs – they become so intoxicated with their own power that they simply do not or dare not contemplate their country's future when their hands shall no longer be at the helm. Few, certainly, have ever made the slightest effort to ensure an effective succession. (The idea of *après moi le déluge* may, in short, be a good deal more commonly held among ageing autocrats than we realise.) Suleiman still had five more years to live; he had devoted his entire life to almost constant campaigning, and for one reason only: to increase the extent and power of his Empire. How could he – so deliberately, so consciously – have arranged matters in such a way as to ensure that after his death that Empire would pass to a drunken debauchee, of all the thirty-six Ottoman sultans by far the worst?

~

For the five years after 1560 the eastern and central Mediterranean was comparatively quiet. There was, inevitably, spasmodic naval harassment of one fleet by another, but there were no large-scale engagements. From the Turkish point of view, by far the most persistent troublemakers were the Knights of St John; they had now adopted a policy of out-and-out piracy, waylaying all the Muslim pilgrim ships that they could find bound for ports near

Mecca and exacting heavy charges before allowing them to proceed on their way. There was still greater anger at the Porte when it was reported that the Knights had seized a ship bringing goods destined for the imperial harem and forced it to unload its cargo in Malta. Whether some of these goods were intended particularly for Suleiman's daughter Mihrimah is uncertain, but she seems to have worked on her father to persuade him that outrages such as this could no longer be tolerated.

In 1564 the Sultan celebrated his seventieth birthday. He had had plenty of time to regret his merciful treatment of the Knights after his seizure of Rhodes in 1522. He had granted them his safe conduct from the island only in return for a promise never again to take up arms against him; never had a promise been so flagrantly or so repeatedly broken. Now that the Knights had been settled for some thirty-five years in their new home they were becoming as persistent a nuisance as ever they had been. Clearly the time had come to expel them from Malta, just as he had expelled them from Rhodes. And there was another reason too. Malta occupied a key position in the central Mediterranean, forming a natural stepping-stone between Turkish-held Tripoli and Sicily, which was ruled by Philip of Spain. Once it had fallen into the hands of the Sultan it would provide the perfect springboard for the conquest of that most desirable island – after which Turkish landings in south Italy would have followed as surely as night follows day.

Charles V had been fully aware of this when, in 1530, he had made Malta available to the Order. What better means could he hope for, at no cost to himself, of protecting the southern approaches to his empire? The Knights, it is true, had not been initially enthusiastic: they had considered the possibility of a move to Malta six years earlier, and had sent out eight commissioners to find out what it had to offer. 'The island', the commissioners had reported, is merely a rock of soft sandstone called tufa, about six or seven leagues long and three or four broad;* the surface of the rock is barely covered by no more than three or four feet of earth. This also is stony, and most unsuited for growing corn or other cereals. It does however produce quantities of figs, melons and other fruits. The principal trade of the island consists of honey, cotton and cumin seed. These the inhabitants exchange for grain. Except for a few springs in the centre of the island there is no running water, not even wells, so the inhabitants catch the rainwater in cisterns. Wood is so scarce as to be sold by the pound, and the inhabitants have to use either sun-dried cow-dung or thistles for cooking their food.

Malta was not, clearly, an island designed to withstand a siege. On the other hand, it boasted three immense advantages: a limitless supply of mellow, honey-coloured building stone; a fine tradition of quarrymen, builders, stonemasons and carvers; and perhaps the most astonishing natural anchorage in the world. To this day the first sight of Grand Harbour, seen either from a vessel entering it or from the heights of Valletta, cannot fail to catch the breath. It was unquestionably that anchorage that finally decided the Knights, after eight years' homelessness, to accept the Emperor's offer of a permanent lease.

The Knights never forgot that they were first and foremost Hospitallers; for well over five centuries the care of the sick had been their *raison d'être*. No sooner had they settled in Birgu (now known as Vittoriosa), the northern of the two long headlands on the far side of Grand Harbour opposite Valletta, than they set about building a hospital.† Its predecessor in Rhodes had been famous throughout Christendom and visited by the

---

* It is actually hard sandstone, and roughly eighteen miles by nine.
† This first hospital still stands in Triq Santa Scholastica. It is now a convent of Benedictine nuns.

sick of every nation in the western world, and they were determined that a similar institution in Malta should be equally celebrated – as indeed it soon became. Their second priority was defence: the fortification of their superb harbour and their navy. Shipbuilding was no easy task on a treeless island; thanks, however, to massive imports of timber from Sicily, over the next thirty years they gradually built up a considerable fleet, until by 1560 their sea power was probably as great as it had been in the old days on Rhodes. It was just as well; when they received the first reports of Suleiman's coming expedition, their navy at least was ready.

Certainly, they had no illusions about the danger they faced. Without vast reinforcements they knew that they would be hopelessly outnumbered, both in men and in ships, and that they could expect little sustenance from their scanty, stony soil. They also knew, however, that that soil would show itself still more inhospitable to a besieging army. Geography too was on their side; whereas Rhodes was only 10 miles from the Turkish coast, Malta was nearly 1,000. The invaders might possibly bring in some provisions from north Africa; none the less, it was clear that the force that the Sultan was to hurl against them had from first to last to be largely self-supporting. Small wonder that his invasion fleet, carrying as it did not only his entire army of some 40,000 men with their horses, cannon, ammunition, siege machinery and military supplies, but also food and water and even fuel for cooking, was said to be one of the largest ever to embark on the high seas. It consisted of well over 200 ships, including 130 oared galleys, 30 galleasses* and 11 tub-shaped merchantmen, which relied, like the galleons, entirely on sail. The remainder was made up

---

* A galleass might be described as a cross between a galley and a galleon. It was designed to carry cargo, and was largely dependent on sail but was also fitted with oars and a fair weight of guns.

of assorted smaller vessels, mostly barques and frigates. Swelling the numbers still further – though emphatically not part of the official expedition – were the privateers, circling like vultures around them.

In 1557, at the age of sixty-three – he was almost exactly the same age as Suleiman – Jean Parisot de la Valette had been elected forty-eighth Grand Master of the Order of St John. A Gascon, he is said to have been outstandingly handsome in his youth and to have spoken several languages fluently, including Italian, Spanish, Greek, Turkish and Arabic. He was also a hard, implacable defender of the Christian faith. As a young Knight of twenty-eight he had fought at the siege of Rhodes; later he had been captured and had endured a year as a Turkish galley slave. He was utterly single-minded in the service of the Order – a man, it was said, 'equally capable of converting a Protestant or governing a kingdom'. Faith, strength, leadership and steel discipline, all were his. He was to need them all in the months that lay ahead.

The Knights, it need hardly be said, had their agents in Istanbul. They knew as soon as anyone when the Sultan began his preparations, and from the moment of his election La Valette had had every able-bodied man in Malta working flat out to be ready for the battle to come. He had appealed for reinforcements of men and materials from the commanderies of the Order that were scattered throughout Christian Europe; even so, at the start of the siege he could count on only some 540 Knights with their servants-at-arms, together with about a thousand Spanish infantrymen and arquebusiers and perhaps four thousand local Maltese militia. He had also ordered emergency supplies of grain from Sicily and additional armaments and munitions from France and Spain. All his water cisterns were full, and he had had no compunction in arranging for the waters of the Marsa – a low-lying region beyond Grand Harbour which he knew must be the principal source of water for any besieging army – to be contaminated with dead animals when the time came.

~

The great fleet appeared off the horizon on 18 May 1565. The Sultan, feeling his age, had regretfully decided not to command it in person as he had the attack on Rhodes, over forty years earlier. Instead he had divided the command in two, the naval force to be the responsibility of Piale, the land army that of his brother-in-law, the veteran general Mustafa Pasha. It was to prove a catastrophic decision: the two men hated each other, Piale openly contemptuous of Mustafa's military skills and Mustafa deeply jealous of the younger man's success and his popularity with the Sultan.

Grand Harbour was obviously far too stoutly defended to be a possible site for disembarkation, and Piale eventually selected the harbour of Marsa Scirocco (now Marsaxlokk) at the south-ernmost tip of the island, some five miles away across country from Birgu. The Knights made no attempt to stop him. They knew that they could have had little impact on so huge a force in the open sea, or even at a beachhead; their one hope lay in their fortifications, from which they had no intention of emerging more than was absolutely necessary. The Turks, once ashore, then advanced towards the city and pitched their camp on the land sloping down to the Marsa, from which they had a commanding view of the whole anchorage. There, stretching out before them, was the long central sweep of water leading to the open sea, with the three narrower creeks leading off to the right and, to the left, the long crest of Mount Sciberras – where Valletta stands today. At its furthest point, guarding the entrance to the harbour, rose the towering walls of one of the

Knights' two most impressive redoubts, the superbly garrisoned Fort St Elmo.

Had Piale elected – as he should have done – to keep his fleet in the south (where it would have been perfectly safe during the summer months), Fort St Elmo would not have loomed large in Turkish calculations. Instead, he decided to bring his ships up the north-east coast and into the harbour of Marsamuscetto (Marsamxett), which runs along the northern side of Mount Sciberras. This provided a good deal more shelter; unfortunately it brought him once again into violent disagreement with Mustafa. It also involved sailing directly beneath the guns of the great fortress, the destruction of which thenceforth became a top priority.

A cursory examination of Fort St Elmo suggested to the Turks that, as a star-shaped fort of a fairly traditional kind, it might not be a particularly tough nut to crack. The principal difficulty would be the dragging of heavy guns for nearly two miles along the ridge of Mount Sciberras, where they would be within range of the guns from the headlands of Birgu and Senglea on the opposite side of the harbour. Trench-digging here was impossible; within a few inches the sappers' spades hit the solid rock. Thus, if the troops manhandling the huge cannon up the slopes and along the crest were to be protected, it could only be by constructing immense earthworks, which would in turn mean bringing up vast quantities of soil from the Marsa. All this consumed the energies of most of the Sultan's army, providing a welcome breathing space for La Valette and his men as they worked around the clock to strengthen still further the defences of their other great redoubt, Fort St Angelo, at the far end of Birgu.

On 23 May the attack on St Elmo began in earnest. Night and day the bombardment continued. A few days later there arrived the most celebrated Ottoman commander on land or sea: the Christians called him Dragut, but he was known to his countrymen as Turgut Reis. After an early career as corsair under Barbarossa he had succeeded him, on Barbarossa's death in 1546, as supreme commander of the Ottoman navy. He had already directed an earlier raid on Malta in July 1547, when he had done considerable damage; now, at the age of eighty, he took personal command of the siege, setting up new batteries to the north and south of the fort, which henceforth was to suffer a still more remorseless bombardment from three sides at once. By the end of the month its walls were showing signs of imminent collapse. Every night under cover of darkness small boats from St Angelo would slip across the harbour mouth to bring the garrison fresh troops and provisions, returning with the wounded for the hospital in Birgu; it was thanks only to them that the fort held out as long as it did. One night, however, a returning boat brought something more: a deputation from the besieged to tell the Grand Master that they could resist no longer. La Valette looked at them coldly and replied that if they were no longer prepared to defend St Elmo he would replace them with others who would, and that these would be led by himself. Ashamed, they returned to their posts. The fort might be doomed, but there was to be no surrender.

Somehow, Fort St Elmo survived for a total of thirty-one days. When at last, on 23 June, the Turks smashed their way in, only about sixty of the 150-odd defenders remained alive. Of these, all but nine were instantly decapitated, their bodies nailed – in mockery of the crucifixion – to wooden crosses and floated across the harbour mouth to the waters below St Angelo. When La Valette saw them, he unhesitatingly ordered the immediate execution of all Turkish prisoners. Their heads were then rammed into the breeches of the two cannon on the upper bastion and fired back into the ruins of St Elmo. There was no mistaking that message. Henceforth no quarter would be asked or given.

The Turks had achieved their first objective. They had done so, however, at the cost of nearly a month of the precious summer and of some eight thousand of their finest troops – almost a quarter of their entire army. Among them had been old Dragut, struck down by a cannonball in the last stages of the siege of St Elmo. Mustafa Pasha is said to have stood among the ruins, gazing through the haze of summer heat across the harbour. 'If so small a son has cost us so dear,' he murmured, 'what price must we pay for the father?'

That father was, of course, Fort St Angelo itself. Behind it was the headland of Birgu, the Knights' fortified city. Beyond the narrow inlet to the south-west lay the neighbouring headland of Senglea. It was on the defence of these two parallel peninsulas, by now completely surrounded by the Ottoman army, that the Order of St John depended for its survival. They were connected by a flimsy bridge across the creek (now known as Dockyard Creek) and by a chain stretched on pontoons across its mouth. At the landward end, a palisade of stakes had been driven into the muddy bottom. No longer, however, after the fall of St Elmo, could the entrance to Grand Harbour be blocked: the Turkish ships were now free to sail along its entire length, with only the guns of St Angelo to hinder them.

But there were consolations too. In order to move into their new positions south of Senglea and Birgu, the Turks would be obliged to drag all their heavy cannon, ammunition and supplies back along Mount Sciberras and then around the harbour, over a good four miles of roads that were little more than cart tracks, in the fierce heat of a Maltese summer. Moreover, on the very day St Elmo fell, ships from Sicily carrying a relief force of perhaps a thousand all told, including forty-two Knights from northern Europe, had managed to land and, a week later, to make their way by night to what is now Kalkara, beyond another creek to the north-east of Birgu. Not only the arrival of the force itself, but also its almost miraculous success in avoiding the Turkish army had an immense effect on the defenders' morale.

But the struggle continued. In mid-July a concerted attack on

Senglea was made from the sea. It was foiled by the courage of the native Maltese, superb swimmers who tipped the Turks from their boats and fought them hand to hand in the water. A hidden gun emplacement completed the rout. On 7 August an Italian gunner with the Spanish army, Francesco Balbi di Correggio, who was later to write a fascinating eyewitness account of the siege, noted:

> General assault – 8,000 on St Michael's,* 4,000 on the port of Castile . . . But when they left their trenches we were already at our posts, the hoops alight, the pitch boiling . . . When they scaled the works they were received like men who were expected . . . The assault lasted nine hours, from daybreak till after noon, during which the Turks were relieved by fresh troops more than a dozen times, while we refreshed ourselves with drinks of well watered wine and some mouthfuls of bread . . . Victory was given us again . . . though not one of us could stand on his feet for wounds or fatigue.

But by this time it was becoming plain that the Turkish army too was weakening. The heat was merciless. Food was short and water shorter still, since the dead animals with which the Knights had deliberately fouled the wells of Marsa had now been supplemented by large numbers of Turkish corpses. By the end of August dysentery had spread through the Ottoman camp, its victims being carried in the blazing sun to the improvised sick tents where they died in their hundreds. The Turks knew, too, that it would soon be the time of the equinoctial gales, which would quickly be followed by the first of the winter storms. Mustafa Pasha was prepared to spend the winter on the island if necessary, in the hopes of starving out the besieged; Piale, on the other hand, would not hear of it. His navy, he argued, was more important than Mustafa's army, and he could not risk wintering his ships without full maintenance facilities. He would be getting the fleet under

---

* Another, smaller fortress not far from Sant'Angelo.

way by the middle of September at the latest; if the army wanted to stay it was up to them, but they would be on their own.

Had Suleiman's forces remained, it is doubtful whether the Knights in their existing situation could possibly have held out. But then, on 7 September, came deliverance: the *Gran Soccorso*, as it was called, the Great Relief, sent by the Spanish Viceroy in Sicily, which had somehow managed to leave Messina despite the violence of a tempest such as had never before been experienced. Its nine thousand men were fewer than La Valette had hoped for, but they were enough. Mustafa hesitated no longer. Suddenly the guns were quiet; the clamour ceased; instead of smoke, there was only dust from the feet of what was left – little more than a quarter – of the once proud Ottoman army as it shambled back to the impatient ships.

But the Christians too had sustained terrible losses. Two hundred and fifty Knights were dead, the survivors nearly all wounded or maimed. Of the city of Birgu scarcely one stone was left on another; vulnerable to fire on every side, strategically it had proved a disaster. And so, when old La Valette limped forward to lay the first stone of his new capital, he did so not on the ruins of the old one but away on the heights of Mount Sciberras opposite, dominating Grand Harbour. As he richly deserved, the city was named after him: Valletta.* Three years later, on 21 August 1568, he died. Sir Oliver Starkey, his secretary – and, incidentally, the only Englishman to have fought at his side throughout the siege – wrote a Latin epitaph, which can still be read in St John's Cathedral. Translated, it reads:

Here lies La Valette, worthy of eternal honour. He who was once the scourge of Africa and Asia, and the shield of Europe when he drove off the heathen by the might of his holy sword, is the · first to be buried in this beloved city, whose founder he was.

---

* Where that second 'l' comes from nobody seems to know.

One of the first buildings to rise up in the new city was, of course, the hospital. Like its predecessor on Birgu, it still stands, but it is conceived on an infinitely more ambitious scale: its Great Ward, 155 metres long, is the longest hall with an unsupported roof in all Europe. By 1700, by which time it could accommodate nearly a thousand patients, its walls were hung in winter with woollen tapestries, in summer with canvases by Mattia Preti.* It is full of light, space and fresh air, elements in which the Knights – virtually alone among the medical men of the sixteenth and seventeenth centuries – always put their trust. Moreover, unlike all the other hospitals of the time whose patients were normally fed from wooden platters crawling with bacteria of all kinds, the Order provided plates and cups of silver, thus dramatically – if unconsciously – reducing the risks of infection. Each item was carefully numbered and stamped on the side with the emblem of the Holy Ghost. Finally, the Knights knew the value of good nursing; every one of them, whatever his seniority, would do his tour of duty in the ward, the Grand Master himself taking his turn on Fridays. For 'our lords the sick' – as they always described their patients – only the best was good enough.

~

'With me alone do my armies triumph!' Suleiman's words when the news of the disaster at Malta was brought to him were all too true. His fleet had remained almost intact; but he had lost well over twenty thousand men – perhaps almost twice that number. Had he assumed sole command, as he had at Rhodes in 1522, there would have been none of that destructive rivalry

---

* Mattia Preti (1613–99) was a painter of the Neapolitan school who spent the last thirty-eight years of his life in Malta.

between Piale and Mustafa; his supreme authority, together with his infinitely superior generalship, would probably have saved the day. His first reaction had been to swear personally to lead a new expedition to Malta the following spring, but he must obviously have thought better of the idea: he was too old, the distance was too great, the logistical problems by now almost certainly insuperable. Instead, he decided to launch one more campaign against Hungary and Austria.

Not that hostilities with the Habsburgs had ever really stopped. At the beginning of the 1550s Archduke Ferdinand had made an ill-fated attempt to occupy Transylvania, where, although Isabella and her young son John Sigismund continued to rule under Ottoman suzerainty, the real power rested with 'Father George' Martinuzzi, a Croatian monk – he subsequently became a bishop and a cardinal – who had been treasurer and chief counsellor to John Zápolya and whom the dying Zápolya had appointed his son's official guardian and Regent of the Kingdom. This time, for once, there had been no question of military force; Ferdinand had quite simply bribed Father George to persuade Isabella to give up the throne, promising him in return substantial estates in Silesia. It was not long before the news reached the Porte; Suleiman was predictably furious. He arrested Ferdinand's ambassador and locked him up in the Castle of the Seven Towers, where he remained for the next two years, dying shortly after his release. Fighting flared up again, but it continued in a curiously desultory way. Negotiations dragged on until both parties were bored stiff; and after the death of Rüstem Pasha in 1561 a peace treaty was confirmed, valid for the next eight years.

Three years later, in 1564, came the death of Ferdinand himself, to be succeeded as Emperor by his son Maximilian II. Once again, there was no need for an election. Maximilian had been elected King of the Romans in 1562; his succession was a foregone conclusion. So, indeed, was his almost immediate attack on Transylvania – after all, as Emperor, was it not his first duty to annihilate the enemy of Christendom? Suleiman was now well past his prime – old and tired, it was rumoured, and sick as well. Besides, Transylvania was a long way from Istanbul. Now, surely, was the time to strike. But what troops did he have to throw against him? Ghislain de Busbecq, Charles V's ambassador, regretfully reported:

> Our soldiers are far from courageous; they refuse to obey orders and have little love for either work or the exercise of arms. As for our generals, most of them are dominated by greed of the most sordid kind. Others are reckless and despise discipline; many give themselves up to the most outrageous excesses of debauchery . . . With all that, can we have any doubt of our future fate?

Whether or not Maximilian shared this depressing view of the situation we cannot tell; he certainly did not allow it to deflect him from his purpose. He gathered together some forty thousand men and flung them against John Sigismund – Isabella had died in 1559 – at first with some success; but the Turks struck back quickly, and Suleiman decided that he had had enough. On 1 May 1566 he left Istanbul for the last time with his Grand Vizier Sokollu Mehmet Pasha – in full state, at the head of an army estimated at three hundred thousand men, with vast quantities of heavy artillery. What was needed now was a major victory – something that would erase all memories of the Maltese disaster of the previous year. The Sultan was, of course, in titular command, though he no longer had the strength to ride a horse. Instead he travelled in a carriage the five hundred miles to Belgrade. The Balkan roads – if they could be so described – were such that the journey took him forty-nine days; a horse would have been not only much faster but infinitely more comfortable. Moreover he, like the Emperor Charles, was a martyr to gout. And the weather, as nearly always on his campaigns, could hardly have been worse. Although it was midsummer, roads were flooded, bridges swept away. The cannon got stuck in the mud, and many of the baggage-carrying camels were drowned.

When at last he arrived at Belgrade, the Sultan wanted only rest; he did not get it. For now the ceremonial began: the welcome by John Sigismund, followed by the all-important exchange of presents: for Suleiman a ruby worth 50,000 ducats, for John Sigismund daggers, sabres and saddles all encrusted with jewels, a magnificent white charger splendidly accoutred, and, at his own particular request, a considerable stretch of territory between Transylvania and the River Tisza. Then there were the troops to be reviewed, the interminable banquets to be sat through, the inspections, the presentations, the common lot of crowned heads everywhere. Altogether there were just three days in Belgrade; then, all too soon, the army was off again.

The Sultan's original plan had been to march on the town of Eylau, which controlled the route leading into Transylvania; but while he was still in Belgrade he received a report that Count Nicholas Zriny, the lord of Szeged, had killed one of the more distinguished officials of the Sublime Porte. Such behaviour clearly deserved punishment, and Suleiman immediately gave orders for the army to march on the city. The weather showed no improvement; the journey was yet another nightmare. Finally, however, on 5 August, he reached Szeged, where ninety thousand men and as many of his cannon as had not been abandoned in the mud awaited him. Somehow he found the strength to clamber on to his horse and order the start of the siege; then he made for his tent.

The siege of Szeged lasted a little over a month. Hardly had it begun when the city went up in flames; resistance was thereafter confined to the fortress, where the Count held out with dogged determination. Then, finally, when all the outer bastions were in Turkish hands and he and his six hundred remaining men were surrounded in the central keep, he dressed himself magnificently – 'as if for a feast', it was said – and marched his men out in a heroic but suicidal last stand. Few were left alive; Zriny himself was badly wounded, but was not left to die of his wounds. His head was rammed into the mouth of a Turkish cannon immediately before it was fired – an unpleasant end, but at least a quick one.

A few hours later, Suleiman murmured to his Grand Vizier, 'The great drum of conquest is not yet to be heard'. It was ordained, alas, that he should never hear it. He died in his tent, possibly of a stroke but more probably of a heart attack, on the night of Saturday, 7 September 1566. He was seventy-one. Sokollu acted fast. The important thing, he realised, was to ensure the peaceful succession of Prince Selim, who was at the time the acting Governor of the city of Kütahya in western Anatolia. He was well aware, on the other hand, that once the army – and in particular the janissaries – got to know of the Sultan's death, all discipline would collapse and there would be chaos in the camp. Those few who were already aware of it – including the doctors – he therefore executed at once: the Sultan, he announced, was suffering from a severe attack of gout, and had requested him temporarily to assume the supreme authority. Meanwhile he sent a messenger to Selim, urging him to come at once to Szeged.

One man only he took into his confidence: the chief standard-bearer, Cafer Ağa. This man, who was later to marry Sokollu's daughter, was a gifted forger and could imitate Suleiman's signature to perfection. The generals, continuing to receive their daily orders just as they always had, suspected nothing; letters were sent out to the princes of Europe, the Shah of Persia, the Khan of the Crimea, the Ottoman provincial governors – all of them signed with Suleiman's usual flourish – announcing his victory. Another letter was addressed to the Governor of Buda, accompanying what was left of Zriny's head with a request that it be forwarded to the Emperor Maximilian. To keep the army occupied, Sokollu claimed that the Sultan had ordered the defences of Szeged to be repaired with all possible speed, and that a large mosque should be built in the centre of the city, where he intended to give thanks just as soon as the severe swelling of his foot would allow.

For forty-three days the army remained in the camp, with heavily armed sentries continually on guard outside the Sultan's tent preventing all but the Grand Vizier from entering. Only then did Sokollu give the order for departure on the long journey back to Istanbul. The Sultan, he announced, would be travelling in a closed litter. 'From time to time,' writes the chronicler Ibrahim Peçevi,*

> Sokollu approached the throne, pretending to make a report to the Sultan. He also gave the impression of discussing the report with him after he had read it out ... Many rumours were circulating, but the skilful tactics of the Grand Vizier managed to dissipate suspicions. No one knew for certain whether the *padishah* was dead or alive.

Selim, meanwhile, on receipt of Sokollu's letter, had immediately left Kütahya and, without stopping in Istanbul, had ridden on to meet his father's funeral cortège. He finally caught up with it as it was approaching Belgrade. Only then did the Grand Vizier reveal to the army as a whole that the Sultan had indeed drawn his last breath. Summoning the professional readers of the Koran to the imperial tent, he bade them recite the appropriate prayers. The full funeral service began the following morning, shortly before dawn. Selim himself appeared at sunrise, dressed entirely in black. Approaching the carriage

---

* Ibrahim Peçevi (1572–c.1650) was an Ottoman provincial official who became a historian after his retirement. His two-volume history of the Empire – alas, still untranslated – is the chief source of our knowledge of the period from 1520 to 1640.

on which his father's body had been laid, he silently raised his arms to heaven as the imams intoned further prayers for the dead. When these were over, he withdrew once more to his tent.

The army was already grumbling. It was a long-standing tradition that the janissaries and other regiments received what were known as 'accession gifts' every time one sovereign succeeded another. Only after these had been duly distributed were their recipients – though still deeply dissatisfied by the inadequacy of the distribution – sufficiently appeased to continue their march. And when at last they reached Istanbul, violence broke out again. Two distinguished officials, the *kapudan pasha* – the chief admiral – and Pertev Pasha, the second vizier, were dragged from their horses and beaten to within an inch of their lives; Sokollu himself escaped only by hurling gold coins at his would-be attackers. Order was eventually restored, but only after a number of executions and a promise from the new Sultan that the janissaries' pay would be substantially increased.

Suleiman's tomb was ready; it had been designed in the year of his death by the greatest of his architects, Mimar Sinan, and stands in the small garden behind the great mosque – the Suleimaniye – that Sinan had already built in his honour.* Relatively few visitors to the mosque seek it out – a pity, because it is a lovely little building, domed, octagonal and surrounded by a charming arcade on columns. Inside, the walls are covered with vast quantities of superb Iznik tiles, twice as many as can be found in the immense mosque itself. Its only defect – for which Sinan cannot be blamed – is overcrowding, for Suleiman's coffin has been joined, not only by that of his favourite daughter,

---

* The complex surrounding the mosque also included a hospital, a medical college, a primary school, four schools for the teaching of the Koran, public baths and a public kitchen for the serving of food to the poor.

Mihrimar, but also by those of two later sultans, Suleiman II and Ahmet II. Roxelana was luckier; she has been allowed to keep a separate tomb of her own, standing a little way to the east. It is naturally smaller and simpler than her husband's, but the tiles inside are even finer – a good deal better, it must be said, than she deserved.

~

Of all the celebrated men of history, two only are known as 'the Magnificent'. One is Lorenzo de' Medici, the other is Sultan Suleiman. Lorenzo symbolises the Florentine Renaissance; but even though the Islamic world experienced no reawakening comparable to that which occurred in Italy, there can be no doubt that the Sultan presided over a Golden Age. This was touched on briefly in the first chapter, when he was first introduced; since then, however, we have seen him principally as a military leader, and it is perhaps time to expand a little on the cultural gifts he bestowed on his subjects. He encouraged every form of artistic creativity except sculpture – at which, as a pious Muslim, he was obliged to draw the line. Two-dimensional painting, on the other hand, he encouraged, and particularly the art of portraiture. We possess a surprising number of admirable portraits of him – Titian himself painted at least five (though he never clapped eyes on his model), and there is the splendid pencil portrait by Dürer in Bayonne. We are told that no fewer than thirty painters – mostly miniaturists – worked permanently at the palace.

Their output was, of course, entirely secular. Religious painting – which produced such a glorious harvest in the Christian world – was forbidden; for the rest, opinion was divided. The trouble lies in a passage of the Koran* which states that Allah is the only *musavvir* – a word that means 'creator' but which is unfortunately used, both in Arabic and Turkish, with the meaning of 'painter'. Must Allah therefore be not just the only creator but the only painter too? In much of the Islamic world the jury is still out, but the Turks had already settled for a compromise. Paintings, however secular, could never be hung in mosques or in public rooms. Private apartments of sultans or other important persons were, however, another matter. They might contain portraits or ideal landscapes; scenes of pageantry or processions before the Sultan were especially popular. Love scenes, however, were generally to be avoided.

Architecture was largely dominated by Sinan. A Greek Christian brought up in the *devşirme* system,† he began life as a military engineer, building bridges, aqueducts and caravanserais; as such, he took part in the siege of Rhodes, in the Belgrade campaign and, of course, at the Battle of Mohács. He was nearly fifty when he was appointed Court Architect; only later, after the Sultan had fully recognised his genius, did he start work on the vast religious buildings – mosques and *medreses,* hospitals and charitable foundations – for which he is famous. Of mosques alone he managed to build 146 before he died in 1588, which was his ninety-ninth year.

But – and this is characteristic of the age in which he lived – everything he built was devoted to religious or utilitarian purposes. We search in vain in the Turkish world for palaces or for great houses, such as the Sultan's contemporaries were building in Europe. In Ottoman lands there was never a Fontainebleau or a Chenonceau, never a Nonsuch or an Escorial; the 'palace' of Topkapı where the Sultan lived is in fact nothing of the kind:

---

* LIX. 24.

† The regular conscription and conversion of Christian children for service in the Sultan's administration or in one of the palace regiments.

it is simply a group of pavilions, many of them of a single storey. Only the harem – a seemingly endless labyrinth of rooms and corridors which, extended haphazardly over the centuries, remains utterly devoid of any overall plan – occasionally strives towards elegant decoration as opposed to quiet distinction; and the harem, as we know, was for its inhabitants little more than a gilded cage.

And then there are the decorative arts: the carpets – an art developed by the Turks while they were still nomads, long before they appeared in Anatolia in the eleventh century; the textiles – brocades, satins and velvets, mostly woven in Damascus, Baghdad, Bursa and in Istanbul itself, whose workshops were the only ones permitted in the sixteenth century to use gold and silver thread; and finally the ceramics – the plates and vases, the ewers and cups and lamps and, above all, the tiles, employed in their hundreds of thousands to adorn the interiors of the mosques, drenching them in light and colour. All the best came from the workshops of Iznik – the ancient Nicaea – which reached their peak around 1550. Their designs are mostly animals and birds, flowers and fruit, and quite often that glorious swirling Arabic calligraphy, so beautiful that it provides a perfect substitute for painting within mosques and holy places, making it the Muslim decorative art *par excellence*.

Suleiman the Magnificent, the tenth and greatest of the Ottoman Sultans, was a statesman, a legislator and a patron of the arts; first and foremost, however, he was a soldier, and he died as we are told good soldiers wish to die, with his troops on the field of battle. There are those who argue that he should not have kept his eyes fixed so determinedly on Europe, that he would have achieved far greater conquests had he turned them to the east, following in the footsteps of Alexander the Great. With his vast army and his limitless wealth he could almost certainly have vanquished Babur, his almost exact contemporary, who, with his victory at Panipat in 1526, had founded the Moghul

Empire in north India. There had, in fact, been one Ottoman expedition in 1538 which had gone so far as to besiege Diu, the large Portuguese fortress on the west coast of the subcontinent; but it had failed – owing largely to the stupidity and incompetence of its commander, Hadım Suleiman Pasha, a eunuch of Greek origin aged over eighty and so fat that it took four men to raise him from his seat* – and thereafter the Sultan seems to have lost interest.

So it was Europe that remained his objective, and it was in Europe that he died. And when, on that fateful September evening – it was a Saturday – he took his last breath, the Ottoman Empire began that remorseless decline that was to continue for the next three and a half centuries.

---

* 'He was', notes André Clot with commendable understatement, 'probably not the ideal choice.'

9

Worth Celebrating

T HE DEATH OF Suleiman before the walls of Szeged brings
our story to its end. Of the four princes who together
constitute the subject of this book, only he completed his three
score years and ten; none of the other three reached even sixty
– Francis dying at fifty-two, Henry at fifty-five, Charles at fifty-
eight. But there: lives were, as we know, shorter in the sixteenth
century, and they differed from our own in many other ways as
well. To take but one example, the three Christian rulers were
– in ways that we can hardly imagine today – all dominated by
their religion. Henry VIII spent seven years of his life arguing
with the Pope about his divorce from Catherine of Aragon
before he finally rejected the whole concept of papal supremacy
and established the Church of England; Francis I, whom we
tend to think of primarily as a flamboyant Renaissance prince,
was burning heretics in the Place Maubert as early as 1523 –
though the persecutions became much worse after the *affaire des
placards* in 1534, and were ultimately to develop into the hideous
Wars of Religion that were to continue till the end of the
century; Charles V fought the Reformation with all his strength,
did his unsuccessful best to prevent it spreading through the
states of north Germany, was responsible for the burning of

many a heretic at the stake and spent his last years in a Spanish monastery.

Suleiman, as a Muslim, cannot obviously be properly compared with the other three; many writers testify to his piety, and there can be no doubt that he conscientiously obeyed the call to prayer and the other requirements of his religion, as did virtually all his Muslim subjects; but Islam is – to its credit – a simpler faith than Christianity, and we somehow feel that the Prophet Mohammed loomed less large in the Sultan's day-to-day thinking than did Jesus Christ in that of the princes of the west. He did, however, possess one quality that was signally lacking in Francis and Charles and increasingly uncertain in Henry. That quality was tolerance, an instinctive respect for the beliefs of others and a readiness to allow them their own customs, traditions and forms of worship. In Suleiman's dominions tolerance was absolute; if only his fellow princes had followed his example, how much happier Europe would have been.

In other ways, too, the Sultan was the odd man out. The three westerners were all related by marriage – Henry was Charles's uncle through Catherine of Aragon, his sister was married to Francis's cousin Louis XII, Charles and Francis were brothers-in-law – and though none could be said to have known each other well, they had at least met. Charles had visited England twice: once in May 1520 (and he had seen Henry again in Picardy a month later, immediately after the Field of the Cloth of Gold), and in the summer of 1522 he was in the country for several weeks. He was to meet Francis at Aigues-Mortes in July 1538, and again when the two travelled across France together in December 1539 and January 1540. Henry and Francis had met, first, at the Field of the Cloth of Gold and then again (with Anne Boleyn) in 1532. None of the three Christian princes, however, had ever encountered Suleiman, who remained to all of them a somewhat shadowy figure. To Henry, indeed, he was of relatively little importance. 'One should', he observed, 'be more apprehensive of a certain other person than the Great Turk, of one who devises worse things against Christendom than the Sultan' – pointing darkly across the Channel. Cardinal Wolsey went even further: the Turks were so remote, he said, that they really did not affect England at all.

For neither the Emperor nor the King of France, on the other hand, was it possible to forget Suleiman for very long. The Sultan was keeping up a relentless pressure on the eastern borders of the Empire – in 1529 besieging Vienna itself – and although Charles's brother Ferdinand was bearing the brunt of the aggression, it was obviously the Emperor who was ultimately responsible for the safety of his Hungarian subjects. Nor was the danger confined to eastern Europe; the corsairs of the Barbary Coast – who also owed allegiance to Suleiman – constituted an ever-present danger to the coasts of Spain, the Balearic Islands and Sicily, a danger so great indeed as to persuade Charles personally to take part in two expeditions to north Africa: that which captured Tunis in 1535 and that of 1541 which so humiliatingly failed to take Algiers. More important than any of this, however, was the simple fact that the Emperor was by definition the protector of Christendom, to whom the Ottoman Sultan represented Antichrist. In his youth Charles had dreamed of a glorious pan-European Crusade that would drive the infidels back to the Asiatic steppe from which they had come, allowing Constantinople once again to take its place as a Christian capital. In his later years he had come to accept the fact that this could never happen – a dream it would remain; but he personally could never have treated Suleiman with anything but bitter hostility, and he never forgave his brother-in-law for the increasingly friendly relations that he maintained with the Sublime Porte.

Francis, naturally, viewed the Sultan in a rather different light. He was penned in by the Empire: Spain on one side, the Low Countries, Germany and Austria on the other. He could not forget that he had spent more than a year as Charles's prisoner, while his two sons had passed four precious years of childhood in captivity as hostages for their father. The former Duchy of Burgundy constituted another running sore in his relations with his brother-in-law, as did his claim to Milan. It was no wonder that the two were almost constantly at war with each other. What the King desperately needed was an ally against the Emperor; and Suleiman, who alone was able to exert pressure on the Empire from the east, was ideal for his purposes. The Sultan's one disadvantage was his religion. From time to time the Pope would start talking about Crusades, and Francis, as the Most Christian King, would be obliged to pay lip-service to any call on the armies of Christendom. But lip-service it remained: it was perfectly plain that, for any number of reasons, sixteenth-century Europe was incapable of launching a Crusade of the kind that had been possible three or four centuries earlier – and Francis soon became adept at smoothing over any signs shown by the Sultan of a ruffled temper. We read with something approaching astonishment of the Franco-Turkish siege of Nice in 1543, and of how the old pirate Barbarossa and his entire fleet then wintered in Toulon until the following April. On occasions such as these, eyebrows were raised all over western Europe and Francis had a good deal of explaining to do; but somehow – even after Barbarossa had, on his return journey, ravaged several islands that were indisputably imperial territory – he managed to get away with it.

Of the four great principals in our story, Suleiman was, as we have seen, the last survivor. Already, on the western political stage, there had been a major change of cast. The age of the giants was gone: the second half of the sixteenth century consequently possessed a flavour remarkably different from that of the first. It boasted one monarch, in the magnificent shape of Queen Elizabeth I, as great as – or perhaps even greater than – any of our four protagonists; but only one of her contemporary rulers was of any real interest to her – her brother-in-law, Philip of

Spain – and Philip was lugubrious, sanctimonious and more devout than even his father had been, though nowhere near so intelligent. In France, Henry II, Francis II, Charles IX and Henry III formed a dismal quartet indeed; it was only with the arrival of Henry IV in 1589 that things cheered up. In the Empire, Charles's brother Ferdinand and Ferdinand's son Maximilian were curiously dull; after them Rudolf II was colourful enough, but he was to spend most of his life studying alchemy and astrology in Prague. As for the Turks, it is sad to have to record that while Suleiman could – and should – have been succeeded by his son Mustafa, who possessed all his father's qualities and who would surely have led the Empire on to further triumphs, his eventual successor – Selim II, always known for very good reason as 'the Sot' – was to prove the nadir of the Ottoman line. With him, the demoralisation of their once formidable Empire was well under way, as was its long, slow but steady decline.

But the first half of the century – now that *was* worth celebrating. Has there, in all European history, been a half-century like it? Here, packed into the space of just fifty years, are the High Renaissance, Luther and the Reformation, the exploration of the Americas, the panoply and pageantry exemplified by the Field of the Cloth of Gold and, above all, those four magnificent, memorable monarchs – each of whom, individually, left his indelible imprint over the land he ruled and who together transformed the civilised world.

Acknowledgements

I AM MORE THAN grateful to Georgina Laycock, Caroline Westmore, Lyndsey Ng and Ruby Mitchell, all of John Murray, for their hard work; to Juliet Brightmore for her brilliant performance with the illustrations; to Douglas Matthews, for yet another superb index; and, as always, to my wife Mollie, for her constant encouragement and eagle-eyed proofreading.

Illustration Credits

akg-images: 2 above/Album/Oronoz, 6 below left/Archives CDA/St-Genès, 12 above/painting by Marco Vecellio (detail)/Cameraphoto, 13 below/design for tapestry (detail) by Jan Cornelisz Vermeyen/photo Erich Lessing. Alamy: 1 above left/The Artchives, 1 below left/Masterpics, 6 below right/portrait attributed to Corneille de Lyon/© FineArt, 8 below/painting (detail) by Pierre-Denis Martin/© Heritage Image Partnership Ltd, 9 below/© Marka, 11 above/© Images & Stories, 12 below left and below right/© GL Archive, 13 above/engraving by Agostino de' Musi/© liszt collection, 14 above/Heritage Image Partnership Ltd, 15 above/painting by Matteo Pérez d'Aleccio/© Heritage Image Partnership Ltd, 15 below/The Art Archive, 16 below left/Interfoto. Bridgeman Images: 3 above/Sonia Halliday Photographs, 3 below/Pictures from History, 7 above/Universal History Archive/UIG, 8 above/watercolour by Joris Hoefnagel/Private Collection/photo © Mark Fiennes, 9 above/Bibliothèque National Paris, 10 above/panel by follower of Joachim Patenier, 11 below/painting by Pieter Snayer/Private Collection/Photo © Rafael Valls Gallery London, 14 below. © The British Library Board: 7 below/Royal 2 A. XVI, f.63v, 16 above right/Add.7880, f. 53 v. Mary Evans Picture Library: 1 above right/Imagno, 2

Bibliography

Brandi, K., *The Emperor Charles V*, trans. C. V. Wedgwood, London, 1949

Bridge, A., *Suleiman the Magnificent, Scourge of Heaven*, New York, 1983

Clot, A., *Suleiman the Magnificent: The Man, His Life, His Epoch*, London, 1992

Eggenberger, E., *A Dictionary of Battles*, London, 1967

Hammer-Pugstall, J. von, *Histoire de l'Empire ottoman depuis son origine jusqu'à nos jours*, Paris, 1835–48

Kinross, Lord, *The Ottoman Centuries*, London, 1977

Knecht, R. J., *Francis I*, Cambridge, 1982

Lacey, R., *The Life and Times of Henry VIII*, London, 1972

Loades, D., *Henry VIII*, Stroud, 2011

MacCulloch, D., *Reformation: Europe's House Divided, 1490–1700*, London, 2003

Mattingly, G., *Catherine of Aragon*, New York, 1942

Michelet, J., *François I et Charles Quint 1515–47*, Paris, 1880

Motley, J. L., *The Rise of the Dutch Republic*, London, 1855

Pollard, A. F., *Wolsey*, London, 1929

Russell, J. G., *The Field of the Cloth of Gold*, London, 1969

Scarisbrick, J. J., *Henry VIII*, 2nd edn, New Haven, CT, 1997

Seward, D., *François I: Prince of the Renaissance*, New York, 1973

Starkey, D., *Henry: Virtuous Prince*, London, 2008

Terrasse, C., *François I, le roi et le règne*, Paris, 1943–8

Tyler, R., *The Emperor Charles the Fifth*, London, 1956

Williams, N., *Henry VIII and His Court*, London, 1971

Index